The Cross and the Flag

Other Books of Interest from St. Augustine's Press

Maurice Ashley Agbaw-Ebai, *Light of Reason, Light of Faith: Joseph Ratzinger and the German Enlightenment*

Maurice Ashley Agbaw-Ebai, *The Essential Supernatural: A Dialogical Study in Kierkegaard and Blondel*

Maurice Ashley Agbaw-Ebai and Matthew Levering, Editors, *Africae Munus: Ten Years Later*

Maurice Ashley Agbaw-Ebai and Kizito Forbi S.J., Editors, *An African Perspective on the Thought of Benedict XVI*

Maurice Ashley Agbaw-Ebai and Kizito Forbi S.J., Editors, *Benedict XVI: Rethinking Africa*

George Gänswein, *Who Believes Is Not Alone: My Life Beside Benedict XVI*

Roberto Regoli, *Beyond the Crises: The Pontificate of Benedict XVI*

Marin Schlag, editor, , *Holiness through Work: Commemorating the Encyclical Laborem Exercens*

Peter Kreeft, *The Philosophy of Jesus*

Peter Kreeft, *Socratic Logic (3rd Edition)*

Jean-Luc Marion, *Descartes's Grey Ontology: Cartesian Science and Aristotelian Thought in the Regulae*

Josef Pieper, *In Tune with the World*

Sister M. Pascalina Lehnert, *His Humble Servant: Sister M. Pascalina Lehnert's Memoirs of Her Years of Service to Eugenio Pacelli, Pope Pius XII*

John Paull II, *John Paul II LifeGuide: Words to Live By*

Roger Scruton, *The Meaning of Conservatism: Revised 3rd Edition*

Roger Scruton, *The Politics of Culture and Other Essays*

Joseph Bottum, *Spending the Winter: A Poetry Collection*

D. C. Schindler, *God and the City*

The Cross and the Flag
Papal Diplomacy and John Paul II's Struggle Against the Tyranny of the Possible

JOHN TANYI NQUAH LEBUI

ST. AUGUSTINE'S PRESS

South Bend, Indiana

Manufactured in the United States of America.

1 2 3 4 5 6 29 28 27 26 25 24

Library of Congress Control Number: 2024937896

Paperback ISBN: 978-1-58731-143-7

∞ The paper used in this publication meets the minimum requirements of the American National Standard for Information Sciences – Permanence of Paper for Printed Materials, ANSI Z39.48-1984.

St. Augustine's Press
www.staugustine.net

In memoriam
Papa Tanyi Ake Francis, Magdalene Nanga Tanyi, Api Rita Tanyi, Sixtus Ongene Tanyi, Uncle Joseph Assandack, Mama Beltha Andela, and Chief Max Bikelle (old Lion).

CONTENTS

ACKNOWLEDGEMENTS

This project is the culmination of a process that has been shaped by many agents and forces over the years. In life and in death, Pope John Paul II, my patron saint, has had an enormous influence on my life. In 2007, as a young missionary in the coastal region of Kenya, Sr. Angelina Munyao gave me a precious gift entitled, "John Paul II: A Quarter of a Century." It was a big, old cassette that was popular in Africa before the advent of CDs and DVDs in the continent. "A Quarter of a Century," is a documentary on the papacy of John Paul II. I became enamored of "A Quarter of Century," and without any hyperbole, I have watched it not less than five hundred times over the years. This particular documentary definitely sowed the seed for the desire and realization of this book. After the death of Pope John Paul II, Fr. Maurice Agbaw-Ebai introduced me to the writings of George Weigel. Without doubt, Weigel is the most authoritative interpreter of John Paul II in the anglophone world, and my reading of his extensive writings on the pope and his papacy, especially *Witness to Hope*, definitely whetted my appetite for this project. Perhaps, I have read all of Weigel's books on the papacy of John Paul II.

Special appreciation goes to Hekima Institute of Peace Studies and International Relations (HIPSIR), Nairobi, Kenya, where my knowledge and skills of international relations and diplomacy were honed. I am indebted to my former professors at HIPSIR, including: Professors C.A. Mumma Martinon, Philip Nyingu'ro, Gasper Sunywa, Robert Mudida, Omoka Wanakayi, Robert White, Sahayaraj Thangasamy, Benson Mulemi, Jada Patrisio, Peter Wanyande, and Patrick Maluki. The faculty, staff, and seminarians at Pope John XXIII National Seminary have been incredibly supportive to me in the realization of this project. I am grateful to the Rt. Rev. Brian Kiely, the rector of the seminary, members of the faculty: Msgr. William Fay, Msgr. James Mongelluzzo, Msgr. Peter Conley, Msgr. Robert Oliver, Dr. Antony Keaty, Fr. Bill Murphy, Fr. Vincent Daily, Fr. Paul Miceli, Fr. Joseph Zwosta, and Fr. Steve Linehan, Fr. Scott Surrency, OFM, Michael Bellafiore, S.J., and Dr. Bernadine Kensinger.

This book is a product of primary and secondary research. I had profound interviews with scholars of papal diplomacy and some persons who knew, worked, and interacted with Pope John Paul II. Their informed articulation of John Paul's diplomacy only improved the quality of this work. I thank these persons who amidst busy schedules made time for the interviews. Special recognition goes to Archbishop Alain Paul Lebeaupin (former nuncio to Kenya), Bishop Francis Lysinge, Bishop Maurice Muhatia Makumba, Dr. George Weigel, Msgr. William Fay, Msgr. William M. Helmick, Prof. Norman Tanner, S.J., Prof. Aquiline Tarimo, S.J., Prof. Benezet Bujo S.J., Prof. Jean-Marie Quenum, S.J., Prof. Laurenti Magesa, Prof. Jada Patrisio, Fr. Anthony Murphy, MHM, Fr. Maurice McGill, MHH, and Fr. Hans Burgman, MHM.

I cannot thank enough the friends and scholars who painstakingly reviewed the manuscript and whose intelligent suggestions only improved the quality of this work. In this regard, I am wholeheartedly grateful to Msgr. James Mongelluzzo, Dr. Maurice Agbaw-Ebai, Prof. Tracey Rowland, Thomas Fallati, Stephen Mullaney, John Williams, William Burns, Patrick Long, Eugene Wirba, Jared Rottinghaus, and Faith Mutua.

I continuously give praise to God whenever I think of my siblings, parents and relatives, who have been a wonderful blessing in my life. I always felt the support of my family throughout the writing of this manuscript. Special appreciation goes to Mama Angela Bikelle Tanyi, Chief Tanyi Ake Francis, Loveline Tanyi, Baiye Samuel Tanyi, Lilian Tanyi, Ake Aurelien Tanyi, Raphael Ndem Tanyi, Ndem William, Joseph Tanyi, Justice Therese Bikelle, Andrew Bikelle, Jackson Bikelle, Angele Bikelle (Shushu), Mama Susan Bikelle, Aunty Janet Bikelle, Magdalene Tanyi Nanga, Francis Ongene Tanyi, Ongene Esther Sandra, Yensi

Kuwan Sonia, George Tanyi Ezikpe, Michael Kalu Ezikpe, David Ezikpe, Jason Baiye Tanyi, Eliot Baiye Tanyi, Liam Baiye Tanyi, Lucy Eyabi, Anyi Ndem Larissa Ndem, Larry Ndem, Baiye Ndem, Anyi Ndem Tanyi, Boniface Ayi Tanyi, Shellan Abang, Nchang Emerentia Suh (Manyi), Rose Betek, Mama Sylvia Nakintije, and Papa Ernest Nakintije.

During this project, I fully understood the veracity of the African adage, "It takes a village to raise a child." The emotional, psychological, financial, academic, and physical support I received from friends played a vital role towards the completion of this book. Questions such as: "How is the writing?," "How far with the book?," "When am I getting a copy of the book?," and "When is the book going to be published" only gave me the extra motivation to burn the midnight oils in order to cross the finishing line. Ipso facto, the following friends contributed in a small and big ways: Fr. Fons Eppinck, MHM, Fr. Hubbs Stockmann, MHM, Bishop Joseph Willigers, Fr. Innocent Akum Wefon, MHM, Fr. Joseph King, MHM, Fr. Anthony Ndichia Ndang, MHM, Fr, Sylvester Ponje, MHM, Fr. Christopher Eboka, Fr. Augustine Tazisong, Fr. Bomki Matthews, S.J., Fr. John-Baptist Nzamcho, S.J., Fr. Joycelyn Rabeson, S.J., Fr. Gabriel Mmasi, S.J., Fr. Thomas Oates, Fr. Fr. Paul Nkongho, Fr. Edmund Ugweoegbu, Fr. Joseph Gaudet, Fr. Steve Koen, Fr. Gerry Fraser, Fr. John Morris, Fr. Casmia Bello, Fr. Kelvin Sakwe, Fr. Denis Tameh, Fr. Jim Morris, Michael Okuku, John Ewu, Barrister Godlove Ebai, Nkengafac Kesley, Clifton Mastran, Rajesh Ravi, Greg. Dougherty, Victor Andreozzi, Gregory Zingler, Nelson Tlatelpa, Barry Mungeon, Alex Olszewski, PeterClaver Kiviiri, James DiVasto, Edgar Serrano, Sinclair Cushmore, Gustavo Correa, Fr. Jose Perez, Vincent Vu, Anh Vu, Andrew Tsui, John Ippolito, Joseph Gonzalez, Francis Awokang, Marion Blanchette, Charles Tupta, Eric Mukatia, Sharon Inziani, Chief Etta Fidel, Harrison Teke, Susan Nungari, Pat Bruen, Dacta Peter (Small Peter), Kelvin Hongla, Harrison Ouafor, Wankah Claude, Shum Victor, Philip Emase, Afoh Kenneth Ndi, Frankline Nki Abungwo, Sr. Anne Njume, Sr. Cecila Foleng, Sr. Madelene Formilack, Sr. Anne Schoettelkotte, Sr.

Agnes Olayode, Stephen Gust, Mary Cahill, MaryAnn Harold, Maurice Mashiwa, Gideon Wafula Wakesa, Agunda Denis, Jackson Sokoine, Sharon Inziani, Samuel Mulle, Esther Shikuku, Ndanu Mung'ala, Alma Pelletier, Sr. Pauline Fortin, Nancy Gavenda, Judy Ware, Mary Warren, Monica Brenton, Joseph Stella, Caroline Mengeto, Ashu Felix, Fualem Donald, Stanley Doh, Diporrah Ombachi, Oben Relindis, Briget Aroke, Dr. Hilary Aroke, Carolyn Jupiter-Mcintosh, Deacon John Beagan, Marita Beagan, Virginia Greeley, Eva Mwakazi, Joy Nandhego, Agbor Tarh, Divine Lereh, Samuel Mwiwawi, Deo Nchamga, Cecilia Fombin, Philomena Che, Cecilia Fonge, and Njila Francis. There are definitely some names and people who assisted me in this project but haven't been acknowledged here. Be assured of my appreciation and indebtedness to you all.

President Bush, whom John Paul II criticized for the U.S.-led invasion of Iraq, *inter alia,* said, "Pope John Paul II left the throne of St. Peter in the same way he ascended to it—as a witness to the dignity of human life. In his native Poland that witness launched a democratic revolution that swept Eastern Europe and changed the course of history.... We will always remember the humble, wise, and fearless priest who became one of history's great moral leaders. We are grateful to God for sending such a man, a son of Poland who became the bishop of Rome and a hero for the ages." President Mohammad Khatami of the Islamic Republic of Iran sent a message of condolence to the Vatican, "Pope John Paul II was a disciple of religious mysticism, philosophic deliberation and thought, and artistic and poetic creativity." Khatami, who met the pope in 1999, continued, "By emphasizing his experience and teachings, [he] earnestly tried to utilize them in the path of the triumph of truth, justice, and peace." Unable to regard his royal wedding as a compatible event on the same day (Friday) the mortal remains of John Paul II were to be interred, Prince Charles of the United Kingdom postponed his marriage to Camilla Parker Bowles until the following day (Saturday), so that he could represent at the pope's funeral in Rome his mother, Queen Elizabeth II of Great Britain, Northern Ireland, and other Commonwealth realms.

Upon learning that Jesus Christ was a Galilean, Pontius Pilate sent him to Herod since Herod was tetrarch of Galilee. The passion and death of Jesus became an instrument of reconciliation since "Herod and Pilate became friends that very day, even though they had been enemies formerly" (Luke 23:12). Likewise, in his simple wooden casket, Pope John Paul II continued sowing seeds of peace and togetherness, at least temporarily, when his funeral "miraculously" brought archenemies in international diplomacy to the same benches and kneelers in St. Peter's Square. Since heads of state and governments sat alphabetically according to the French spelling of their country's name, and diplomatic protocol, diplomatic faux pas during the ceremony did not go *incognito.* President Robert Mugabe of Zimbabwe shook hands with

Prince Charles of the United Kingdom. Since the Israeli and Syrian delegations were seated next to each other, President Bashar Al-Assad of Syria reached out to Israeli President Moshe Katsav. "I told him [Bashar Al-Assad] 'Good morning' and he shook my hand," Katsav said. Even though it was ferociously denied by Iranian President Mohammed Khatami, his Israeli counterpart, President Moshe Katsav, claimed they shook hands during John Paul's funeral, "The President of Iran extended his hand to me, I shook it and told him in Farsi, 'May peace be upon you'" (*The Guardian*, April 9, 2005). President Katsav sat only two seats away from President Khatami, amidst strained relations.

After bitter disagreements and insults over the U.S.-led invasion of Iraq in 2003, U.S. President Bush and French President Jacques Chirac found themselves seated in the same row only separated by their wives. Presidents Bush and Chirac shook hands and Chirac even kissed the hand of U.S. Secretary of State, Condoleezza Rice (Soltis, 2005). Andy Soltis, American chess grandmaster and columnist, captured the moment when he entitled his April 8, 2005, piece for *New York Post*: "Magic 'Spell' Unites Bush and Chirac."

John Paul II's funeral saw the largest gathering of world leaders in history. It was more than any moment of international diplomacy. No UN General Assembly, since its inception in 1945, has managed to bring such a huge number of dignitaries under one roof as was the case during the funeral of John Paul II. President Paul Biya of Cameroon, who seldom attends summits of heads of state, was one of the first world leaders to arrive in the Vatican. Zimbabwean strongman Robert Mugabe defied a European Union travel ban to attend the funeral. Taiwanese President Chen Shui-bian made an unprecedented appearance in the Vatican. "Presidents, princes, patriarchs, kings; the new leader of a war-torn democracy sitting here, the angry ayatollahs of a yearning nation there, the Dalai Lama, dictators. They were all there, at St. Peter's, witnessing, watching, hearing" (Noonan, 2005:223).

Ecumenical Patriarch Bartholomew I was in the honorary first seat in the section reserved for delegations from churches not in full communion with the Roman Catholic Church. It was the first time an ecumenical patriarch attended a papal funeral since the Great Schism of 1054 A.D. The then-Archbishop of Canterbury, Rowan Williams, was also present—the first time such had been witnessed since the Church of England broke with the Catholic Church in 1534 A.D. Noteworthy also was the presence of Patriarch Abune Paulos, who became the first head of the Ethiopian Orthodox Tewahedo Church to attend a papal funeral. As a result of the unprecedented number of representatives from Christian churches and other world religions, Peggy Noonan picturesquely described the funeral as "... the greatest evangelical event since Gutenberg printed the Bible" (2005:222). In another instance, the same distinguished writer, Peggy Noonan, labelled John Paul II's funeral, "... the first great moment of the twenty-first century." According to her, the pope's funeral was a watershed moment for Europe. "Europe came. Europe took to the streets. Millions of pilgrims spontaneously came to his funeral....That was Europe rising up, and coming, and weeping. That was Europe showing that there may be more going on in the European heart right now than statistics can express, or reflect. One sensed that Europeans may, just may, have come back from that funeral a newly heartened people" (Noonan, 2005:199).

Why was the death and funeral of Pope John Paul II the main religious and diplomatic event of 2005? Why all the encomia? A straightforward answer to these questions is that Pope John Paul II was the most influential personality of the second half of the twentieth century or perhaps the entire century. More still, he remains the most consequential pope in five centuries. He was the most recognizable spiritual leader in the world, a spokesperson for the religious community, an ally of the poor, the voice of conscience for the world, and the highest moral authority on earth.

Saint John Paul II restored the medieval grandeur and influence of the Holy See in international politics. Through her soft power, the Holy See and the Vatican became the moral superpower of the careening billiard-ball international system, the diplomatic and geographical center of the world, and the prime drawing room of diplomacy. This explains why senior Vatican commentator John L. Allen Jr. recorded that, in the weeks leading up to the U.S.-led invasion in Iraq in 2003, "diplomatic heavy-weights, shuttled in and out of the Vatican like clients at a popular deli: Tony Blair, Joschka Fisher, Silvio Berlusconi, Jose Maria Aznar, Mohammed Reza Khatami (speaker of the Iranian parliament and brother of the country's president), Kofi Annan, and even Tarik Aziz" (Allen, 2005). These dignitaries flocked into the Vatican for a cup of coffee with the pope and to hear his final verdict on Bush's planned Iraqi invasion. During his reign, right-wing dictators tried to demonstrate how popular they were with the Holy Father by joining him on his cavalcades and taking Holy Communion from his hands, but then, months later, were either toppled or suffered serious reverses.

In 1986, Pope John Paul II unprecedentedly brought together to Assisi leaders of other religions, including practitioners of the African Traditional Religion and Voodooists from West Africa, Buddhist monks, the Tibetan Dalai Lama, and Shamans, not to "pray together" but "to be together and pray" (John Paul II Assisi Address, 1986). In about 27 years, he made 104 international journeys to almost every country on the planet, circumnavigating the world at least 30 times, or more than 2.8 times the distance between the earth and moon. At World Youth Day 1995, five million people gathered at Luneta Park in Manila, the Philippines capital, an event recognized by Guinness World Records as the largest crowd ever— a record only surpassed 20 years later, when six million people attended an outdoor Mass celebrated in Manila by Pope Francis in January 2015.

Goal of this Book

Contrary to the wisdom and spirit of Mark Anthony's funeral oration for Caesar, my primary intention is not to praise Pope Saint John Paul II. It is not a chronicle or litany of the achievements of John Paul II. Any encomium or vilification is simply a necessary concomitant effect of this academic inquiry. The overall goal of

Theoretical Framework

Theories are analytical tools for understanding, explaining, and making predictions about a given subject matter or phenomenon. The theoretical underpinnings informing the arguments in this book are the Multi-Track diplomacy of Louise Diamond and John McDonald, and James Rosenau's idiosyncratic level of analysis.

Multi-Track Diplomacy

Multi-Track diplomacy is a conceptual framework developed by John McDonald and Louise Diamond in the United States in the mid-1990s. This conceptual framework is principally an expansion of Track One and Track Two diplomacies, which have traditionally been the dominant tracks in international diplomacy. With the changing nature of conflicts at the end of the Cold War, coupled with the inadequacies of the traditional Tracks One and Two diplomacies in the management of intrastate conflicts, Diamond and McDonald expanded the dual tracks of diplomacy to include other tracks suitable for managing post-Cold War conflicts and new security dangers such as cyber threats. The Cold War interstate conflicts have been overshadowed by intrastate and proxy wars with different natures and forms (genocide, civil wars, and ethnic cleansing), and hence the need for new conflict management methodologies. The establishment of the Institute for Multi-Track Diplomacy (IMTD) in 1992 was a significant step in the Multi-Track Diplomacy system. Multi-Track diplomacy has nine tracks.

The Holy See is indisputably a special case under international law and officially engages in Track One diplomacy, or peacemaking through diplomacy. In the memorable Protocol of March 19, 1815, the Congress of Vienna confirmed the status of the Holy See, at that time the oldest continually existing agent of international diplomacy, as a *"permanent* subject of *general* customary international law *vis-à-vis* all states, Catholic or not." (Kunz, 1958:308). The juridical personality of the Catholic Church and the Vatican City under international law is distinct from that of the Holy See. The Vatican City is a distinct independent geographical entity. On the other hand, the Holy See is a non-geographical sovereign entity recognized in international law. The Holy See refers to the area governed by the bishop of Rome, which includes the Vatican City State and the universal Catholic Church. However, they are united by the pope who heads both institutions. The main commonality of the two entities is their moral personality.

The Holy See engages in Track One diplomacy, while the Catholic Church traditionally takes part in unofficial or Track Two diplomacy. One means by which the Catholic Church as a church organization with a non-governmental organization (NGO) status officially engages in Track Two diplomacy, or peacemaking, is through conflict resolution. The phrase "Track Two" was coined by Joseph Montville of the Foreign Service Institute in 1982 to describe methods of diplomacy that were outside the formal government system (Diamond & McDonald, 1996:1). Conflict resolution scholar and practitioner Susan Allen Nan opined, "Track One and a Half diplomacy combines the official influence of Track One with the unofficial approaches of Track Two" (2004:57). Popes officially engage in Track One and Track Two diplomacies. In some instances, Saint John Paul II's diplomacy was a combination of both Tracks (Track One and a Half diplomacy). In another instance, Susan Allen Nan argued, "Unofficial work with high-level officials is a form of Track One and a Half diplomacy" (2002).

Track Three diplomacy, or peacemaking through commerce, hinges on the assumption that international business plays a role in international diplomacy and peace. "Business is not an isolated phenomenon but an integral part of the social and political fabric of international life" (Diamond & McDonald, 1996:52). Track Four, grassroots or citizen diplomacy, is built on the premise that individual citizens or groups of individuals can play a role in international conflict management through private activities. Track Five diplomacy is built on the assumption that training people in skills of negotiation and mediation plays an important role in conflict management. Track Six diplomacy, or peacemaking through advocacy, is based on the hypothesis that peace is not possible without social, political, environmental, and economic justice, and integrity.

Track Seven diplomacy is built on the assumption that love and compassion are means by which conflicts can be resolved. Printed materials and writings of church leaders aimed at instructing their faithful also constitute Track Seven diplomacy. Track Eight diplomacy, or peacemaking through providing resources, is important in understanding the role of the John Paul II Foundation in the Sahel countries as a peace effort. It is informed by the thesis that "those with wealth have a responsibility and an opportunity to make a positive contribution to the world through the judicious use of that money to sponsor worthwhile projects" (Diamond & McDonald, 1996). Conflicts are minimized in the Sahel countries because scarce resources like water, which is a major source of conflict, are provided for by the John Paul II Foundation for the Sahel. He was also the first pope to make extensive use of the media in his diplomacy. In the Multi-Track diplomacy system, the media or peacemaking through information constitutes Track Nine diplomacy.

The Idiosyncratic Level of Analysis

James N. Rosenau propounded the five-dimensional levels of analysis. Levels of analysis refer to the units which researchers, students of international relations, historians, biographers, and hagiographers use to comprehensively explain and predict global phenomena. Charles Kegley defined levels of analysis as "the different aspects of and agents in international affairs that may be stressed in interpreting and explaining global phenomena" (2004:14). Some of the units include: states, individuals, and transnational actors like the pope. (Russett & Starr, 1985:11).

In his seminal paper, "The Level-of-Analysis Problem in International Relations" (1961), J. David Singer pioneered the discourse on levels of analysis when he postulated the state and the international system as units of analysis (Goldstein *et.al*, 2006:133). Singer, among others, pointed out that "in any area of scholarly inquiry, there are always several ways in which the phenomena under study may be sorted and arranged for purposes of systemic analysis" (1961:71). James Rosenau built on Singer's foundation when, in 1962, he published his five-dimensional levels of analysis in his scholarly article, "Pre-theories and Theories of Foreign Policy." He advanced five philosophies of analysis including the idiosyncratic and role levels, governmental politics, the societal level, and the international system. In 1966, Rosenau systematized his levels of analysis in his famous *magnum opus*, *The Scientific Study of Foreign Policy*.

The word "idiosyncratic" may be used interchangeably with the term "individual." The idiosyncratic level of analysis is built on the assumption that individual leaders make foreign policy decisions, and different leaders will make different foreign policy decisions given the same situations due to their unique idiosyncratic variables (Rouke, 1997:127). Rosenau argued that in the exercise of the role occupied by an individual, there is always an allowance or leeway for individual expression, discretion, and interpretation of events made possible by the uniqueness of different personalities and other singular variables (1971:160). *Ipso facto*, Saint John Paul II's idiosyncratic variables are of utmost importance in the analysis of his diplomacy. Historian Ralph Waldo stated that "individuals are the movers of history, and there is properly no history, only biography" (Kegley, 2006:86). Certain historical events are catalysed by individuals and cannot be explained without reference to their idiosyncratic variables. This explains why certain doctrines/neologisms are linked to specific leaders, and not the states they governed, such as the "Nixon doctrine," "Bush Doctrine," "Truman Doctrine," the "Travelling Papacy" of John Paul II, "Reaganomics," "Clintinomics," "Abenomics," "Obamanomics," and the "Trump Doctrine."

Rosenau defined individual variables as "any aspect of an actor which characterized him prior to his assumption of policy

making responsibilities and which did not necessarily character-
ize any other person who might have occupied, through election,
appointment, or other means, the same position" (1971:161).
Some idiosyncratic variables are: age, personal experience, health,
worldview (*Weltanschauung*), past history, ego and ambition, political history, education, temperament, ideology and morality,
personalizing tendencies, and personal policy beliefs, amongst
others (Rouke, 1997:131). In examining the role of the "Prisoner's
Dilemma" factor in Thucydides' *The History of the Peloponnesian
War*, American political scientist Joseph Nye Jr. concluded,
"Human decisions mattered...accidents and personalities make
a difference even if they work within limits set by the larger structure...." (2007:19).

What is the correlation between the levels of analysis and the
conduct of papal diplomacy? A major thesis, widely agreed upon
by scholars of ecclesiastical diplomacy such as Paul Johnson, John
L. Allen, Robert Araujo, and John Lucal and by Vaticanologists
like Peter Hebblethwaite, holds that the direction of papal diplomacy is centered on the personality of the supreme pontiff. There
is a marked continuity in goal and conduct of pontifical diplomacy. However, the style and method of the conduct of papal
diplomacy has continuously been shaped by the idiosyncratic
variables of pontiffs. There is a popular pious belief that Providence watches closely the paths, childhood, and career of an
eventual pope, shaping it towards the Petrine office. This explains
why, upon the election of a new pope, historians and biographers
immediately start sifting through autobiographies to see the hand
of Divine Providence in his early life.

Due to the ingenuity of the idiosyncratic level of analysis in
explaining the conduct of the papal office, I propose *the idiosyncratic theory of the conduct of papal diplomacy*. Notably, the idiosyncratic level of analysis does not solely explain the conduct of
papal diplomacy. The influence of the idiosyncratic variables of
leaders is more pronounced in personalized political systems,
dictatorships, military juntas, theocracies, monarchies, and autoc-
racies than in very institutionalized political systems such as the

United States. The role level is equally important because certain offices like the secretariat of state are very important in the conduct of papal diplomacy. It is for this reason that Church historian Robert Graham stated, "The details of Church affairs are not administered by the pontiff personally but by officials endowed with well-defined authority in their respective domains" (*curia Romana*).

Political scientists such as Jean-Robert Leguey-Feilleux argue that roles have a tendency to inhibit novel behavior (2009:13). The pope is a transnational actor, and the omnipresent 1.3 billion Catholic Christians is a notable societal variable. The apostolic authority of the pope is universal. Robert Graham opined that a pope knows no territorial boundaries because of his religious mission (1959:177). The nature and structure of the international system and, most conspicuously, the Cold War, are important systemic variables, which must not be overlooked in the study of papal diplomacy during the reign of Saint John Paul II. Abraham Lincoln captured the influence of systemic variables in foreign policy decision making while summarizing his presidential career in the following words: "I have not controlled events, but events have controlled me" (Kegly, 2007).

CHAPTER TWO
PAPAL DIPLOMACY

What Is Papal Diplomacy?

Pontificate or papacy simply refers to the reign of a pope. The word "pontificate" is derived from the Latin word *pontifex*, meaning bridge builder. The term *maximus pontifex* means the supreme pontiff or the greatest bridge builder and has its origin from Roman paganism. In his *A Concise History of the Catholic Church*, Thomas Bokenkotter writes, "At first Constantine (emperor) observed an attitude of formal correctness toward paganism. He remained its supreme pontiff, paid homage to the sun god on the official coinage and in general was careful not to alienate the pagan masses and aristocracy of Rome" (Bokenkotter, 2005:40–41). After Christianity became the state religion following the Edict of Thessalonica (380 A.D.) by Emperor Theodosius l, applying the title (supreme pontiff) to the bishop of Rome, the successor of St. Peter, seemed appropriate.

The Italian appellation for pope is "papa." "Father" is its equivalent in English and that explains why "Holy Father" is one of the official titles of the pope. Etymologists will easily deduce that the term "papal diplomacy" means the diplomacy of the pope. Bernard O'Connor (2005) defines papal diplomacy as the first study of the pope from the perspective of international diplomacy. In turn, international diplomacy entails established interstate diplomatic activities and intercourses carried out by special envoys, statesmen, and stateswomen. Such practices and activities have been codified in diplomatic conventions and treatises. Thus, papal diplomacy examines the role of the pope as a transnational actor because of the number of active Catholic Christians in all corners of the world. It looks at the activities of the Holy See *vis-à-vis* international law, and the relations of the Holy See with international organizations and states. Hence, when Pope Pius X repeatedly thought of suppressing papal diplomacy, he meant cutting all ties or limiting the role of the Holy See in the international arena and politics. Robert Graham offers a more elaborate definition of papal diplomacy as a:

> system by which, through accredited public agents, the Holy See carries on stable, formal and reciprocal intercourse with the states. It is the instrumentality by which the supreme authority of the Catholic Church communicates within the framework of standard international practice, with the supreme authority of the states, in the transaction of current or special problems which arise on the part of either Church or State, for the resolution of which the common accord of the ultimate authority of both parties is required. This consensus may take the shape of treaties (concordats) or less formal understandings.... In short, by papal diplomacy is here meant the system of reciprocal permanent representation ... (1958:11–12).

The permanency and longevity of the papal office are extraordinary strong enticements for states to seek diplomatic associations with the Holy See. During the International Conference on Population and Development in Cairo in September 1994, the Clinton administration was conspicuously humiliated when the Vatican delegation successfully opposed the inclusion of the U.S. delegation's language on abortion (Reese, 1998:4). That was an apt example of papal diplomacy.

The key behind-the-scenes role played by the Holy See and Pope Francis that culminated in the 2015 U.S.-Cuba thaw is a glaring example of papal diplomacy. The Holy See was instrumental in the process leading to the re-establishment of diplomatic relations between the U.S. and Cuba after the two countries sought out the Vatican as a trusted broker near the conclusion of their negotiations. In 2014, Pope Francis sent letters to Presidents Barack Obama and Raul Castro requesting them "to resolve humanitarian questions of common interest, including the situation of certain prisoners, in order to initiate a new phase in relations." The Vatican hosted delegations from the two countries and a subsequent breakthrough was achieved. A senior U.S. official told Reuters news agency, "The support of Pope Francis and the support of the Vatican was important to us." Idiosyncratically, Pope Francis' role in the United States-Cuba breakthrough undoubtedly is tied to his status as the first Latin American pope of the Roman Catholic Church.

In his announcement of the new diplomatic relations with Cuba, President Obama thanked Pope Francis for his role in the process, "whose moral example shows us the importance of pursuing the world as it should be, rather than simply settling for the world as it is." The idealists see the world the way it should be while the realists look at the world the way it is. Thus, President Obama's statement indicates his leanings toward the idealism school of politics. In May 2015, the Obama administration removed Cuba from the list of state sponsors of terrorism, a crucial step towards the normalization of relations between Washington and Havana.

On Sunday, May 10, 2015, Cuban President Raul Castro equally thanked the pontiff for brokering the thaw between Havana and Washington and said that the pope so impressed him that he might return to the Catholic Church, despite being a communist. Later, at a news conference with Italian Prime Minister Matteo Renzi, the visibly elated Castro said that he came out of the meeting with the pope "really impressed by his wisdom and his modesty." President Castro said, "When the pope comes to Cuba in September, I promise to go to all his Masses and I will be happy to do so." He then added, "I told the prime minister if the pope continues to talk as he does, sooner or later I will start praying again and return to the Catholic Church, and I am not kidding." Castro jokingly said that in a certain sense he is also a Jesuit since he was educated by the Jesuits before the 1959 revolution. Fidel and Raul Castro were baptized in the Catholic Church. President Castro kept his word and attended Mass when the pope visited Cuba in September 2015.

Papal diplomacy affects public policy at national, regional, and international levels. The obvious task of papal diplomats is to introduce sound moral values in the world. The Church makes sound moral values available by applying Christ's vision to honest human philosophy. The menu of papal diplomacy contains not only relations between the Holy See and other juridical personalities, but also those between the Holy See and national branches of the Catholic Church. This explains why nuncios have double accreditations: to the local Church, and to the host state. The local Churches exist in unity with one another and the mother Church of Rome. The communion of the Church of Rome and other branches of the Catholic Church has, down the line, influenced the life of the Church.

The relationship between the Holy See and other branches of national Churches has not been devoid of criticisms. Some critics hold that local bishops have been reduced to the ranks of branch managers of a multilateral corporation due to the over-centralization of power by the Roman Curia. Saint John Paul II told journalists in 1994 that he was going to Australia and the furthest parts of the world because he is the parish priest of the whole world, and a parish has many branches. Some ecclesiologists were concerned by his pronouncement because they felt that his view of a universal parish priest reduced bishops to papal stooges.

Why then would the pope's statement before his visit to Australia in 1994 raise so many eyebrows, when Canon 333 §1 of *The Code of Canon Law* states, "By virtue of his office, the Roman pontiff not only has power over the universal Church, but also has pre-eminent ordinary power over all particular Churches and their groupings." Does the relationship between the Holy See and other religions and Christian communities constitute papal diplomacy? Was the interreligious Assisi meeting of 1986, convened by

John Paul II, which brought together leaders of other religions, including adherents of the African Traditional Religion (ATR) and Voodooists from Africa, Buddhist monks, Hindus, Jainists, the Tibetan Dalai Lama, and shamans, Shintoists, Sikhs, American Indians, and Christians from both the East and the West, an aspect of papal diplomacy? The religious leaders went to Assisi not to "pray together" but "to be together and pray." The Assisi meeting was an expression of the pope's mission of promoting interfaith unity. During the gathering, two practitioners of the ATR from Africa prayed, "Almighty God, the Great Thumb we cannot avoid in tying any knot, the Roaring Thunder that splits mighty trees, the All-Seeing Lord up on high who sees even the footprints of an antelope on a rock here on earth ... you are the cornerstone of peace."

The publication of the encyclical letter on climate change, *Laudato Si'* (On Care for our Common Home), is an act of papal diplomacy. I was somewhat taken aback by criticisms leveled against the pope for dedicating an encyclical to the problem of climate change. United States Senator Rick Santorum argued that the pope should "leave science to the scientists." Jeb Bush, a 2016 U.S. presidential hopeful, narrowly argued that Pope Francis is unqualified to issue policy recommendations of any kind related to climate change. "The pope should just stick to theology and let the several dozen scientists who support the scientifically disproven point of view on global warming do the talking," Bush concluded. Is caring for the environment and creation and an appeal to humanity to care for our common home outside the realm of theology, morality, diplomacy, and religion? Before the promulgation of the encyclical, a member of Heartland Institute insinuated that Pope Francis would "demean" the office of the papacy and the Church if he published the document and put his moral authority behind fighting global climate change. The writings of a pope to people of goodwill constitute Track Seven diplomacy.

The climate is a common good, as the pope rightly points out in the encyclical. Climate change is an issue of common global concern, affecting people from every geographical longitude and latitude, especially the poor in the developing world. By virtue of being the highest moral authority on earth, the most recognizable spiritual leader, influential international actor, voice of conscience for the world, and leader of at least 1.6 billion Catholics, the pope has the unavoidable mandate to speak out against humankind's abuse of the environment, which thereby affects human flourishing. The pope has the moral responsibility and prerogative to invite everyone to have an urgent ecological conversation and conversion, since the earth is becoming an "immense pile of filth," due to human activities.

The pope ought to weigh in on the debates on climate change because its worst impact is felt by people in developing countries who do not have the resources to easily adapt to climatic changes. The Church advances a preferential option for the poor, and about 40% of Catholics live in developing countries. Future generations will inevitably bear the brunt and dire consequences of the abuse of the earth by the present generation. Thus, climate change is a justice and human rights issue, since its matrix goes against the logic of intergenerational justice and solidarity, human rights, and sustainable development. Woe to the pope should he fail to take to task big multinational enterprises and developed nations exacerbating the problem of climate change because of their market models which tend to promote mass production and extreme / compulsive consumerism.

Those who criticized the pope for writing about climate change did not only lack a proper understanding of papal diplomacy, but were also ignorant of the fact that Jorge Mario Bergoglio chose the papal name "Francis" for a significant reason. Saint Francis of Assisi was an insatiable lover of God's creation. Saint John Paul II named Francis the patron saint "of those who promote ecology" in 1979. It is without doubt that ecological consciousness informed Bergoglio's choice of the name "Francis" upon his election as pope and environmental protection is therefore a major theme of his pontificate.

The pope's moral authority gives him the leverage and soft power in the ideological and political tussle of climate change because, "when a pope in Rome pushes the boulder into the sea, the waves roll up on every side." Climate change is a dire global problem requiring a revolution and urgent action. The pope's proposal for dialogue has inevitably influenced international and public policy. "Diplomacy also takes on new importance in the work of developing international strategies which can anticipate serious problems affecting us all" (Francis, 2015:175).

A Historical Survey of Papal Diplomacy

Any attempt to chronicle a compendium of official and unofficial diplomacy (Track One and a Half diplomacy) in the last two millennia without recourse to the historical relevance of the "Holy See" would be a pursuit of a fool's errand. The Holy See (*Sancta Sedes*) is the institutional embodiment of the authority of the pope within the Church. The term "see" is derived from the Latin appellation *sedes*, which refers to the seat or chair of Saint Peter. In line with Canon 361 of *The Code of Canon Law*, by function and extension, the Holy See does not only refer to the pontiff, but also includes the Secretariat of State, the Council for the Public Affairs of the Church, and other institutions of the Roman Curia, as well as the residence of the pope. So, the pope cannot be considered as distinct from the Holy See since, *inter alia*, the Holy See also includes the sovereign pontiff. Napoleon Bonaparte's conviction that had there been no papacy, one would have been invented out of necessity, is not an overstatement, since the Holy See has been in the forefront of many major diplomatic landmarks in the last two millennia. British historian Thomas Babington Macaulay (1800–1859) magnificently captured the significant longevity of the papacy in one of his essays:

> THERE is not, and there never was on the earth, a work of human policy so well deserving of examination as the Roman Catholic Church. The history of that Church joins together the two great ages of human civilization. No other institution is left standing which carries the

mind back to the times when the smoke of sacrifice rose from the Pantheon, and when camelopards and tigers bounded in the Flavian amphitheatre. The proudest royal houses are but of yesterday, when compared with the line of the Supreme Pontiffs.... The republic of Venice came next in antiquity. But the republic of Venice was modern when compared with the Papacy; and the republic of Venice is gone, and the Papacy remains. The Papacy remains, not in decay, not a mere antique, but full of life and useful vigor.... She saw the commencement of all the governments and of all the ecclesiastical establishments that now exist in the world; we feel no assurance that she is not destined to see the end of them all. She was great and respected before the Saxon had set foot on Britain, before the Frank had passed the Rhine, when Grecian eloquence still flourished in Antioch, when idols were still worshipped in the temple of Mecca ... (Whale, 1980:9).

Interestingly, Lord Macaulay was not even remotely Catholic when he wrote such a lofty historicity of the papacy. The nature, roles, functions, and features of papal diplomacy today are products of long historical evolutions and vicissitudes. The papacy has had to adjust, readjust, change, adapt, and reinvent itself over the last two millennia. That piece of information would not be a cause of alarm should St. John Henry Newman's sagacity be remembered, "Here below, to live is to change, and to be perfect is to have changed often." The exact genesis of the Holy See's diplomacy is a bone of contention among scholars. Araujo and Lucal (1994:3) trace the commencement of the Holy See's participation in international affairs to Christ's commissioning of His Apostles to preach the Good News to the utmost bounds of the earth (Matthew 28:16–20). Critically, that mandate was missionary in nature, but out of it sprang up the Holy See's immersion in diplomacy. Thus, Vatican diplomacy must be understood in the context of that ecclesiological mission of the Church.

Some scholars argue that the "Edict of Milan" (313 A.D.) marked the official immersion of the Holy See in international politics. In support of that line, scholars of global politics Keith A. Hamilton and Richard Langhorne write, "With the conversion of the Roman Empire to Christianity, the traditional universal authority of Rome was joined by a new and sacred role as representative of God; and gave to both the empire and emperor a limitless scope" (2005:15). Since nature knows no vacuum (*natura non facit vacuum*), with the split of the Roman Empire in the fourth century and the failure of the Holy Roman Emperor, the pope assumed the role of a temporal leader of part of the Roman Empire. The Holy See's assumption of temporal responsibility, coupled with her divine ecclesiological mission, immensely shaped her diplomacy.

In the early ecumenical councils of the Church, convened, ironically, by emperors, empresses, and regents, and not the popes, the Holy See sent legates as papal representatives. Pope Sylvester I was represented by the Roman priests Vitus and Vicentius as his legates at the Council of Nicaea in 325 A.D. (Tanner, 1990:2). There were papal representatives to the emperors of Constantinople beginning in 453 A.D., but they were not thought of as ambassadors (Cardinale, 1976). In medieval times, the pope and the Holy Roman emperor were the two main influential actors in *Republica Christiana*. By the end of the sixteenth century, the pope was arguably the most influential leader in Christendom or the Commonwealth of Nations due to the failure of the Roman emperor to hold states together, as well as the numerous attacks and opposition they faced from successive popes (Araujo & Lucal, 1994:18).

The fall of Constantinople to the Turks in 1453 marked a turning point in the history of papal diplomacy. The fall meant that *Republica Christiana* was threatened, and a rapid rescue action was needed. The Peace of Augsburg in 1555 A.D. did not help the course of papal diplomacy. It actually signified the end of the medieval community of Christendom. Its principle, *cuius regio eius religio* ("the religion of the king is the religion of the land"), invited Christian rulers to take more responsibility for religious affairs within their own territories. The phrase *nullus alius quam rex possit episcopo demandare inquisitionem faciendam* ("no other than the king can command the bishop to make an inquisition") was born from this history.

The Treaty of Westphalia (1648) signaled the end of Christendom. It established the normative structure, or constitution, of modern world politics. The end of the Commonwealth of Nations also marked the end of the role of the pope as the unifying unit in Christian Europe. The emergence of sovereign states is the principal legacy of the Peace of Westphalia. According to historian Carl Conrad Eckhardt, the Treaty of Westphalia marked the secularization of politics because the Catholic and Protestant princes ignored the protest of the pope against the treaties of Münster and Osnabruck, which subsequently surfaced as fundamental laws of Europe (Araujo & Lucal, 1994:39).

With the Treaty of Westphalia, the Holy See shifted its role from being the leader of the *Republica Christiana* to that of the highest moral authority in the world, practicing neutrality and more pacifism in international affairs. Pope Innocent X dismissed the Westphalian settlement as "Null, reprobate and devoid of meaning for all time" (Baylis *et.al*, 2008:23). One can surmise that the pope's blatant attack on the Peace of Westphalia was for the very reason that it curtailed some of the authority and power enjoyed by the pope in Christendom.

Seemingly contrary to the view of his Jesuit confreres (Araujo and Lucal), Robert Graham argued that the Treaty of Westphalia excluded the papacy from a direct role in the political community, but it failed in its mission to entirely laicize diplomacy (1959:163). With the evolution of sovereign states, slogans such as *rex in regno suo est imperator* ("the king is emperor in his own kingdom") became the maxims. European writers such as Hugo Grotius and Thomas Hobbes argued that it was not God but the king who was truly sovereign. Nevertheless, papal diplomacy declined after the Peace of Westphalia in 1648.

The history of pontifical diplomacy has been intermittently picturesque and grotesque due to historical vicissitudes during the last two millennia. Evidential records reveal that Christianity was the main unifying factor of Europe and the pope was the most influential figure in Christendom. There were times when the pope was the main arbiter and judge of legal relations among sovereigns. During the suzerain papacy, all concordats and treaties were subject to papal approval or annulment (Araujo & Lucal, 1994:21). Pope Boniface VIII managed to subject all Christian kings to the papacy so that they had to pay tributes (Burgman, 2010:213).

After his excommunication in 1077, Holy Roman Emperor Henry IV was forced to visit Pope Gregory VII's residence at Canossa, where he waited for three days to present himself barefoot in the snow to receive the pope's absolution. Pope Gregory was a no-nonsense, austere pontiff and was once addressed by one of his associates as "my holy Satan." Although popes invested and excommunicated kings, kings also made and unmade popes. This explains why, in his analysis of Caesaropapism, political scientist Francis Fukuyama recorded that of the twenty-five popes who held office immediately before 1059 A.D., twenty-one were appointed by emperors and five were dismissed by them (2011:264–65).

On the other hand, papal involvement in secular affairs has been considered anachronistic by some temporal powers down through the ages. This explains why pontiffs have often struggled to assert their independence, while temporal powers have systematically devised myriad mechanisms to lord power over the Church and maintain their independence from the papacy (papal supremacy): *Gallicanism, Febronianism, Caesaropapism, Regalism, Erastianism,* and *Jurisdictionalism* (Kent & Pollard, 1994:3). Pierre Pithou's eighty-three propositions contained in the Liberties of the "Gallican" Church aimed at limiting the power of the papacy. Its famous device was: "One faith, one law, one king" (Murray, 2003:5). *Febronianism* was devised to expand the authority of the national churches at the expense of the primacy of the papacy (Graham, 1959:222). In his *History of the Popes,* Freiherr von Pastor (1854–1928) wryly noted that *Febronianism* handed the Church to secular arms. The practical meaning of Caesaropapism is that political authorities have the power of appointment over ecclesiastical ministers, and this was the case throughout Europe during the early medieval epoch (the investiture conflict) (Fukuyama, 2012:263). It was informed by the principle of *imperator est episcopus rerum externarum* ("the emperor is the bishop of external things").

The Congress of Vienna of 1815 asserted the important role of the Holy See in international diplomacy. Riots in 1848 compelled Pope Pius IX to flee to Gaeta in the Kingdom of Naples. While in the Eternal City, the constituent assembly of February 9, 1849, declared that the papacy had forfeited her responsibility as a temporal ruler (Graham, 1959:180). This was the first phase of the "Roman Question." The French Revolution of 1789 did not do the papacy any good either. Napoleon's ambitions to put an end to the papacy only added salt to its already deep wounds. Italian nationalism, which led to the sequestration of the Papal States (1870), a symbol of the pope's sovereignty, could not leave the historical role of the Holy See in diplomacy unscathed.

Pope Pius IX's retreat within the Vatican walls, during which he was euphemistically referred to—chiefly by himself—as the "Prisoner of the Vatican," was his final reaction to all the ignominious twists of pontifical diplomacy in the 19th century. The medieval influence of the papacy became a relic of its former self within the tiny square of the Vatican City in the last quarter of the nineteenth century. Even more ironic is that the death agonies of the Papal States freed pontiffs from the horrendous social responsibilities of those States. In a typical Augustinian and Catholic paradox, it was a *felix culpa* (happy fault), "O happy loss of Papal States." *Felix culpa* is a Latin phrase that comes from the words *felix*, meaning "happy," and *culpa*, meaning "fault." The phrase, "*O felix culpa*," is derived from the writings of Saint Augustine of Hippo regarding the Fall of Man, the source of original sin, "For God judged it better to bring good out of evil than not to permit any evil to exist" (*Melius enim iudicavit de malis benefacere, quam mala nulla esse permittere*). The phrase also appears in the *Exsultet* of the Easter Vigil, "O happy fault, O necessary sin of Adam, which gained for us so great a Redeemer" (*O felix culpa quae talem et tantum meruit habere redemptorem*).

At the Paris Conference of 1856, which put an end to the Crimean War, Count Cavour raised the issue of the "Roman Question." By 1870, the Papal States were confiscated and Pope Pius IX famously called himself "a prisoner of the Vatican" and did not venture out of Rome thereafter. Thus, the "Roman Question" was fully in existence. The Italian government attempted to compensate the papacy for its loss of territorial possession in what came to be known as the "Laws of Guarantee" (1871), but it was rejected by Pope Pius IX. Church historian Robert Graham noted that the "Laws of Guarantee" conferred nothing upon the pope which he did not already possess by virtue of international law (1959:197). The situation remained unfixed until 1929, when the Lateran Treaty was signed.

During the period of the "Roman Question" (1870–1929), Italy worked tirelessly to ensure that the Holy See did not take part in multilateral conferences for fear that the Holy See would use those forums and platforms to table the issue of the seizure of the Papal States. This explains why, when the Queen of the Netherlands invited the Holy See to the Hague Conference of 1899, Italy threatened to stage a boycott of the conference if the Holy See was represented. At the end of the deliberations, however, a letter from the Holy See was read to the Conference delegates, the Italian threat notwithstanding. Nevertheless, even without any territorial jurisdiction during the six decades of the Roman Question, many nations and states continued their diplomatic relations with the Holy See (Graham, 1959:93). The Holy See and various states entered into concordats, and popes acted as arbitrators in a number of territorial disputes (Morley, 1980:9). French journalist André Frossard beautifully expresses some blessings (*felix culpa*), which came with the loss of Papal States, "It was an interesting trade-off, that the papacy had to divest itself of its territorial heritage for the sake of a united Italy and watch those lands shrink to the forty-four gilded hectares of Vatican City, while at the same time its power literally expanded right up into the skies—the more real estate the papacy lost, the more influential the office became" (1990:50). The practice of the "Prisoner of the Vatican" started by Pope Pius IX was continued by successive pontiffs until the election of Paul VI in 1963.

The saintly Pope Pius X (1903–1914), repeatedly thought of suppressing papal diplomacy during his pontificate. Due to all the twists in pontifical diplomacy, Haron-Feiertag non-infallibly concluded his eulogy of papal diplomacy with these unequivocal words of condolence, "Papal diplomacy is dead, may its soul rest in peace" (2009:2). However, the prestige of the papacy rose tremendously in the 19th and 20th centuries. Pope Benedict XV (1914–1922) worked hard to put an end to the First World War, but to no avail. However, his "Peace Note" of 1917 resonated with the Fourteen Points Speech of U.S. President Woodrow Wilson, which led to the formation of the League of Nations in 1919. The Decrees and Constitutions of the Second Vatican Council (1962–1965) have been important in the history of Vatican diplomacy in the second half of the last century. The prestige of papal diplomacy rose even higher during the pontificate of Saint John Paul II (1978–2005), even though the Holy See is a unique case under international law.

The Unique International Juridical Personality of the Holy See

Giovanni Cardinal Lajolo defines the Apostolic See as "the institutionalized manifestation of the pope's supreme authority over the whole Catholic Church and his sovereign authority to act in the name of the Church" (2005:3). It is a unique entity since the Church understands itself to be a divinely initiated institution. The Holy See is a spiritual entity since it transcends geographical boundaries and it is not bound by territoriality.

The pope engages in diplomacy not as a temporal sovereign, but as the highest moral authority in the world. It was with the emergence of nation states during the Peace of Westphalia and its clear definition in the Congress of Vienna (1815) that the pope assumed his very singular role of engaging in diplomacy solely on the basis as head of the Catholic Church. In the analysis of Graham Robert, "The papacy was exercising a form of sovereignty long before that word took on the clear-cut political and juridical meaning it was later to have" (Weigel, 2001). In his address to the 34th General Assembly of the United Nations in 1979, Saint John Paul II explained that the Holy See had been endowed with sovereignty for many centuries. The pontiff then stated the rationale behind the sovereignty of the Apostolic See in the following words: "The territorial extent of that sovereignty is limited to the small State of Vatican City, but the sovereignty itself is warranted by the need of the papacy to exercise its mission in full freedom, and be able to deal with any interlocutor, whether a government or an international organization, without dependence on other sovereignties."

The unique international legal personality of the Holy See is of central importance to the exercise of papal diplomacy. Both the State of Vatican City and the Holy See are subject to international law since both have international juridical personalities. However, both are distinct subjects of international law. The Holy See is a non-territorial institution, while Vatican City is a state. The Holy See preexisted the State of Vatican City since the Church and popes have been in existence for over 2000 years, but Vatican City only came into existence in 1929. John Francis Morley, renowned Seton Hall University Professor of Religious Studies, insightfully distinguished both entities, "The Holy See may be considered the juridic personification of the Church, and Vatican City may be viewed as a state created to assure the absolute and visible independence of the Holy See" (1980:10). Of course, the Holy See and the State of Vatican City are subject to the authority of the pope, who exercises temporal authority as head of Vatican City and spiritual authority as head of the Holy See (Morley, 1980:10). John Morley expresses this beautifully in saying that "the pope combines in himself a unique amalgam of spiritual and temporal authority" (1980:11).

It is important to note that it is the Holy See that engages in international diplomacy, not the State of Vatican City. This explains why the term "Holy See" and not the "Vatican" is used in all the documents of the United Nations pertaining to matters of diplomacy, except in texts related to the International Telecommunications Union and the Universal Postal Union, where the term "Vatican City State" is employed. The Holy See engages in international diplomacy on behalf of the Vatican City State under the formula, "acting on behalf and in the interest of the State of Vatican City" (Lajolo, 2005:6). According to John Allen Jr., the Holy See is the technical term for the Vatican as a global diplomatic entity, with sovereign status and the capacity to enter into formal relations with other states. Heads of state do not send ambassadors to the Vatican, but to the Holy See, since the pope is not just the governor of Vatican City State, but also the spiritual head of the Catholic Church worldwide (2002:217). Papal diplomacy scholars Robert Araujo, S.J. and John Lucal, S.J., point out that it is technically incorrect to use the term "the Vatican" when speaking of the Holy See because it would be analogous to "using a geographic place name for a political entity, such as 'Westminster' for the British Government, or the 'Quai d'Orsay' for the French Foreign Ministry" (2010:51).

The State of Vatican City (*Stato della Città del Vaticano*) was a creation of the Lateran Treaty of 1929. Perhaps a statement from Dag Hammarskjöld, the revered former U.N. chief, succinctly expressed the distinction between both entities, "When I request an audience from the Vatican, I do not go to see the King of Vatican City but the head of the Catholic Church" (Allen, 2004:25). The metaphor of Cardinal Renato Martino could not clarify the relationship between the Holy See and the Vatican any better, "Vatican City is the physical or territorial base of the Holy See, almost a pedestal upon which is posed a much larger and unique independent and sovereign power: that of the Universal Church, respected and esteemed by many, suspected and combated by others, yet always present by its stature, its history, and its influence in the international forum" (Allen, 2004:26).

Robert Araujo, S.J. and John Lucal, S.J., describe the relationship as follows, "Both the Holy See and Vatican City are sovereign
subjects of public international law that are indissolubly united
in the person of the pope, who is both head of state and head of
government in that he possesses fully legislative, judicial, and executive powers" (2010:50). As explicit in Article 3 of the 1929 Lateran Treaty, the Holy See has "full ownership, exclusive
dominion, sovereign authority, and jurisdiction" over the city
state of the Vatican City. Article 24 of the treaty spells out the international aspects of the Holy See and Vatican City:

> With regard to the sovereignty belonging to it in inter-
> national matters, the Holy See declares that it remains
> and shall remain outside all temporal rivalries between
> other states and shall take no part in international con-
> gresses summoned to settle such matters, unless the
> parties in disputes make a mutual appeal to its mission
> of peace; in any case, however, the Holy See reserves
> the right of exercising its moral and spiritual power.
> Consequently, the Vatican City shall always and in any
> event be considered as neutral and inviolable territory.

The Vatican City State is a sovereign state with almost all the
normal attributes of a secular state. It has its own currency, banks,
military in the name of Swiss Guards, and independent radio sta-
tion (Vatican Radio). However, Vatican City State is an anomalous
state because, unlike other states, its sovereignty is ordered to a
sovereign entity of a spiritual nature (Holy See) (Lajolo, 2005:5).
The Vatican City State, *vis-à-vis* international law, frees the Holy
See from pundits against her full participation in international
diplomacy due to not having a territory. However, the Holy See
engages in diplomacy not by virtue of having an inconsequential
or puny territorial endowment of 108.7 acres, but by virtue of the
status of the pope as the highest moral authority in the world.
The Vatican's 108.7 acres of territoriality is mainly centered
around the Basilica of St. Peter and the Vatican Palace, as well as

several other pieces of property throughout Rome (Morley, 1980:9). This territorial endowment affords the pope the independence and space to carry out the mission of the Church without any external influence. After the Lateran Treaty of 1929, Pope Pius XI once said of the Vatican City: it is "the body reduced to the minimum necessary to serve the soul and keep life in being" (Binchy, 1941:270).

The Holy See has an idiosyncratic sovereignty claim. Araujo and Lucal beautifully describe the unique sovereignty status of the Holy See, "What makes the Holy See unlike other sovereigns is that fact that its sovereignty is not restricted to a specific territory. The places where the Holy See exercises its authority transcend a particular territory because it is exercised throughout the world, and this is a reason why the sovereignty of the Holy See has sometimes been described as 'supranational'" (2010:53). The spiritual sovereignty and not the temporal sovereignty of the pope is the basis of his diplomatic recognition among the community of nations. The pope engages in diplomacy because he is the representative of God on earth. In introducing his wife Raisa Maximovna to Pope John Paul II during his visit to the Vatican in 1989, Mikhail Gorbachev, the then head of the atheistic Soviet Union, uttered the following words, "Raisa Maximovna, I have the honor to introduce the highest moral authority on earth" (Weigel, 1999:602).

The Holy See was still an active participant in international diplomacy in the years of the "Roman Question" (1870–1929) even though some states suspended their diplomatic relations with the Holy See during this period. Indeed, the diplomatic corps accredited to the Holy See increased after the seizure of the Papal States in 1870. By 1890, there were 18 permanent diplomatic missions at the Vatican. On the eve of World War I (1914), the number dropped to 14, but quickly rose to 24 by 1921. By the time the Lateran Treaty was struck in 1929, there were 27 permanent diplomatic missions at the Vatican (Graham: 1959:25).

According to Robert Graham, "Vatican diplomacy rests essentially, however, upon the spiritual sovereignty of the Holy See and not upon dominion over a few acres in the heart of Rome" (1959:15). States desire representation at the papal court not because the pope is a territorial sovereign, but because of his role as head of the Roman Catholic Church (Vischer, 1974:625). The status of the Holy See defies the positivist theory of international law, which posits that territoriality is an essential prerequisite for diplomatic engagements by states. That is why Canon 113 §1 of *The Code of Canon Law* states that the legal personality of the Holy See is God-given, or based on divine law, "The Catholic Church and the Apostolic See have the status of a moral person by divine disposition." In October 1965, Pope Paul VI explained to the United Nations General Assembly, the nature and purpose of the Holy See's sovereignty:

> He is your brother, and even one of the least among you, representing as you do sovereign States, for he is vested-if it please you so to think of Us-with only a mute and quasi symbolic temporal sovereignty, only so much as is needed to leave him free to exercise his spiritual mission and to assure all those who treat with him that he is independent of every worldly sovereignty. He has no temporal power, no ambition to compete with you. In point of fact, We have nothing to ask for, no question to raise; at most a wish to express and a permission to request: to serve you, within Our competence, disinterestedly, humbly and in love .... Whatever your opinion of the Roman Pontiff, you know Our mission: We are the bearer of a message for all mankind.

Even though the Holy See is, to some extent, a unique case under international law, it shares some similarities with the Order of Malta, officially known as the Sovereign Military Hospitaller Order of St. John of Jerusalem of Rhodes and of Malta. The origin of the Order dates back to 1048 A.D. Robert Graham argues that the sovereignty of the Order, like the sovereignty of the Holy See, does not rest on territoriality for diplomatic participation. In 1798,

Napoleon, on his way to Egypt, seized the ancient seat of the Order. The sovereignty of the Order is largely ceremonial in nature (1959:26). The head of the Order holds the title of the Grand Master.

Even without any clear-cut territory, the Order of Malta is now settled in Rome with extra-territorial status, just like many universities in the early days of scholasticism in medieval Europe. Philip Ochieng, one of the most widely read persons on the planet, stated, "The term *scholasticism* refers to the Church's theological '*philosophy* that characterized the European Dark Ages, based wholly on the writings of Aristotle, after *scholastic Rome* had posthumously baptized this pre-Christian Greek pundit as an *honorary Christian*'" (*The Daily Nation*, Saturday January 28, 2012).

As of 2022, the Order has diplomatic relations with 112 sovereign states, many of which are non-Catholic. In the third Ordinary Consistory of his pontificate, held on November 20, 2010, Pope Benedict XVI gave the red berretta to Paolo Sardi and appointed him papal representative to the Order of Malta. Notwithstanding, the Order of Malta as a subject of international law is not in the same league as the Holy See, since the pope is a very influential transnational actor. Many states have diplomatic relations with the Order for reasons of tradition, and, in recent times to ease the humanitarian work of the Order.

Atypical Diplomacy:
Diplomacy Unlike Conventional Interstate Diplomacy?

The Holy See has been at the helm of international diplomacy for the last two millennia. However, the diplomacy of the Holy See is singular in nature, and ought to be understood in its own right. It is an "atypical diplomacy." According to international law scholar Rebecca Wallace, the Holy See is an anomaly (1992:76). Many factors account for the incongruity of the Holy See within the fabric of conventional categories of juridical personalities. Papal diplomacy is an "atypical diplomacy," since it cannot be smoothly packaged in the categories of conventional diplomacy and in the framework of international law. The reason for this peculiarity is that papal diplomacy preceded the Peace of Westphalia (1648), which laid the foundation stone for conventional diplomacy in most of its present facets. "Neither the Holy See nor the Vatican City State conveniently fall within traditional explanations of statehood, international personality, or sovereignty" (Araujo & Lucal, 2010:51).

Conventional diplomacy, as conceived and practiced today, gradually took shape after the Peace of Westphalia in 1648, which led to the emergence of nation-states like Poland, Spain, and Portugal. It is important to note that the Holy See was already an active actor in the international diplomatic arena long before the idea of Westphalian states (nation states) was conceived. Since medieval times, the episcopal see of Rome has been recognized as a sovereign entity. However, the uniqueness of ecclesiastical diplomacy does not undermine the audacious heritage of the Holy See as the oldest existing diplomatic entity and moral superpower in the world (Stake, 2006:11).

The Holy See established the earliest permanent diplomatic exchange with the State of Venice in 1500 A.D. Thus, any attempt to snugly knit papal diplomacy into conventional categories is analogous to fitting old wines into new wine skins. It is very important to bracket Rome aside in the study of the practice of diplomacy. In the words of the Protestant Friedrich Kolle in 1938, "Rome was for a long time the best school of diplomacy, the post where apprentices should be sent at the beginning and ambassadors at the climax of their careers." Such sentiment had been raised earlier by the Iron Chancellor Bismarck (Graham, 1959:22). As early as the 16th century, during which time Rome was the diplomatic and geographical center of the world, Cardinal Richelieu's wise advice reads, "It is necessary to act everywhere, near and far, and above all in Rome" (Madison, 1961:95). Some of the factors which show the singularity of papal diplomacy are the aim of papal diplomacy, its personality and nature, instruments of foreign policies, and its diplomatic agents.

CHAPTER THREE
BILATERAL AND MULTILATERAL DIPLOMACY
OF THE HOLY SEE

The Holy See, as a non-state sovereign entity and full subject of international law, has traditionally been an active player in multilateral, or summit diplomacy. She takes part in most conferences organized by the United Nations. In October 1965, Pope Paul VI was the first pontiff to address the U.N. General Assembly, while Saint John Paul II did the same in 1979 and in 1995. Vatican delegates were very vocal in the Conference on Population in Cairo in 1994, and in the Conference on Women and Gender in Beijing in 1995. The Holy See was a founding member of the International Atomic Energy Agency (IAEA) and of the Organization for Security and Cooperation in Europe (OSCE). She enjoys an observer status at the Organization of American States (OAS), and the African Union (AU), and is represented in the Arab League. The Holy See was one of the first diplomatic entities to be admitted to the Executive Committee of the Program of the UN High Commissioner for Refugees (UNHCR) (Lajolo, 2005:21).

Ordinarily, diplomatic relations involving the Holy See are mutual and bilateral; however, the Holy See claims the right, independent of any secular authority, to send its representatives into every part of the world (Morley, 1980:13). The Holy See maintains 180 permanent diplomatic missions abroad, of which 73 are non-residential. She has 106 concrete missions, some of which are accredited not only to the host state, but also to one or more other states or international organizations. Prior to December 2010, she had "relations of a special nature" with the Russian Federation and the Palestinian Liberation Organization (PLO). Today, Russia has full diplomatic relations with the Holy See. Following a treaty negotiated by the Holy See and the State of Palestine in March 2015, the Holy See has now switched its diplomatic recognition from the Palestine Liberation Organization to the State of Palestine. "This is a very important recognition as the Vatican has a very important political status that stems from its spiritual status," said President Abbas' senior aide, Nabil Shaath. "We expect more EU countries to follow" (Winfield, 2015).

China terminated diplomatic ties with the Holy See in 1951 after the communist takeover in 1949. The government in Beijing is preoccupied with the notion of uncompromised sovereignty, and thereby eschews any external interference. This explains why China constantly cracks down on bishops appointed by Rome and insists on the prerogatives of the government in Beijing in the appointment of bishops. The Holy See's establishment of diplomatic ties with Taiwan exacerbated the sour relations between the Holy See and China because of the Chinese traditional "one-China policy." The relationship is much more cordial, however, since the seemingly secretive "provisional" agreement between the Vatican and Beijing was sealed on September 22, 2018, and extended for two more years on October 22, 2020. Even though the full content of the said deal is as hidden as the holy grail, one of its key points is said to be the involvement of the Vatican and Beijing in the appointment of bishops in China. Ordinarily, it has been the prerogative of the pope to appoint bishops worldwide without much input from national governments. Through this agreement, the Vatican is seemingly placing the things of God on Caesar's altar. The Vatican and churchmen like the revered Polish Primate Stefan Wyszyński worked hard to limit state interference in the management of the Church's affairs in communist eastern Europe. In 1953, at the height of communist oppression of the Church in Poland, Wyszyński sent a bold letter to Bolesław Bierut, Poland's communist leader, in which he unwaveringly refused to subordinate the Church to the authorities, declaring the famous "Non possumus!" (We cannot.)

Cardinal Joseph Zen, retired bishop of Hong Kong, has been a staunch critic of the accord. Cardinal Zen's bone of contention is that the Vatican struck such an important deal with a cunning and secretive government without any input from prelates in China who are on the ground and understand the situation better than the Vatican's Secretary of State, Cardinal Pietro Parolin, and other curialists. Further, Zen claims that neither he nor other bishops in China know the content of the agreement. "Never appease a dictator" is an important maxim in international politics. Appeasement of dictators has often proven disastrous and costly throughout history. It is the hope of many that the said agreement is not an appeasement of Beijing.

The Holy See does not maintain diplomatic relations with Saudi Arabia or Vietnam because of ideological differences. Although Saint John Paul II participated in summit or conference diplomacy, he was keen on the establishment and reestablishment of bilateral diplomatic ties. At his election in 1978, the Holy See had diplomatic relations with 84 states. At the end of his papacy in 2005, the Holy See had diplomatic relations with 174 diplomatic entities. There is no facet of diplomacy, from environmental, media, and cultural, to private diplomacy, which is beyond the competence of the Holy See. However, the diplomacy of the Holy See has some peculiarities and does not fit snugly into the categories of conventional diplomacy. It is diplomacy unlike conventional interstate diplomacy.

The Goal of Papal Diplomacy

Realists, such as Hans Morgenthau and Kenneth Waltz, argue that states engage in diplomacy and behave the way they do because of national interests (1948). Whatever their form of government, "states act in their national interest" (Nye, 2007:49). The legal maxim states that, "The safety of the state is the supreme law" (*salus rei publicae suprema lex*). Satow defined diplomacy as "the civilized pursuit of state interests ... directed to the defense of national welfare" (1911:22).

The foreign policies of states are said to be effective and efficient if they can influence the behaviors of other units in the international system. As early as 515 A.D., Emperor Anastasios wrote, "There is a law that orders the emperor to lie and to violate his oath if it is necessary for the wellbeing of the empire" (Wozniack, 1984:196). Ermolao Barbaro the Younger (1454–1493), Venetian humanist and diplomat, similarly asserted, "The first duty of an ambassador is … to do, say, advise, and think whatever may best serve the preservation and aggrandizement of his own state" (Craig & George, 1995).

Liberalists such as Michael Doyle and Robert Keohane posit that universal interest is the rationale for the foreign policies of states. Unlike liberalists or idealists, realists look at soft power as a luxury in international diplomacy. Some diplomats think that hard power via punishment, war, threats, and sanctions is the best recipe for managing conflicts in what scholars like George Alexander, Robert Art, and Patrick Cronin call coercive diplomacy or gunboat diplomacy (2007:299). The realist school holds that humanitarian intervention and assistance, which states dish out due to *moral imperatives*, is informed by the principle of national interest and reputational pressures. In his *Discourses*, Italian diplomat and author Niccolò Machiavelli argued that princes were obliged to strive for a *reputation* for integrity in their dealings with others, since a faithful *reputation* led princes to be courted even by enemies (Berridge, 2001:14).

The oscillating nature and double standards in states' foreign policy formulation and implementation is informed by national interest. Traditionally, informed by George Washington's famous Farewell Address (1796), and the *Monroe Doctrine* (1823), the United States foreign policy was isolationist and non-interventionist. In his last address to the nation, George Washington, America's first president, admonished the country to steer clear of permanent alliances, and to practice neutrality and non-intervention in its foreign relations, "The great rule of conduct for us in regard to foreign nations is—in extending our commercial relations—to have with them as little political connection as possible." This partly explains why the United States did not join the League of Nations.

The Monroe Doctrine was articulated on December 2, 1823, in President James Monroe's seventh annual message to Congress. The European powers, according to Monroe, were obligated to respect the Western Hemisphere as the United States' sphere of interest. At the same time, the doctrine noted that the United States would neither interfere with existing European colonies nor meddle in the internal affairs of European countries. In 1821, John Quincy Adams, Secretary of State to James Monroe, and the real architect of the Monroe Doctrine, declared:

> Wherever the standard of freedom and independence has been or shall be unfurled, there will be America's heart, her benedictions, and her prayers. But she does not go abroad in search of monsters to destroy. She is the well-wisher to the freedom and independence of all. She is the champion and vindicator only of her own.

U.S. foreign policy only became interventionist during the World Wars. During the Cold War, the U.S. top foreign policy was dubbed "Containment." It was a policy designed to prevent the spread of communism. Democracy was not a top policy priority of the U.S. during the Cold War (1947–1989). This explains why the U.S., via the Military Assistance Program (MAP), supported friendly tyrants, such as Mobutu Sese Seko of former Zaire and Manuel Noriega of Panama, whom they later ousted when the Cold War ended. A Machiavellian principle states that "there are no permanent friends and foes in diplomacy and politics, but only permanent interests." Osama Bin Laden, the most wanted man on the U.S. red list until his death, was formerly an ally of the United States.

With the demise of the Cold War, western democracy became a top priority of U.S. foreign policy. The Machiavellian realist principle of the end justifying the means explains why states exhibit double standards in diplomatic practices. For a long time, Egypt, under the despot Hosni Mubarak, was one of the main beneficiaries of U.S. aid in Africa because of its strategic position in the Middle East and control over the Nile. However, according to human rights watchdog Amnesty International, Egypt had a very bad record of human rights abuses in Africa, especially during Mubarak's three decades of dictatorship (1981–2011).

Marxist and neo-Marxist theorists such as Immanuel Wallerstein taught that class interest is the main preoccupation of the various classes of production such as the bourgeoisies, the comprador bourgeoisies, and the proletariats (Dougherty & Pfaltzgraff, 2001:428). The foreign policies of dependent states are reactionary and not proactive because of their dependence on those at the core. The sovereignty of states at the periphery is consistently trampled by states at the core. Dependency theorists such as Andrè Gunder Frank define dependency as a scenario whereby "the growth and expansion of some economies (in the periphery) is conditioned by the growth and expansion of others (in the core) in the global economy."

Unlike for secular states, national interest is not in any way the main preoccupation of the Holy See. Addressing the ambassador of Georgia to the Holy See on December 6, 2001, Saint John Paul II succinctly stated the main mission of the Holy See, "The Holy See's approach is distinctive because it is not tied to national interest of any kind, but seeks instead the common good of the whole human family" (Dupuy, 2004:98). According to papal diplomacy scholars such as Valerio Valeri, the Holy See's diplomatic activities are informed by Catholic interests, which basically constitute upholding the absolute values of peace, respect for life, human rights and dignity, common good, dedication to the principles of justice and charity, and religious tolerance among others (Valeri, 1956:23–24).

Robert Graham observes that the Holy See is a religious society whose goals are to be found in the supernatural and the world beyond (1959:6). While addressing a symposium on papal diplomacy on November 12, 1998, Saint John Paul II stated, "Papal diplomacy has no other goal than to promote, to extend around the world and to defend human dignity and all forms of human social life, from family, the workplace and the school, to the local community and to regional, national and international life" (Dupuy, 2004:97).

Furthermore, papal diplomacy is informed by the Holy See's ecclesiological mandate and not by issues of state survivability, security, and national interests. *Ecclesiology* is a Greek word for the study of the nature of the Church. The Holy See will certainly not engage in any diplomatic activity which is contrary to her ecclesiology, upholding the absolute values (Kwitny, 1997:10). However, Canon 3 of *The Code of Canon Law* states that "canons of the Code do not abrogate, nor do they derogate from, agreement entered into by the Apostolic See with nations or other civil entities. For this reason, these agreements continue in force as hitherto, notwithstanding any contrary provisions of this Code."

In his address to the Diplomatic Corps accredited to the Holy See on January 14, 1980, Saint John Paul II maintained that the guiding principle of the diplomatic activities of the Holy See is succinctly summed up by the Second Vatican Council: "The Church, by reason of her competence, is not identified with any political system. It is at once the sign and safeguard of the transcendental dimension of the human person" (*Gaudium et spes*, n.26).

The Holy See's Foreign Policy Instruments

Foreign policy is the externalization or extension of domestic policies. It refers to the externalized policies of states. Foreign policies guide the behavior of states in the external milieu or beyond territorial borders. The goal of foreign policy is to promote the interests of a single political community or state in world politics by influencing the behavior of other units in the international system. Foreign policy is an attribute possessed solely by states. International regimes and actors, such as the World Bank, Law of the Sea, the United Nations, and multinational corporations do not have foreign policies. States pursue foreign policies via diplomatic, military, cultural, and economic instruments, among other means.

Realists posit that military instruments such as war, military assistance programs, and military bases are the most important foreign policy instruments. Traditionally, the test of a great power was "strength for war" (Mufson, 2001). As American political scientist Joseph Nye Jr. writes, "War was the ultimate game in which the cards of international politics were played and estimates of relative power were proven" (2002:24). The realists employ slogans such as "power is might and might is right." Liberalists such as Woodrow Wilson and Michael Doyle argued that diplomacy should be the pivotal instrument of foreign policy. Constructivists and primordialists remain adamant that cultural instruments such as international exchange programs and scholarship schemes matter in the economy of foreign policy.

The Soviet Union probably named its Cold War scholarship program after the legendary Congolese Prime Minister, Patrice Lumumba, because of his pro-Soviet Union leanings before his assassination. Lumumba was executed on January 17, 1961, by Belgian police Commissioner Gerald Soete. Lumumba's body was later sawed and doused in acid by his executioner to obliterate any evidence. His assassination has gone down as Africa's "most important assassination of the 20th century." The culpability of U.S. President Eisenhower's administration in the assassination scheme is corroborated by CIA director Allen Dulles' confession, "… we conclude that his (Lumumba's) removal must be an urgent and prime objective" (Mutunga, *Daily Nation*, January 28, 2012). The Democratic Republic of Congo achieved her independence from Belgium in 1960. At the time of independence, there were only a handful of Congolese university graduates. Although Lumumba was intelligent and visionary with foresight and charisma, he barely went past primary education. The lack of technocrats and other qualified personnel at the time of independence partly explains the decades of unending wars in the oil-rich Democratic Republic of Congo.

The concept of soft and hard power is the brainchild of Robert Keohane and Joseph Nye Jr. Hard power is pursued via inducements ("carrots") or via sanctions and threats ("sticks"). In 2011, the United States' embassy in Kenya made public the names of some government officials who could not be granted U.S. visas allegedly because of their efforts to slow down constitutional reforms in Kenya. That is an apt example of hard power. Joseph Nye Jr. defines soft power as "the art of getting others to want what you want" (2007:62). Elements of Nye's definition of soft power resonate with Vance Packard's definition of leadership, "The art of getting others to want to do something that you believe should be done" (Lewis, 2007:4). Soft power co-opts people rather than coerces them (Nye, 2002:28).

According to Nye, the recipes of soft power include resources such as the attraction of ideas and the art of packaging political agendas in ways that shape the preferences of others as the constructivists posit. The art of shaping the preferences of others is based on resources such as culture, ideology, and institutions. In his encyclical *Redemptoris Missio* (The Church's Missionary Mandate), Saint John Paul II laid emphasis on the Holy See's soft power in the following words: "The Church proposes, she imposes nothing ... she respects individuals and cultures, and she honors the sanctuary of conscience" (1992).

Hard and soft power are distinct, related, and not mutually exclusive. While hard power twists the arms, soft power twists the minds and hearts of people. The moral authority of the pope and the international prestige of the papacy are essential resources of the Holy See's soft power. According to Nye Jr., "The soft power of the Vatican did not wane as the size of the Papal States diminished in the nineteenth century" (2007:63). *Ipso facto*, the soft power of the Holy See is not simply a reflection of its hard power.

The efficacy of soft power does not diminish because it is less transferable, non-tangible, and less coercive. In the words of former German Chancellor Otto von Bismarck, *"imponderabilia"* (soft power) "often have more influence in politics than gold or military force." Church historian Robert Graham concluded that "the imponderables represented by the moral authority of the Holy See were an important factor in his ultimate decision to liquidate

the Holy See in these relations, perhaps more so than in the case of the ordinary foreign minister, for the papal Secretary of State is more than just a foreign minister" (1959:127). Pope Pius IX's *motu proprio* of June 12, 1847, outlined the main role of the Secretary of State as follows: "The Secretariat of State is the center of all the matters that are treated by the various ministers; it is the organ for the publication of the laws and for the transmission of the orders emanating from the sovereign, as well as for relations with the sovereign himself on appeals against the acts and decisions of the various dicasteries (papal organs)" (Graham, 1959:136).

It is no secret that Pope Francis has been very determined to reform the Roman Curia. Responding to journalists on the return flight from his pilgrimage to the Holy Land on June 3, 2014, the pontiff said that he wanted to "combine the dicasteries, for example, to streamline the organization a bit." This was one of the changes studied in the reform of the Curia and in the governance of the universal Church. The supreme pontiff has selected a council of eight cardinals, the "C8," to assist him in reforming the Curia.

As part of the reform agenda, Pope Francis has created the Secretariat for the Economy to oversee all economic activities of the Holy See and the Vatican City State. It is, after the Secretariat of State, the second dicastery named a *secretariat*, an indication of its importance relative to other parts of the Curia. George Cardinal Pell, the former archbishop of Sydney, Australia, was named the Secretariat's premier Prefect. As of 2022, Juan Antonio Guerrero, S.J., is the Prefect of the Secretariat for the Economy. A key mandate of this Secretariat is to bring about some financial sanity in the Vatican by carrying out "economic audit and supervision" of offices of the Roman Curia, the Vatican City State, and institutions connected to the Holy See. The new Secretariat is also tasked with the responsibility of making "policies and procedures regarding procurement and the allocation of human resources" for the Curia and Vatican City State (Reese, 2014). The conduct of papal diplomacy has not been immune to criticism.

Objections to Papal Diplomacy

Although the Holy See is the oldest existing diplomatic entity, its participation in international diplomacy has perennially been a subject of criticism by some institutions and individuals. The very fact that popes engage in international diplomacy has been dubbed anachronistic and oxymoronic by a plethora of stakeholders and scholars. *Inter alia*, critics, skeptics, and cynics base their reservations on the fact that by feasting from the sanctuary of God and on the altar of Caesar simultaneously, popes contradict Jesus' wise counsel to the Pharisees and the supporters of Herod to "give unto Caesar what belongs to Caesar and to God what belongs to God" (Matthew 22:22).

Critics hold that the pope is a spiritual leader who should not be actively involved in temporal affairs, or in the words of Robert Audi and Nicholas Wolterstorff, "No religion in the public square." It is the raison d'être why in a famous one-on-one with French Premier Pierre Laval, in the 1930s, Josef Stalin, the communist chief, bemused by the pope's temporal and spiritual influence, exclaimed, "How many divisions has the pope?" Such sentiments were repeated by Winston Churchill of England (Pollard & Kent, 1994:2). American Catholic philosopher Michael Novak once asserted that Stalin feared the "moral power" of the pope more than he feared Hitler (Roth, 2002:238).

Why does the pope send and receive diplomats while other leaders of world religions do not enjoy such prerogatives? John L. Allen Jr. wryly notes, "If the archbishop of Canterbury, or the president of the Lutheran World Federation, visits Madras or Jakarta, he has to catch cabs like everyone else. If the pope visits, he's a celebrity" (2004:20). The pope is arguably the most recognizable spiritual leader in the world, with the strongest bully pulpit and the most significant presence in the mass media. The pope is head of the Catholic Church, which is one of the largest and oldest institutions in the world. The pope sends and receives diplomats because he is a head of state, the Vatican City State. Most if not all religious leaders in the world are not heads of state.

According to John Allen Jr., the pope plays a unique, even if un-declared and sometimes controversial, role as a spokesperson for the religious community (Allen, 2002:20). The London Tablet has called John Allen Jr. "the most authoritative writer on Vatican affairs in the English language," and renowned papal biographer George Weigel has labelled him "the best Anglophone Vatican re-porter ever" (CRUX, 2015).

The great Indian anti-colonial national Mahatma Gandhi once said, "Anyone who says they are not interested in politics is like a drowning man who insists he is not interested in water." Aris-totle taught that human beings are political animals. Thus, even those dubbed as the leadership of the Church are still political an-imals. Although the Holy See engages in international diplomacy, she maintains the "principle of neutrality" when dealing with dis-putes between nations, which makes her the ideal mediator. This explains why she enjoys the privileged position as the only non-state permanent observer at the United Nations. However, is there a facet of life which cannot be informed by ethics and an ap-peal to the consciences of people, and which is the primary mis-sion of the Holy See's diplomacy?

While celebrating Mass in Victory Square during his first visit to his native Poland in 1979, Saint John Paul II unequivocally stated the role of the Church and the Holy See in international diplomacy and other facets of life in the following words, "One cannot exclude Christ from the history of man in any part of the world at any geographical longitude or latitude. Excluding Christ from the history of man is an act against man. Without Him it is impossible to understand the history of Poland" (John-Stevas, 1982:39–40). Can one exclude Christ from the conduct of interna-tional diplomacy? After the pope voiced that conviction in Poland, the applause from the crowd was overwhelming and lasted several minutes unremittingly. At that point, the commu-nist-controlled Moscow TV, which was broadcasting the Mass live, cut off its live feed. Communism was ignominiously de-feated, harassed, and humiliated in its own backyard without the slightest use of force.

In his *The Drama of Atheist Humanism* (1944), Henri de Lubac defended papal diplomacy using a quote by Dostoevsky, "Man cannot organize the world for himself without God; without God he can only organize the world *against man*. Exclusive humanism is inhuman humanism" (De Lubac, 1963:ix). Fascism, Nazism, and communism are expressions of atheistic humanism. According to de Lubac, Europe today is experiencing a civilizational crisis because of atheistic humanism, whose goal is to jettison God from the activities of the state. It is for that very reason that Saint John Paul II insisted unrelentingly, although without much success, on the insertion of the "Invocatio Dei" clause in the preamble of the European Constitution (Kaiser, 2006:xx). The pope wanted the word "God" mentioned in the European Constitution, since Christianity played a role in the formation of present-day Europe. This is one concrete example of how the pope engages in diplomacy as the representative of God on earth and to steer the conscience of humankind. Papal biographer George Weigel argues that the Church constantly asks the world to consider the possibility of its conversion (1992:17).

Papal diplomacy scholars John F. Pollard and Peter C. Kent argued that during Vatican II (1962–1965) there were some voices advocating for the elimination of papal nuncios and representatives, and that they be replaced by local bishops or episcopal conferences. The critics argued that local ecclesiastical officials could perform the same functions. John Morley points out that it is theoretically possible to cede such roles and functions to local ecclesiastics. He argues that local Church leaders, however, oftentimes do not have the needed preparation and training to perform such tasks (1980:12). The diplomats of the Holy See are trained in the reputable Pontifical Ecclesiastical Academy, and are among the best-trained in the world. Furthermore, many of the issues between Church and state are transnational in nature and involve international law and so, *ipso facto*, are beyond the competence of local ecclesiastical authority (Cardinale, 1974:20).

On March 11, 1985, the Holy Office issued a *Notification on the book "Church: Charism and Power" by Father Leonardo Boff, O.F.M.*

The Holy Office found Boff's book wanting in the following ecclesiological areas: the structure of the Church, the concept of dogma, the exercise of sacred power, and the prophetic role. The *Notification* concludes: "In making the above publicly known, the Congregation also feels obliged to declare that the options of L. Boff analyzed here endanger the sound doctrine of the faith, which this Congregation has the task of promoting and safeguarding." Brazilian theologian Leonardo Boff was subsequently invited to Rome for a "colloquy," or conversation, about his book. The invite offered him the possibility of a dialogue for the sake of clarification. When Cardinal Ratzinger of the Holy Office sent his secretary, Joseph Clemens, to fetch Boff from a Franciscan house in Rome, Boff jokingly asked, when he climbed in the car with Clemens, if handcuffs would be necessary.

Although he did observe a year of canonical silence as instructed by the Holy See, Leonardo Boff did not only demand a recall of all nuncios by the Holy See, but also for the dissolution of papal sovereignty. Perhaps as a gesture of retaliation after his license to teach as a Catholic theologian was withdrawn, Boff's lynching satire read, "Ecclesiastical power is cruel and merciless. It forgets nothing, it forgives nothing. It demands everything" (Kaiser, 2006:127). In Marxist parlance, Boff called for "class struggle" inside Catholicism to redistribute authority.

After his tumultuous dealings with the Vatican concerning the orthodoxy of his writings, Bernard Häring satirically asserted that he preferred his days in Hitler's courts to the halls of the Holy Office. Häring suggested that the Holy Office go on sabbatical for few years. The renowned German theologian recommended that "Amnesty International should have a look inside the Vatican. The Holy Office is a poisoned lake where healthy fish cannot swim. It is a combination of ignorance and arrogance, run by ecclesiastics who are career terrorists" (Kaiser, 2006:178). However, such views did not go far and were swiftly forgotten.

In 2000, the liberal group Catholics for a Free Choice organized a campaign aimed at revoking the Holy See's diplomatic status. The campaign was cleverly entitled, "The See Change

Campaign." The U.S. Congress vetoed the campaign and only California Democratic Rep. Pete Stark voted in favor of the campaign (Allen, 2004:46). These critiques notwithstanding, the Holy See is still a major player in the field of diplomacy. The fact that members of the Catholic Church live in states across the world makes the Church's diplomacy not only legitimate but also an effective means of fulfilling its role (Cardinale, 1974:18). There is hardly any major public policy upon which the Holy See is not expected to make a pronouncement. Vaticanologist John Allen Jr. recorded that in the weeks leading up to the U.S.-led invasion in Iraq in 2003 "diplomatic heavyweights, shuttled in and out of the Vatican like clients at a popular deli: Tony Blair, Joschka Fisher, Silvio Berlusconi, Jose Maria Aznar, Mohammed Reza Khatami (speaker of the Iranian parliament and brother of the country's president), Kofi Annan, and even Tarik Aziz" (2004:21). All those dignitaries flocked into the Vatican for a cup of coffee with the pope and to hear his final judgment on Bush's planned Iraqi invasion. Pope John Paul II was a ready guide to all men and women of good will. He spoke the language that everyone understood, the human language (Onaiyekan, 2016:317).

CHAPTER FOUR

JOHN PAUL II, IDIOSYNCRATIC VARIABLES,
AND PAPAL DIPLOMACY

A Biographical Outlook of John Paul II

In Freudian psychoanalysis, the behavior, actions, attitudes, and orientations of human beings are understandably shaped and molded by their early childhood experiences. A brief exploration of Saint John Paul II's biography and curriculum vitae in this book is more than just biographical information. The pre-papal themes and experiences in the life of Saint John Paul II immensely shaped his conduct of pontifical diplomacy. That is why George Weigel wrote, "Thus in marking the accomplishment of Pope John Paul II, the historian does no disservice to the man or his memory by acknowledging the contexts that produced the conditions for the possibility of John Paul II" (2010:479).

The man now known as Saint John Paul II, Karol Józef Wojtyła, was born in the small Polish city of Wadowice on May 18, 1920. Wadowice was once referred to as "Galician misery" by a Polish writer because the people there often lived on the edge of starvation. The Galician was the Austro-Hungarian section of Poland. Wojtyła was born on a significant day in modern Polish history. Jane Barnes captures it beautifully:

> May 18, 1920, a day called the Polish Miracle. On that day, Marshal Jozef Pilsudski struck a deciding blow in the war against the Soviet Union and seized Kiev. It was Poland's first major military victory in over two centuries. It set in motion events which briefly restored

Poland's independence. Mindful of the nation's turning point, Karol's father gave his new son Pilsudski's middle name. Some people said he also called Karol "Jósef" after Mary's self-sacrificing husband. The confluence of history and religion were significant, as was the moment of Karol's birth (Barnes, 1999).

The history of Poland, if defined by conventional chronology, was conspicuously melancholic due to its shameful legacy of repeated invasion, occupation, resistance and, oftentimes, no internationally recognized borders, occasioned by her incapacity for good governance and diplomacy. Before 1918, the Polish state had not appeared on the map of the world for 125 years, although the Polish nation survived through its religion, culture, people, language, and literature (Weigel, 2010:448).

Just like the history of Poland, Wojtyła's early years were seemingly unfortunate. He was conceived during a time of war pitting the newly independent Republic of Poland against the Soviet Republic (Bernstein & Politi, 1996:17). Death was a constant theme in Wojtyła's early childhood. Most of his maternal uncles and aunts died before Wojtyła was grown enough to know them, "She [Emilia Kaczorowska] watched four of her brothers and sister grow sick, languish and die" (Barnes, 1999). Wojtyła's elder sister, Olga, died in 1914, six years before he was born. She died before she could be christened. Wojtyła's sickly convent-educated mother, Emilia Kaczorowska, took up sewing to help with the family finances. Due to her poor health, she could not devote enough time to the young Wojtyła. According to papal biographers Jane Barnes and Helen Whitney, "She [Wojtyła's mother] was often in bed, suffering from inflammation of both heart and kidney. She was increasingly nervous, melancholy, silent" (1999). She died on April 13, 1929, when Wojtyła was eight. "He found out when he came home one day from grade school. A neighborhood woman came out and hugged him and told him his mother was in heaven" (Noonan, 2005:128). Wojtyła said that the mother was "the soul of home" (Barnes & Whitney, 1999). Interestingly, before she passed on, Emilia prophetically prognosticated, "My Lolek will become a great person." Owing to his diminutiveness, Wojtyła was fondly referred to as "Lolus" and later "Lolek" by his parents and friends. A decade after the death of his mother, Wojtyła wrote a poem about her: "O Mother, my extinct beloved."

Wojtyła's handsome elder brother, Edmund, contracted scarlet fever from a patient while serving as a doctor and died on December 4, 1932. He was a "victim of his profession," as young Karol later wrote in his epitaph. Lolek later revealed to French journalist, André Frossard, "My brother's death probably affected me more deeply than my mother's, because of the peculiar circumstances, which were certainly tragic, and because I was more grown up" (Bernstein & Politi, 1996:27). Edmund's death was a very painful one for Wojtyła. He was close to him and both shared a passion for theatre and soccer.

Sr. Emilia Ehrlich, an Ursuline nun who was Pope John Paul II's English tutor and personal librarian, observed some regular religious coincidences in the death litany in the life of the pope:

> There is an odd regularity to his life. Whenever he has a big religious experience, someone dies or is stricken. His mother died while he was preparing for his first Holy Communion. His brother died when he was preparing to be confirmed. His father died while he was considering the seminary. His great friend, Father [Marian] Jaworski, lost an arm just before he became a bishop or cardinal, I can't remember which. Then there was Bishop [Andrzej] Deskur, who had his stroke just before he was elected pope. What would be great moments for anyone else also [involve] tragedies for him. It is almost as if he were being orphaned again and again (Weigel, 2017:123).

His widowed father, a retired military man known as "the Captain," ensured that Lolek received the love and discipline he could provide. Before Lolek was born, his father had joined a

secret resistance movement which was training riflemen to overthrow the Austro-Hungarian Empire occupying Poland at the
time. On August 30, 1914, Austrian policemen broke into the Wojtyła apartment, humiliatingly beat Karol in front of his wife, and
dragged him off to jail to face charges of stealing weapons and
ammunition from the army. He escaped execution only by feign-
ing madness. That experience prompted the first of a number of
heart attacks that she eventually suffered. Karol Wojtyła Sr. died
in 1941, three months before Wojtyła's twenty-first birthday. Emotionally confiding in French journalist and essayist André
Frossard, Saint John Paul II observed, "at twenty, I had already
lost all the people I loved and even the ones that I might have
loved...." (1982:13).

The circumstances surrounding Wojtyła's childhood paint a
melancholic picture. However, early biographical records portray
a jovial, gregarious, intelligent, pious, and extroverted chap. As
part of his career discernment, Wojtyła matriculated at the prestigious Jagiellonian University to study the Polish language and
letters in 1939. His vocation to the priesthood was slow in coming,
as he later confessed to Frossard, and the defining moment came
only during his meeting with Cardinal Adam Stefan Sapieha,
archbishop of Krakow. Prior to embracing his call to the priesthood, Wojtyła worked in a Solvay chemical plant with a meager
salary during the Nazi occupation (Formicola, 2002:16).

"Clandestinity" and Saint John Paul II's biography are not
mutually exclusive. With the seminaries closed and outlawed
during the war, Wojtyła's subsequent papacy was formed by his
experience as a clandestine seminarian. Clandestine university
student, clandestine member of the Living Rosary under the tutelage of Master Tyranowski, and a clandestine member of the
Rhapsodic Theatre was the predicament of the future pope. "It
was as if Tyranowski had seen his protégé safely onto the path of
destiny before quietly slipping away" (Leighton, 1980:82). On the
feast of All Saints, November 1, 1946, Wojtyła was ordained a
priest by Cardinal Sapieha. Upon returning from his studies in
Rome in June 1948, he was surprisingly appointed vicar of a rural

parish in Niegowić, and it was there that his longtime dedication to the youth ministry started taking root. Seemingly with the hand of Divine Providence, the young Wojtyła swiftly grew in the ecclesiastical ranks and favor. On July 4, 1958, while on a kayaking holiday in the lakes region of northern Poland, Pope Pius XII appointed him as an auxiliary bishop of Kraków. Following the death of Archbishop Eugeniusz Baziak, Pope Paul VI appointed Bishop Wojtyła archbishop of Kraków on January 13, 1964. Wojtyła's participation and contributions to the Second Vatican Council's Decree on Religious Freedom (*Dignitatis humanae*) and the Pastoral Constitution on the Church in the Modern World (*Gaudium et spes*) increased his stature and prestige among the Church's hierarchy. On June 26, 1967, Pope Paul VI created him a cardinal.

Pope Paul VI had great admiration for the young Polish cardinal and appointed him to many commissions and synods in Rome after the Second Vatican Council. Some papal historians hold that he was prepared for the papacy by Paul VI. His international travels gave him a first-hand lesson and knowledge of the joy and suffering of people in various corners of the globe. The year of three popes (1978) saw the surprise election of Wojtyła as pope against all odds. On the intrigue and probing of Franz Cardinal König of Vienna, Wojtyła's former "boss" and primate of the century, Stefan Wyszyński, wrote him off as a "young actor" and a "poet," not papal material. Just like Pope Saint Pius X in 1903, Wojtyła momentarily burst into tears when it became evident that the lot had fallen on him in the Sistine Chapel on October 16, 1978. His election to the papal office was seen by many as a fulfilment of the 19th-century prophesy of the distinguished Polish poet and playwright, Juliusz Slowacki. In 1848, he wrote a prophetic poem, entitled "The Slavic Pope." Here is an excerpt from the poem:

Amidst all the discord,
God sets an immense bell ringing,
He opens the throne to a Slavic Pope ...

Much energy is needed to rebuild the Lord's world
And that is why a Slavik Pope is coming
A brother of the peoples....

Pope John Paul II's twenty-six-and-a-half-year pontificate of
surprises ended on April 2, 2005, 9:37 p.m. Roman time. Perhaps
in line with the doctrine of predestination, papal biographer Tad
Szulc advances that, due to Saint John Paul II's special, extraordinary, and singular biography, a modicum of speculation that
his pre-papal life was a preparation for the Petrine ministry cannot be denied (1995:53). This explains why David Willey's picturesque summation of Wojtyła's biography is a significant verdict,
"He was fifty-eight when he was elected pope, not an age when
a man changes in character or outlook. So, his family, education,
student days, and career as priest, bishop and then cardinal in
Krakow are of more than mere passing biographical interest"
(1992:27). According to Willey, those early themes of his life resur-
faced in his diplomacy as pope. Thus, Saint John Paul II's biography is an important and recurrent component in the analysis of
the role of his idiosyncratic variables in pontifical diplomacy
(1978–2005). He was promptly beatified by Pope Benedict XVI on
Sunday May 1, 2011, the first time in the history of the Church
that a pope beatified his immediate predecessor. John XXIII and
John Paul II were canonized at the Vatican on Sunday, April 27,
2014, by Pope Francis, in an unprecedented ceremony witnessed
by another living pope, Benedict XVI.

Popes, the Church, and Idiosyncratic Variables

Maurice McGill, MHM, former General Superior of the Saint
Joseph's Missionary Society (1988–2000), in an interview with this
author, pointed out that the word "idiosyncrasy" has a negative
connotation. However, "idiosyncratic variable" is a specialized
term in international relations that is not necessarily derogatory
and is repeatedly used by political scientists in textbooks, jour-
nals, and annals of foreign policy analysis. Idiosyncratic variables

include, among other things, nationality, age, religious affiliation, past experience, world view, education, personal gifts, dispositions, and temperament.

Political scientist James Rosenau defined idiosyncratic variables as those aspects that characterized a person prior to occupying a particular position of decision-making. Personality is a subset of the idiosyncratic variables. A common thesis agreed upon by experts of the Holy See's diplomacy and *Great Man* theorists such as Thomas Carlyle, and seconded by many interviewees, holds that the personality and idiosyncratic variables of popes and political actors impinge on their diplomacy (Kellerman, 1986:3–57). In the analysis of writer Rubenstein Richard, a plausible credit to John Cornwell's controversial study of Pope Pius XII in *Hitler's Pope* is the importance he levied on the pope's family background (idiosyncratic variable) for a proper understanding of the pontiff's role before and during the war (2002:178). In contrast, there is another school of thought with proponents like Herbert Spencer, who argue that the personality of leaders is not pivotal and important in diplomacy.

Spencer and his school harness their skepticism of the efficacy of *personality* in diplomacy on a number of controversial reservations. First, they argue that political actors are randomly distributed in roles and that therefore their personalities are cancelled out. Second, political actions are determined more by the actor's political environment (action dispensability) than their own characteristics (actor). Third, individuals are typically unable to have much effect on political outcomes (Greenstein, 1992:352). However, albeit the discrepancy, there is a consensus that the personality and, in a broader sense, the idiosyncratic variables of leaders impact their foreign policies in a plethora of ways and to varying degrees. This accounts for the numerous single-case-personality analyses and studies of many leaders.

In 1956, a study was carried out on the impact of President Woodrow Wilson's personality in his diplomacy entitled, *Woodrow Wilson and Colonial House: A Personality Study.* Tucker's *Stalin as Revolutionary: A Short Study in History and Personality* is another case in point. The great thinker, Francis Fukuyama, understood the role of the personality of leaders in their policies when he analogously pointed out that "liberal ideas have no force independent of the human actors who put them into effect, and if Andropov or Chernenko had lived longer, or if Gorbachev himself had a different personality, the course of events in the Soviet Union and Eastern Europe between 1985 and 1991 would have been quite different" (1992:47).

Tanzanian theologian Laurenti Magesa, in an interview with this author, argued that the idiosyncratic variables of popes are more pronounced in their foreign policies than those of other heads of state. His argument anchors on the premise that, unlike popes, world leaders are answerable to congresses, parliaments, senates, and constitutions. For instance, although Woodrow Wilson was the chief protagonist for the formation of the League of Nations in 1919 (particularly through his "Fourteen Points" Speech), conspicuously, the U.S. was not a founding member because the U.S. Congress vetoed her admission into the League against the will of President Woodrow Wilson. "What man in power, if he is a man, wants to see his power checked?" A pope is not subjected to checks and balances and constitutions like other heads of state.

In canon law parlance, according to Jada Patrisio, lecturer of canon law at the Catholic University of Eastern Africa, the person of the pope is above the law. The inclinations of a pope inevitably affect the image of his diplomacy. Although not a sacrosanct verdict, historian Michael Walsh opined that "the Vatican is Western Europe's last dictatorship with no independent civil service. All its officials hold their post at the will of the pontiff. All will have been promoted by him" (2011:7). The Church is not a democracy, and, as Saint John Paul II customarily added, "no one from below can decide on the truth" (Blaire, 2006:17).

The dogma of "Papal Infallibility," defined during Vatican I (1869–70), states that the pope, when speaking "ex-cathedra" relating to matters of faith and morals pertaining to the Universal Church, is infallible. One of the bishops courageously stood up to Pius IX, asserting that such a dogma had no precedent in ancient Church Tradition and so could not be defined. Pius IX responded, "Traditio sono io. Sono io la chiesa" (I am tradition. I am the Church) (Kaiser, 2006:xii). Pio Nono (Pius IX) also said that "the Council {Vatican I} may have declared me infallible, but it also led me to bankruptcy" (Szulc, 1995:202). Pope Pius IX's personalization and embodiment of Tradition and the Church in his personhood speaks volumes of the importance of a pope's personality and inclinations in the running of the Catholic Church.

Contrary to the positions of Laurenti Magesa and Jada Patrisio, the youthful Archbishop Muhatia M. Maurice of the archdiocese of Kisumu in Kenya, in an interview with this author, argued that the pope's personality, unlike in the case of world leaders, does not play a vital role in his diplomacy. In his analysis, he advanced that the burden and responsibility of the good offices of the pope weigh heavier on him than on other heads of state. The pope is the Vicar of Christ, and his actions and policies do not only affect Catholics but also every human being, since the pope is the highest moral voice on earth and God's representative among His people.

Canon 333 of *The Code of Canon Law* states, "The Roman pontiff not only has power over the universal Church, but also has preeminent ordinary power over all particular Churches and their groupings." The pope does not act arbitrarily, but his decisions are precariously scrutinized, sifted, and weaved. Archbishop Muhatia argued that the pope is the most consultative leader in the world. He has representatives at all levels and corners of the world, such as nuncios, bishops, and, to an extent, priests and every Catholic Christian, and they advise the pope accordingly, depending on the subject. Martin Wight, the great British scholar of international relations, talked of a "massive international bureaucracy" of the Catholic Church (1977:22). Owing to their culpable ignorance of the history and essence of the Church, writers such as Michael Walsh claim that popes and the Vatican are dictatorial. The fact that the Church is not a democracy does not mean that the pope is dictatorial.

The main goal of the Church is to reveal the Truth in the person of Jesus Christ, and truth is not dependent on the vote of people or public acclamation for its veracity, although, in the early Church, public acclamation was the main criterion for sainthood (*santo subito*) and, on a few occasions, for elevation to the episcopacy. A case in point was the appointment of Ambrose as archbishop of Milan in 374 A.D. Ambrose of Milan, who later became an outstanding Doctor of the Church, was a popular political figure and governor of Aemilia-Liguria in northern Italy. Towards the end of the fourth century, the diocese of Milan was marred by conflicts between the Catholics and the Arians. Things only became worse upon the death of Bishop Auxentius of Milan in 374 A.D. In his capacity as governor, Ambrose went into the church where the election of the new bishop was taking place, so as to prevent any uproar from the conflicting factions. Surprisingly, as Ambrose was addressing the assembly, a shout "Ambrose, Bishop" was taken up by everyone in the Church. Within a week of his appointment in 374 A.D., during which he spent most of the time in hiding, Ambrose was baptized, ordained, and consecrated bishop of Milan.

Truth supports the vote of the people, and that is why the Church is not a democracy, argued Archbishop Muhatia. In his *Reflecting on Our Priesthood*, Francis Cardinal Arinze, who practiced the Ibo tribal religion in Nigeria as a youth, cautions priests on the danger of introducing secular democracy in the Church. The Nigerian cardinal and curialist wrote, "... the priest should not try and introduce a type of secular democracy which does not agree with the divinely constituted hierarchical nature of the Church" (2008:37). Francis Fukuyama could have been impeccably correct in his analysis that the Polish Church was more independent than other branches of the Catholic Church in Soviet Republics (1992:19). However, Fukuyama's analysis, using the yardstick of secular democracy, that the Church as a whole had liberalized after Vatican II in the 1960s, is highly misrepresentative of the way the Church operates.

Reflecting on the democratic nature of the Catholic Church, Dutch historian and poet Hans Burgman, MHM, wrote, "We are stuck with it, there is no alternative, for the only alternative is democracy; and democracy is incompatible with a religion as ours, because God's Will is not determined by a majority vote ... democracy is not about counting noses but about the shared responsibility of the people" (2010:151). The Church discerns the will of Christ and not the opinion of people. For more than two millennia, the Church has seldom relied on the wisdom of crowds. The personality of the pope is important, but it is not the only informing variable in his diplomacy. The pope, according to Archbishop Muhatia, is also guided by canon law.

In 2002, Giovanni Cardinal Battista Re spoke at a conference in Milan regarding the place of democracy in the Church. He explained that, in a democracy, the people are sovereign, whereas the Church is ruled by a pope whose authority is "instituted from above." Battista Re graphically explained that, in the Church, the people are protected from themselves by "the hierarchical constitution of the Church," which "must not be seen as a limitation to the freedom and spontaneity of Christians, but as one more manifestation of God's mercy toward men." How so? The hierarchical constitution can remove the Church from the "variations, mutations, and competitions that occur in history" (Kaiser, 2006:10). Etymologically, the word "hierarchy" means "rule by the holy," and in an extended sense, "rule from above." Just before the 2005 conclave, George Cardinal Pell of Sydney told Robert Blaire Kaiser that "there's nothing wrong with hierarchy." In Pell's view, the hierarchical Church has existed for two thousand years, and it seemed to be doing just fine.

Why all the fuss about democracy in the Church? Why are high-voltage critics of the caliber of Hans Küng, Eamonn Duffy, and Robert Blaire Kaiser so obsessed with the notion of a democratized Church in its *modus operandi* and *modus vivendi*? Is democracy compatible with the nature, tradition, history, and essence of the Church? Samuel Huntington's 1968 book, *Political Order in Changing Societies*, contested the view that "all good things necessarily go together." Must the Church and democracy be intertwined and move together? When the Cold War ended in 1989, political scientist Francis Fukuyama proclaimed that liberal democracy is the best form of human organization. He concluded that the end point of human development was the triumph of democracy over communism.

Democracy is still the most popular form of human organization, since at least 70% of the world's population practice some form of democracy today. "The Third Wave of democracy that began in the early 1970s saw the number of electoral democracies around the world go from 35 to 120 by 2013" (Fukuyama, 2014:33). However, in his 2014 masterpiece, *Political Order and Political Decay,* Fukuyama questions the universal applicability and globalization of democracy. In the last 25 years, China and the "Asian Tigers" (developmental states) have achieved phenomenal economic growth without real recourse to democratic principles. Thus, democracy is not the only means to prosperity and happiness. Fukuyama also identifies weaknesses, moral and political decay, in advanced democracies. He boldly stated that political decay is more advanced in America, the cradle of democracy, than in other thriving democracies. "Modern liberal democracies are no less subject to political decay than other types of regimes" (Fukuyama, 2014:28).

Fukuyama accepts that there is a connection between democracy and prosperity. However, he cautiously does not infer an automatic causal relationship between those two variables. While Western models of development have been impressively successful at delivering justice and prosperity, "each society must adapt them to its own conditions and build on indigenous traditions." The Catholic Church builds on indigenous age-old traditions and must not conform to contemporary democratic aspirations and practices. That notwithstanding, it should not be forgotten that "the rule of law was most deeply institutionalized in Western Europe, due to the role of the Roman Catholic Church. Only in the Western tradition did the Church emerge as a centralized, hierarchical, and resource-rich actor whose behavior could dramatically affect the fortunes of kings and emperors" (Fukuyama, 2014:11). Turning the Church into a democracy as understood in the secular world was beyond the competence of Pope John Paul II.

An analysis of the novelty-laden papacy and diplomacy of Saint John Paul II without recourse to his personality and past experience would be grossly deficient. That is why John Paul II remarked, "I don't think the eminent cardinals knew what kind of personality I am, and therefore what kind of papacy they were getting" (Bernstein & Politi, 1996:424). However, the danger of psychologizing and identifying clinical fallacies befalls any researcher or scholar who analyzes the diplomacy of leaders only from the spectrum of personality and idiosyncratic variables without cognizance of situational determinants and other factors (Greenstein, 1992:363).

Papal historian David Willey noted during Saint John Paul II's pontificate, "The origins and nationality of the Polish pope have always deeply colored his policies and decisions ..." (1992:26). In line with Willey's argument, Bernstein and Politi (the Vaticanista of *La Repubblica*) asserted that, "The great themes of the life and papacy of Pope John Paul II are to be found in the birth, childhood, and youth of Karol Wojtyła: the devotion,... the familial ties to Judaism ..." (1996:23). In another instance, they argued that Wojtyła "had been an actor, poet, playwright, and philosopher, and all these aspects of his personality came together in the supreme role of his life as pontiff" (1996:13).

Professor of Romantic Literature John Whale acknowledged the prime role of Saint John Paul II's idiosyncratic variables in his Petrine office in the following words, "Pope though he may be, he will remain a man, marked by his own personal history and experience, who addresses his fellow men. His documents are a personal witness" (1982:99). More still, in an interview with George Weigel in 1997, Saint John Paul II acknowledged that if the Holy Spirit had seen fit in the October conclave of 1978 to call the archbishop of Krakow to the bishopric in Rome, then that must mean there was something in the experience of Krakow that was of value to the universal Church (Weigel, 2010:13).

Irish historian Eamonn Duffy believes that, in recent times, the relationship between the pope and the people of God has been obscured because the papacy has been surrounded by "a superhuman mystique and an aura of sanctity." Notably, he is convinced that popes are men like other men, with likes and dislikes, prejudices and presuppositions, virtues and vices, all of which shape, for good or ill, their actions and their policies (Kaiser, 2006:xvii). After examining the role played by Pope Saint John XXIII to avert a nuclear war during the Cuban Missile Crisis in 1962, Paul VI's efforts to end the Vietnam War in 1975, and John Paul II's role in helping to bring about the fall of communism in 1989, John Allen Jr. made the following summation, "The point to be gleaned from these three examples—John XXIII, Paul VI, and, John Paul II—is that the personal background and interests of the man who becomes pope can, under the right circumstances, change history" (2002:20).

Plausibly, there is a strong correlation between Vatican diplomacy and John Paul II's idiosyncratic variables. Logically, correlation does not always imply causation, even though some scholars are constantly observing correlations between events and syllogistically inferring causation from them. Correlation does not equal causation. Anglican Bishop Alexander Kipsang Muge was an outspoken critic of the Daniel arap Moi's dictatorship in Kenya in the 1980s. In 1990, then-Minister of Labor Peter Habenga Okondo warned the bishop that should he step into Busia in connection with a planned trip, he would not leave alive. However, the justice and human rights crusader was not a man to succumb and cringe under such threats. On August 14, 1990, he decided to go to Busia for a crusade. On his way back to his Eldoret base, the outspoken cleric died in a road accident. Bishop Muge's death was attributed to an ordinary accident. However, many people inferred a correlation and causation between Peter Okondo's threats and Bishop Muge's fatal road accident.

Even though induced/planned accidents are instruments used in eliminating political opponents and critics of dictatorships and regimes in Africa, could we empirically ascertain and verify causation between Okondo's threats and Muge's fatal accident? Is it just a case of *post hoc, ergo propter hoc* argument/fallacy? It is quite possible that the inferred causation between Okondo's threats and Muge's death could just be based on patterns in a series of coincidences. *Post hoc, ergo propter hoc* is a Latin phrase for "after this, therefore, because of this." The term refers to a logical fallacy (of the questionable cause variety) that because two events occurred in succession, the former event caused the latter event. Since event Y *followed* event X, event Y must have been *caused* by event X.

The relationship between Vatican diplomacy and John Paul II's idiosyncratic variables is not that of causation (cause and effect), but of contributory and associational incidents and factors (Whale, 1980:15). The principle of causality is measured by the yardstick of cause and effect, but the causal effects of John Paul II's idiosyncratic variables on his diplomacy are not exactly empirical. It thus poses methodological challenges of empirical verification, just as is the case with other human and social sciences. Besides, it is not possible to verify causality through empirical data only.

John Paul II's idiosyncratic variables are important in analyzing his diplomacy; however, other factors cannot be underestimated. "Diversity in continuity" is the hallmark of ecclesiastical diplomacy. Popes seldom contradict the policies of their predecessors, but in the words of Archbishop Muhatia, "no pope is a photocopy of his predecessor." In an interview with this author, Alain Paul Lebeaupin, a former apostolic nuncio to Kenya, argued that Saint John Paul II did not necessarily change the entire diplomacy of the Holy See, but his personality shaped papal diplomacy during his pontificate. Archbishop Lebeaupin was a seasoned diplomat of the Holy See and, among other others, was Apostolic Nuncio to the European Union (2012–2020).

The Traditions, Councils, Magisterium, nature of the international system, quality of the counselors and advisers, and flow of information are important factors in understanding and explaining John Paul II's diplomacy and *munus regendi* (the mission to govern). In his book *Orthodoxy*, Christian apologist G. K. Chesterton defined "Tradition" as "giving votes to the most obscure of all classes, our ancestors. It is the democracy of the dead." Reflecting on the papacy of John Paul II, George Weigel wrote, "The dramatic renovation of the papacy was not accomplished by personal *fiat* or by reason of a singular personality, but by a pope who is self-consciously the heir and legatee of the Second Vatican Council" (1999:846).

In the words of Archbishop Muhatia, John Paul II ascended the papal chair with a lot of his past history and experience with him. Thus, in examining some of the innovations in the conduct of papal diplomacy during his papacy, such as World Youth Day (WYD), international pilgrimages, new *Ostpolitik*, diplomatic ties with the State of Israel and other diplomatic entities, reorganization of the Curia, and the use of the media, Saint John Paul II's idiosyncratic variables are astonishingly vital. American Catholic priest and author Thomas Reese argues that variables such as age, nationality, state of health, language skills, and media ability are important factors taken into consideration for the election of a pope (1996:95–98).

The Idiosyncratic Variables of Leaders and International Diplomacy

Foreign policy formulation and implementation is a multiple task process with a number of factors at interplay. It is for this reason that former U.S. President George W. Bush, in his published memoir, *Decision Point,* revealed to the public the environment under which he made some of the controversial decisions during his tenure as president. However, amidst the multiple factors involved in foreign policy formulation and implementation, political analysts are of the consensus that the personality and idiosyncratic variables of leaders are important components of that process. The idiosyncratic variables of leaders may impact positively or negatively on their foreign policies. Renowned American author John Stoessinger wrote, "A leader's personality is a decisive element in the making of foreign policy.... It matters very much, in short, who is there at a given moment" (1985:xv).

Leaders elected at relatively youthful ages are more prone to adventures, risks, revolutions, and miscalculations. Looking at the variations in foreign policies, Nye Jr. asserts, "Revolutionary leaders often view their predecessors' foreign policies and even the whole international system as illegitimate" (2007:50). Old age is associated with wisdom and maintenance of the status quo (incremental politics). For example, one cannot successfully explain the demise of communism in Eastern Europe and the disintegration of the Soviet Union in 1991 without paying attention to the relative youthfulness of Mikhail Gorbachev, who was the communist chief in 1989. Gorbachev was the only leader of the communist Politburo born after the Bolshevik Revolution of 1917. He was fifty-four years old when he rose to power in 1985, and the youngest since the election of Stalin in 1922 at the age of 44. His youthfulness in initiating revolutions was expressed in his *Perestrioka, Glasnost,* and *Demokratization.*

Mikhail Gorbachev became the first and last communist chief to visit the Vatican. His predecessors were atheists, and Gorbachev, although not a practicing Christian by 1989, was baptized in the Orthodox Church and was, to an extent, a moral person. That historic visit influenced the Vatican's relation with the Politburo. It is for this reason that once the news of the removal of Gorbachev reached John Paul II while celebrating Mass in Heroes Square in Budapest 1991, he immediately offered words of encomiums and support to Gorbachev. John Paul II's main concern was that the patient diplomacy, dialogue, and the rapport between the Holy See and the Soviet Union should not fall into decline. "I remember with gratitude my meetings with President Gorbachev, in particular, I appreciate the sincere desire that guided him and the high aspiration that animated him in promoting the rights of man, of man's dignity, and his commitment to the good of his country" (Zavattaro, 2003). The Russian ambassador to Hungary was present in Heroes Square, but once he heard that the pope was to offer words of encouragement to Gorbachev, he got up and left, an apparent "emergency" necessitating his abrupt departure.

The personal experience of leaders may sometimes consciously or unconsciously impact their foreign policies. For instance, the election of Jacques Chirac to the French presidency in 1995 had a tremendously positive impact on the relations between Paris and Washington. According to political analysts, Chirac's personal U.S. experience contributed to his pro-U.S. policies. In 1953, Chirac had a glorious experience at Harvard as a student. "Chirac when he was young had studied at Harvard and worked behind the counter scooping ice cream at a Howard Johnson's roadside restaurant in Massachusetts" (Dickey, 2019). Subsequently, as president, he developed a close relationship with the Clintons. English-born American political activist Pamela Harriman stated, "Although Chirac carries the banner of the Gaullist party, he is very pro-United States" (Rouke, 1997:132). However, it is safe to say that President Chirac sharply departed from U.S. policy under President George W. Bush. In 2003, Chirac publicly and vehemently opposed the U.S. planned invasion of Iraq and worked hard to prevent the United Nations Security Council from endorsing the war. His criticisms of the Bush administration caused some francophobia in the United States, leading to the hilarious renaming of "French fries" as "freedom fries." *World News* editor, Christopher Dickey, was probably right in his assessment that "[Jacques Chirac] was in many ways the French president with the greatest affinity for the United States, yet without question he was the one most reviled by Americans" (2019).

According to neurosurgeon Bert E. Park, physical and mental health is an important variable in the policy making of leaders (1994). Scholars of political science argue that the ratification process of the Treaty of Versailles and the subsequent failure of the U.S. to join the League of Nations was associated with Woodrow Wilson's state of health and the cataclysmic stroke he suffered in October 1919. The U.S. might have joined the League in 1919 had Woodrow Wilson been willing to compromise with senators. Weinstein argued that Wilson's hardline stand, obduracy, and obstinacy were due to his stroke, which can cause one to exhibit "diminished emotional control, greater egocentricity, increased suspicion and secrecy, and lapses in judgment and memory (that) are common manifestations of cerebral arteriosclerosis" (1981:323).

President Julius Nyerere's moral rectitude and uprightness impacted Tanzania's diplomatic image. Tanzania, to an extent, is seen as the cradle of democracy in Africa. The establishment of the

Arusha Tribunal on its soil could partly be explained by the positive image of Tanzania in the international scene. In contrast, President Idi Amin's (1971–1979) disgraceful moral behavior contributed to the negative image of Uganda in the international scene. A leader's state of mind may also impact negatively on his/her foreign policy judgments and calculations. Stalin and Hitler have a legacy of being hard-core despots, and their diplomacies were very personalized. One cannot account for the outbreak of World War II without examining the "Hitler Factor." Some scholars of international relations argue that the despotism in the foreign policies of Hitler and Stalin was influenced by their acute mental problems.

According to psychologist Fritz C. Redlich, Stalin consistently suffered from clinical paranoia, while Hitler was mentally disturbed with some minor and major disorders, although not conclusively or legally insane (Rouke, 1997:129). International politics scholar John Rourke supports Redlich's observation of Hitler's disturbed state of mind in his subtle conclusion that, "Whatever Hitler's legal mental state may have been, the drug combinations he used would almost certainly generate a high-low cycle, producing euphoria and delusions of grandeur followed by paranoia and irrational anger" (1997:129). Medical practitioner Hugh L'Efang (1970) argued that if there had been a more sober Hitler during World War II, the war would have gone on longer than the actual time it ended in 1945.

CHAPTER FIVE

OSTPOLITIK AND THE FALL OF EASTERN EUROPEAN COMMUNISM

Continuity in diversity is the hallmark of Vatican diplomacy. Tradition in the Vatican is hard to shake (Noonan, 2005:14). "We think in centuries here" is one of the Roman witticisms. Sir D'Arcy Osborne, British Minister Plenipotentiary to the Holy See (1936–1947), once commented, "The atmosphere of the Vatican (is not only) supranational and universal ... it is also fourth-dimensional and, so to speak, outside of time.... They reckon in centuries and plan for eternity" (Chadwick, 1986:315–16). Yet notwithstanding its hallmark of continuity, change in the Holy See's diplomacy is often brought about by change of tactics, strategy, and personnel.

Rosenau's idiosyncratic level of analysis is built on the premise that different leaders will pursue different tactics, policies, and strategies given a similar situation due to varying personality types and unique experiences. After the Bolshevik Revolution (the October Uprising) of 1917, the Holy See consistently pursued diplomacy with the successive Soviet regimes with the aim of obtaining religious freedom, along with respect for human rights and dignity for Christians in Eastern Europe. Religious freedom was not respected in communist Eastern Europe, and the Church's autonomy was systematically defied and abused. The Holy See's diplomatic rapprochement with Eastern Europe and the Soviet Union became known as *Ostpolitik*. Etymologically, the German word *Ostpolitik* refers to the German policy toward the Soviet Union and Eastern Europe, especially the expansionist views of Adolf Hitler in the 1930s and the normalization program of the West German government in the 1960s and in the 1970s. In this book, *Ostpolitik* is the name given to the Vatican's policies towards the Soviet Union and its Eastern European satellite states, aimed at improving the condition of Christians behind the Iron Curtain.

In an interview with the author, Radoslaw Malinowski, a conflict resolution researcher, said that communism was an evil system. Successive pontiffs have consistently sought to address the situation in Eastern Europe via different diplomatic tacks, as informed by their personalities, worldviews, diplomatic experiences, and nature of the international system. However, many writers hold the view that from the evening of Wednesday, October 16, 1978, with the election of Karol Wojtyła as pope, there was a marked shift and change in *Ostpolitik*, which could be explained by his Polish nationality and piety, direct experience of communism, worldview, and Christian fearlessness, *inter alia* (John Paul II Difference).

During the pontificate of Pope Pius XI (1922–1939), the Holy See pursued a dual diplomacy in Eastern Europe. The Holy See's diplomacy simultaneously aimed for a *modus non moriendi* (that it may not die) as well as a *modus operandi* (way of functioning). Via *modus non moriendi,* to keep the Church alive and going, Pius XI carried out some clandestine ordinations of bishops. Pius XII succeeded Pius XI in 1939. Owing to Pius XII's philosophical and theological convictions and his personal experience of the barbarities and absurdities of communism, his *Ostpolitik* was informed by realistic politics of confrontation and excommunication. Eugenio Pacelli (Pius XII) was one of the henchmen of Pius XI charged with the task of establishing a *modus vivendi* (agreement between opposing parties) with communist regimes held together by Josef Stalin. The end result was futility.

Pius XII had served as apostolic nuncio to Germany and obtained reliable knowledge and experience of the cruelty and barbarity of the communist and Nazi regimes in the whole German world. He learned the art of diplomacy the hard way. Perhaps influenced by the *Munich Analogy* of 1938, that dictators are not to be appeased, Pius XII was not ready to continue the game of appeasing the sadistic regime of Stalin to establish a *modus vivendi*. Stalin's original ethnic Georgian name was Ioseb Besarionis dze Jughashvili. The name "Stalin" was his Bolshevik nom de guerre (Weigel, 2010:30). Boris Pasternak once described Stalin as a "pockmarked Caligula" (Andre & Mitrokhin, 2001:3).

Caligula is the diminutive form of the Latin "Caliga," meaning "little soldier's boot." The young Gaius Julius Caesar Germanicus, at the age of two, earned the affectionate nickname "Caligula" while accompanying his father, Germanicus, on a campaign tour in the north of Germania, although he later grew to dislike the name. The soldiers were amused because Gaius wore a miniature army uniform, boots, and armor, and thus nicknamed him Caligula. Caligula succeeded Tiberius Caesar as Roman emperor in 37 A.D. at the age of 24, and has, perhaps unfortunately, gone down in history as Rome's most tyrannical emperor. Indeed, Tiberius had a spot-on prophesy about his heir (Gaius), "I am bringing up a viper for the Roman People and a Phaethon for the world" (Wiseman, 2013:x). The young Gaius once told his grandmother Antonia, "I can do anything to anybody" (Wiseman, 2013:x). Caligula spent most of his time proudly indulging in adulterous and incestuous sexual activities, especially with his sister, and insisted on being treated as a god. He was carefully assassinated by Chaerea and companions during the Palatine Games on January 24, 41 A.D. (Wiseman, 2013:12–17).

Pope Pius XII's confrontational approach, which also saw a flurry of clandestine ordinations, was informed by his legitimate fear (also shared by U.S. General George Marshall) that communism, if not attacked head-on, would spread to Western Europe, especially with the election of communist deputies in many European parliaments like Greece and Turkey after the Second World War. Pius XII's confrontational diplomacy towards communist Europe was very much influenced by his experience as a seasoned papal diplomat.

Eugenio Pacelli was ordained a priest on Easter Sunday, April 2, 1899. Two years after his ordination (1902), he made a no-return delve into the Vatican diplomatic service in different capacities until his death in 1958. In 1901, Mariano Cardinal Rampolla, Vatican Secretary of State, offered Pacelli a position in the Vatican foreign office. From 1904–1916, Pacelli served at the Vatican's Department for Extraordinary Ecclesiastical Affairs, together with Secretary of State Pietro Gasparri. During that time, Pacelli assisted Pietro Gasparri in codifying the 1917 *Code of Canon Law*.

In 1911, Pacelli was appointed under-secretary. Progressively, on June 23, 1920, he became nuncio to Germany and, practically, to the whole German Empire. It was then inevitable for Eugenio Pacelli to rise to the rank of Secretary of State on February 7, 1930, a post he held until his election as pope in 1939, in one of the shortest conclaves in the history of the Church. It is said that two days after Pacelli's birth, Monsignor Iacobacci held the baby Pacelli in his arms and prognosticated, "Sixty-three years from today the people in St. Peter's and all Rome will loudly praise this *bambino*" (Rychlak, 2000:3). Pacelli was elected pope on his sixty-third birthday on March 2, 1939. He went on to be pope for 19 years, until his death on October 9, 1958. In 1958, Giuseppe Angelo Roncalli (Pope John XXIII), succeeded Pius XII as pope. He was also an experienced diplomat of the Holy See. Roncalli was apostolic visitor to Bulgaria and delegate to Turkey and Greece. Similar to Pius XII, John XXIII had experienced the persecution perpetuated by the communist regimes in Bulgaria and other republics, but opted for diplomacy of dialogue, unlike the diplomacy of confrontation pursued by his predecessor, Pius XII.

John XXIII's diplomacy of dialogue, or "medicine of mercy," was informed by his experience of the Cuban Missile Crisis (CMC) of October 1962. The fourteen days of the CMC was the most dangerous epoch during the Cold War. The U.S. and the Soviet Union were at the brink of a nuclear war of mutually assured annihilation. The immediate cause of the CMC came on October 14, 1962, when a United States Air Force U-2 plane captured photographic proof of Florida-facing Soviet missile bases under construction in Cuba.

John XXIII played a crucial role in brokering a peace deal between U.S. President John Kennedy and Soviet Premier Nikita

Khrushchev and, by October 28, 1962, the CMC came to an end. Angelo Giuseppe Roncalli (Pope Saint John XXIII), in his capacity as apostolic delegate to Turkey during World War II, saved the lives of many Jewish people *en route* to Palestine by shrewdly issuing them Catholic baptismal cards. He knew the horrors of overt conflicts and so opted for dialogue with the communist regimes in Eastern Europe during his pontificate (1958–1963). His diplomacy of dialogue or rapprochement with Eastern Europe was continued by his successor Paul VI. Paul VI had extensive experience in the diplomatic service of the Holy See until 1954 when he was appointed archbishop of Milan by Pope Pius XII, surprisingly without the usual red cardinalate hat. Perhaps he was not made a Prince of the Church when appointed archbishop of Milan because he was not a staunch supporter of Pius XII's confrontational diplomacy. His worldview saw Pius XII's diplomacy as grossly undiplomatic and ecclesiologically deficient (Weigel, 1992:75).

Paul VI was a gentle personality who pursued the traditional cautionary diplomacy of the Holy See. Paul VI's diplomacy was "snail diplomacy" because of his emphasis on a "step-by-step" approach. Snails are very cautious and will inevitably withdraw their antennae if stepped on or when in the face of impending danger. The danger of such concessionary diplomacy was elegantly captured by one historian, "Imagine Christians being torn to pieces by wild beasts while St. Peter conducts a 'dialogue of love' with 'Nero'" (Weigel, 2010:181).

Theoretically, Paul VI's cautionary diplomatic tack was that of concession to concession, whereby the communist regimes took the lead and the Vatican followed (Whale, 1982:251). It was reminiscent of the "Constantinian arrangement" (Caesaropapism) where the Church duly collaborated with the state following the Edict of Milan of 313 A.D. by Emperors Licinius and Constantine. Constantine called himself proto-apostolos (the first apostle) and arranged for his burial in the Church of the Apostles (Malishi, 1987:43–44). Theologian Vito Mancuso opines that the Edict of Milan actually signaled the beginning of state sponsorship of Christianity at the expense of other religions. In his book, *Let's Not Forget God: Freedom for Our Faith,* Angelo Cardinal Scola offers trenchant, albeit disputed analysis of the Edict of Milan. According to Scola, the Edict of Milan did not make Christianity the State's religion but halted the persecution of Christianity within ancient Roman territories. The Edict prevented anyone from forbidding the free practice of Christianity within the Roman Empire. Cardinal Scola considered the Edict as the birth of religious freedom in the West (Scola, 2014:10).

According to Agostino Casaroli (embodiment of Paul VI's *Ostpolitik*), Paul VI's diplomatic strategy was *salvare il salvabile* (saving what could be saved). George Weigel pointed out that the strategy to "save what was savable" instead made matters worse in Czechoslovakia and Hungary. Even if a *modus vivendi* was not forthcoming, Paul VI's diplomacy sought a *modus non moriendi.* Paul VI did not want the Church and her sacramental life behind the Iron Curtain to cease surviving. Therefore, he felt the need to make provisions for that through negotiations with the Soviet Union. Paul VI believed in the art of diplomacy. He was, of course, a seasoned diplomat of the Holy See before his election as pope. In 1968, during his address to diplomats accredited to the Holy See, Paul VI stated, "To despair of diplomacy, is to despair of man" (Whale, 1982:99).

In the words of the cautionary Casaroli, the Church sought some breathing space in Eastern Europe via a *modus non moriendi.* Renée Formicola, church-state relations expert, pointed out that Paul VI gave his *Ostpolitik* a broader outreach to include concerns such as the rights of peoples in the developing world (2002:38). Contextually, a major conclusion drawn from the *Ostpolitik* of previous popes is that their diplomatic experiences, personality, and worldview shaped and informed their *Ostpolitik*. Logically, Saint John Paul II's *Ostpolitik* was influenced by his singular experiences or idiosyncratic variables, and that is why it is argued that there was a change in *Ostpolitik* on the evening of October 16, 1978, when he was elected pope.

A New Ostpolitik 1978–1989?

Many writers argue that with the election of Karol Wojtyła to the papacy, the Church's outreach in Eastern Europe changed because of the "Wojtyłan Factor." Did *Ostpolitik* change from 1978 onward? No and Yes. No, because *Ostpolitik* was basically the Holy See's diplomacy in Eastern Europe in search of religious freedom and respect for human rights. Under Saint John Paul II until the *annus mirabilis* of 1989, the Holy See continued pursuing *Ostpolitik* with the same goals. More still, Secretary of State Jean Villot died in 1979. For his replacement, John Paul II called on the vastly experienced Cardinal Casaroli, whose name is almost synonymous with *Ostpolitik*, since he had been its chief architect from 1960 under John XXIII and Paul VI, respectively. This explains why Joaquin Navarro-Valls, the director of the Holy See press office (1984–2006), rightly described him as "the memory" in the early years of John Paul II's pontificate. His appointment signaled John Paul II's desire to continue with the old diplomacy of the *Ostpolitik* of his predecessors. Casaroli's skillful diplomacy was seen by Wojtyła as an irreplaceable asset in the struggle against the tyranny of the Soviet Union. Msgr. William Fay, a professor of philosophy and theology at Pope Saint John XXIII National Seminary, has an interesting take on John Paul's work with Casaroli. In an interview with this author, Fay opined, "He [John Paul II] was brilliant about Casaroli. Casaroli was very strong on *Ostpolitik*. He kept him in there to have the east think that things are not going to change that much, while all the while, he was doing something very different. And it was nothing else but showing the face of Christ to the world."

In his posthumously published memoirs *Il martirio della pazienza* ("The Martyrdom of Patience"), Agostino Cardinal Casaroli argued that there was no substantive difference between his *Ostpolitik* and the "eastern politics" of John Paul II, only a difference of "phases" (Weigel, 2000). However, George Weigel argued that there was a change in *Ostpolitik* with the election of Wojtyła in 1978. In Weigel's analysis, John Paul II's *Ostpolitik* was ecclesiologically, strategically, and tactically different from that of his predecessor, Paul VI (2000). Cardinal Stanislaw Dziwisz, the pope's longtime associate, in a 2018 interview spelled out the strategic and tactical differences between the *Ostpolitik* of Paul VI and John Paul II, "Paul VI's *Ostpolitik* was a politics of small steps, a politics of dialogue. But it did not bring much success. Wyszyński and Wojtyła knew that this was not the way to go. That is why they chose the path they did. Not one of direct struggle, but a struggle for man."

The game changed because of the election of a Pole as pope in 1978, and not one of the usual Italian candidates. In diplomacy, personnel is policy. John Paul II's election was perceived by many as a political statement to communism, since he hailed from a country behind the Iron Curtain. "A Pole has become pope. It is a great event for the Polish people and a great complication for us" was the reaction of a communist leader in 1978, upon learning of the election of Karol Wojtyła (Szulc, 1995:286). In the same light, Eastern European historian Andrzej Paczkowski analyzed the election of a Pole as pope in October 1978 as "an event ... whose consequences (were) difficult to overestimate" for Poland, for the future of the Catholic contest with communism, and for the Cold War (Allen, 2001). Ironically, his appointment to the archbishopric of Kraków was impossible without the consent of the communist regime in Poland, who saw him as a lesser evil. George Weigel concluded that themes such as Yalta, Europe, Poland, popular piety, and the impending Polish millennium of Christianity, reshaped *Ostpolitik* under John Paul II (1992:101).

According to Weigel, Pope John Paul II accepted his election to the papacy with the same conviction of the theoretical physicist Albert Einstein, that "God does not play dice with the universe." Only a few days after his election, Karol Wojtyła told a Polish friend as they strolled in the papal garden, "I think that God raised me to be pope to do something for the world. I have to do something for the good of the world, and for Poland." (Kaiser, 2006:43). In another instance, Weigel stated that John Paul II ascended to the papacy with the profound conviction that "the trajectory of his life was being guided by divine providence"

(2010:433). His election to the papacy in 1978 during the height of the Cold War gave his papacy an international curiosity. In an interview with the author, Nuncio Alain Paul Lebeaupin, who headed the Holy See's delegation to Prague on September 3, 1991, for the emergency meeting convened by the Conference for Security and Cooperation in Europe, argued that John Paul II's election was an international event in itself, for he was a pope from a communist country (Poland) at the height of the Cold War, pitting communist Eastern Europe against the United States.

The Cold War began in 1947 and ended abruptly in 1989. It was a period of extreme hostilities between two poles of power: the United States and its allies versus the east—the Soviet Union, its allies, and satellites. British liberal politician and historian Peter Calvocoressi recorded that the term "Cold War" was invented to describe a state of affairs. "The principal ingredient in this state of affairs was the mutual hostility and fears of the protagonists" (2008:3). It was a nuclear, ideological, economic, political, and cultural battle for world power without any overt war or "hot war." In broad understanding, the Cold War was "Western democratic capitalism, or social democracy, versus communist totalitarianism ..." (Waters, 2009:62). The Cold War presented shrewd African leaders with some rare leverage over the protagonists. Tactful leaders like Abdel Nasser of Egypt and arap Moi of Kenya were able to "prostitute" on both camps and obtained rewards. Was John Paul II's election in 1978 a political statement to the Cold War and, more specifically, to communism and the Soviet Union?

In his masterpiece *The End of History and the Last Man*, Japanese-American political scientist Francis Fukuyama argued that history ended with the unanticipated end of the Cold War. The destiny, or *the end of history*, was the triumph of liberal democracy and capitalism over communism, authoritarianism, fascism, and the like. Fukuyama wrote, "... more than that, however, I argued that liberal democracy may constitute the 'end point of mankind's ideological evolution' and the 'final form of human government,' and as such constituted the 'end of history'" (1992: xi). In Fukuyama's analysis, the *end of history* does not denote an end of historical occurrences in world history, but that liberal democracy is the destined satisfying political ideology, and the final point and form of the evolutionary process of systems of government (signalling an end to humanity's sociocultural evolution). Democracy, according to Fukuyama, is the best form of political organization of human beings. It was Winston Churchill, Prime Minister of the United Kingdom (1940–1945), who famously said, "Democracy is the worst form of government, except for all the rest."

It is interesting to note that Fukuyama was not the first historian to declare *the end of history*. Fukuyama's *end of history* thesis was inspired by Alexandre Kojève. Kojève, the renowned Russian-French philosopher, argued that history as such had ended in the year 1806 with the Battle of Jena-Auerstadt, when Napoleon defeated the Prussian monarchy. According to him, the Battle of Jena marked *the end of history* because it was at that point that the *vanguard* of humanity actualized the principles of the French Revolution (liberty and equality). Kojève stated that the progress of history must lead toward the establishment of a "universal and homogenous" state, most likely incorporating elements of liberal or social democracy (Kojève, 1969). However, Karl Marx is probably the best-known *end of his history* propagator. He believed that the direction of historical development was a purposeful one determined by the interplay of material forces, and would come to an end only with the attainment of a communist classless, stateless, and property-less society. However, the concept of history as a dialectical process with a beginning, a middle, and an end was borrowed by Marx from his great German predecessor, Georg Wilhelm Friedrich Hegel.

According to revered U.S. Secretary of State Henry Kissinger, the Cold War was an epoch of "hot peace." The exact opposite of "hot peace" is "cold peace." The latter is defined as a state of relative peace between two countries which is marked by the enforcement of a peace treaty ending the state of war while the government of at least one of the parties to the treaty continues to domestically treat the treaty with vocal disgust. Boutros-Ghali termed the Camp David Accords of September 17, 1978, the Israeli-Egyptian Peace Treaty (1979), and aftermath of the Egyptian-Israeli relations as succinct examples of cold peace.

Saint John Paul II was the first non-Italian pope in 455 years. His worldview and convictions were seemingly different from those of his Italian predecessors as far as the Yalta division of Europe was concerned. "History viewed from the Vistula River basin does look different than history from Berlin, Paris, London, or Washington, D.C. This difference has certainly shaped the potent public presence of the first Slavic and Polish pope" (Weigel, 2000).

John Paul II's predecessors, notably, John XXIII and Paul VI, and even great world diplomats of power politics, such as Henry Kissinger, saw Yalta and communism as permanent features or, in Rosenau's levels of analysis categorization, permanent variables of the international system. In George Weigel's analysis, Paul VI also saw the regimes in Eastern Europe as facts and realities with very long-term futures and life spans. As U.S. Secretary of State in the 1970s, Henry Kissinger warned Americans in the following words, "Today, for the first time in our history, we face the stark reality that the (communist) challenge is *unending*.... We must learn to conduct foreign policy as other nations have had to conduct it for so many centuries—without escape and without respite.... *This condition will not go away*" (1977:302).

Saint John Paul II believed communism was a grave injustice and moral abomination. He was convinced that because communism was built on atheistic humanism, it would inevitably be defeated. Idiosyncratically, Yalta did not invoke good memories for the Poles. At Yalta, Poland lost World War II. It was at Yalta that the Poles fell under the communist rule of Josef Stalin (Weigel, 1992:96). Under the Yalta division of Europe of 1945, John Paul II's native Poland fell under the eastern bloc, a division which patriotic Poles with a good knowledge of Polish history correctly do not accept. With his encyclopedic knowledge of Polish history, John Paul II knew that the Poles were Europeans, and not eastern Europeans since, geographically, Poland falls in central Europe, the heart of Europe. Because of the Yalta division of Europe, the Poles often say they lost the Second World War twice.

In their book *City of Saints*, George Weigel, Stephen Weigel, and Carrie Gress noted, "For Poles have never thought of themselves as a part of 'eastern Europe,' Poland is in *central* Europe, and the center of Poland, its history and culture, is Kraków" (2015:2). Geographically, Kraków is located on the border between Europe's two wings, the Latin west and the Byzantine east. "That location is reflected in the city's striking combination of architectural styles, in which the visitor frequently finds elaborate baroque decorations inside churches crowned with onion domes reminiscent of classic Orthodox church architecture" (Weigel, Gress, and Weigel, 2015:3). Historically and culturally, Kraków is an exceptional city with a rich heritage as a European city. Kraków is one of the principal crossroads of Europe, in the heart of Europe. "Kraków's *Rynek Główny*, the main market square at the heart of the Old City, is the greatest public space in Europe, rivaled only by Piazza San Marco in Venice for size, architectural development, and decorative splendor" (Weigel, Gress, and Weigel, 2015:2).

Historically, Kraków had been Poland's cultural capital for centuries. Poland's culture had played a unique role in shaping its singular history and destiny. The famous library of the revered humanist, Erasmus of Rotterdam, is not found in London, Rotterdam, Paris, or in Brussels—(the self-proclaimed capital of Europe), but in Kraków. Polish Catholic journalist Jerzy Turowicz would argue that Wojtyła became a European—not an Eastern European, or a Central European (1991:108). This selfish division of Europe robbed the Poles of their rich cultural heritage as Europeans.

Karol Wojtyła lived in Kraków for almost 40 years as a student, laborer, curate, professor, archbishop, and cardinal. Idiosyncratically, Karol Wojtyła's Cracovian sensibility and experience immensely shaped his pontifical diplomacy. This is corroborated by Weigel's account that he, "… as Pope John Paul II, would bring a Cracovian sensibility to the world—and in doing so would bend the curve of history in a more human direction while leaving an indelible impression on the life and thought of the Catholic Church.... Thus, in what follows, the story of Karol Wojtyła, St. John Paul II, and the story of Kraków are interwoven in a chronological pilgrimage through the life of a saint that reveals, at the same time, the richly textured life of a city where a boy grew into a man, a priest, a bishop—and an apostle to the world" (Weigel, Gress, and Weigel, 2015:2). *Ipso facto,* one cannot fully comprehend Saint John Paul II's papacy and diplomacy without considering his Cracovian heritage.

Culture (cultural diplomacy), and not military prowess, diplomacy, or economic might, according to John Paul II, is the driving force of history. History should be read, understood, and interpreted according to cultural lines and patterns. That is why John Paul II insistently and consistently raised the point that Christianity was the main unifying factor of modern Europe, not military conquests. John Paul II's idiosyncratic beliefs set the necessary themes for his *Ostpolitik,* thereby making it distinct. Informed by his conviction that Yalta and communism were not permanent realities, Wojtyła prophetically taught that a strong defense of human rights and dignity via diplomatic instruments—public evangelism, a revolution of conscience, rhetorical strategy of persuasion or Track Six diplomacy (activism)—would subsequently undo Yalta and the Soviet Union. "The power of his (John Paul II's) papacy lies in a charism of moral persuasion capable of being translated into political effectiveness" (Weigel, 2000).

Pope Saints John XXIII and Paul VI practiced diplomacy of accommodating the communist regimes and did not consistently and out-rightly criticize their abuses. Although abundant caution does no harm (*abundans cautela non nocet*), prior to 1978 the Vatican was overly cautious in her dealings with the communist regimes in Eastern Europe. The Montini/Casaroli *Ostpolitik* adopted a tacit papal commitment to avoid a public moral critique of Marxist/Leninist systems. This explains why, just before John Paul II addressed the U.N. General Assembly in October

1979, the cautious Cardinal Casaroli meticulously went through the draft text of his speech, eliminating references to religious freedom and other human rights issues that the Soviet Union and its allies might have found offensive (Weigel, 2000). Unsurprisingly, John Paul II, the fearless *defensor hominis* ("the defender of man") and voice of the voiceless, just as systematically restored the cuts.

Three times in the first four days of his papacy, Saint John Paul II vigorously defended religious freedom as the first of human rights and the nonnegotiable litmus test of a just society. It was a theme that had been muted under the *Ostpolitik* of Paul VI and Casaroli (Weigel, 2001). John Paul II unprecedentedly defended human rights in Eastern Europe to the discomfort of the communist regimes. He knew he was the *defensor hominis* ("the defender of man"), whose primary vocation as pope was to strengthen his brethren. Thus, his *Ostpolitik* had a prophetic intonation. Renée Formocola entitled his book, *Pope John Paul II: Prophetic Politician*. The *Ostpolitik* of Pius XII made use of hard power via confrontation and excommunication, while the *Ostpolitik* of John Paul II primarily employed soft power in the name of diplomacy of conscience, or the converting of the minds and hearts of people via public evangelization. In the first year of his papacy, Saint John Paul II made it clear that he intended to pursue, personally, a different track, "a post-Constantinian" strategy of resistance through moral revolution.

Idiosyncratically, John Paul II's *Ostpolitik* was immensely shaped by his Polish nationality. "To understand this pope, you must go back to his Polish roots" was a constant refrain during his papacy (Barnes & Whitney, 1999). Pope John Paul II told his country men and women upon arriving at the airport in Poland on Sunday, June 10, 1979, that "it is not easy for me to leave my beloved countryside of Poland. But if it is God's will, I accept" (Oram, 1979:192). He had a personal experience of the harsh realities of communism and Nazism and, without a doubt, one eyewitness is better than ten ear-witnesses (*plus valet unus oculatus testis quam auriti decem*). The Nazis used Kraków as an important transportation center during the war; their presence was very visible in the city. The main square around the cathedral was renamed Adolf Hitler Platz. Here was the residence of Hitler's general governor, Hans Frank, who ruled with an iron hand.

Agostino Cardinal Casaroli once remarked, "I would like to help this pope but I find him so different." Veteran journalist Peggy Noonan explained why John Paul II was a different type of pope, "He [John Paul II] was from the East, not the West. (But popes come from the West!) He was from the communist bloc. (But popes come from liberal democracies!) He was from Poland. (No one comes from Poland!)" (2005:21). John Paul II's spokesman, Joaquin Navarro-Valls, later explained that the "difference" was the difference between a veteran Vatican diplomat of fifty years (Casaroli) and a man from the front lines (Wojtyła) (Weigel, 2010:179). Karol Wojtyła was a clandestine seminarian in communist and Nazi Poland and knew how unfortunate that experience was. He once said, "My experience as a clandestine seminarian has stayed with me all through my life."

Before becoming pope, Karol Wojtyła understood the nitty-gritty of communism, its theoretical and practical failures, its seductions, and its brutalities. He knew how unjust communism was. Life was rigidly ordered in communist Poland. Apartments were constructed to accommodate only small families. Work was deliberately organized in multiple shifts so that families could hardly be together at the same time. The economy was in disarray. Food shortages were endemic. Less than a third of the Polish people had bathrooms, water, or central heating in their houses. Daily life was spent in queues in front of offices or grocery stores. Schools were designed to create a communist-modeled society. The communist police infiltrated everything and everyone. There was no hope or future under communism (Emilewicz, 2018).

Influenced by his Polish resilience, John Paul II knew how to respond to and resist communism. He knew that the communists attempted to transform human beings behind the Iron Curtain into Soviet robots, who would sheepishly and instinctively respond to the Soviet manifesto. Interestingly, Msgr. William Fay, a former General Secretary of the United States Conference of Catholic Bishops (USCCB), in an interview with this author pointed out that Pope John Paul II used the expression *homo Sovieticus* ("the Soviet man"). Fay asserted,

> The *homo Sovieticus* is the man who has his soul taken from him. He is like the mechanistic man. He goes through the motions of being a man, but he is not a man anymore because he doesn't have his own life with him. Interestingly, the Polish man never became a *homo Sovieticus*, except those who chose it like Jaruzelski and others. They still went to Mass, they practiced their religion. They just said we'll live under your rule but we are not going to become what you want us to become. We are the Polish people and we are very proud of our heritage.

Nowa Huta, a communist city constructed in the outskirts of Kraków, was the symbol and face of the transformation of the Polish society and the Polish person into the *societas Sovieticus* and *homo Sovieticus*. That explains why Nowa Huta is said to be one of the most renowned examples of deliberate social engineering in the history of the world. The *homo Sovieticus* was going to be bound to neither tradition nor Catholicism. To achieve this end, there was no room for a church in the urban vision of Nowa Huta, the so-called "workers' paradise." The communists proclaimed that atheism would be the foundation of this new town. Thus, Nowa Huta became the first town in a thousand years in the history of Poland deliberately built without a church. Despite repeated requests, the communists would not let the inhabitants construct a church in Nowa Huta. However, the *semper fidelis* resistant Poles would not be easily cowed into state-sponsored atheism. Under the able leadership of Bishop Karol Wojtyła, demonstrations and protests were held in Nowa Huta. On December 24, 1959, Bishop Wojtyła started the annual custom of Christmas midnight Mass in an open field in Nowa Huta in freezing winter conditions. In 1967, a permit to build the desired church was granted. The Lord's Ark Church was consecrated by Cardinal Wojtyła in 1977. Very fittingly, the Ark of Our Lord was finally planted in the middle of the Workers' Paradise (Emilewicz, 2018).

Karol Wojtyła had seen Primate Stefan Wyszyński put under house arrest several times by the communist regime in Poland because of his fierce defense of the autonomy of the Church and the rights of the human person. The year 2021 marks the 120th anniversary of Cardinal Wyszyński's birth and the 40th anniversary of his death (1981). Interestingly, since history is full of ironies, the Polish parliament declared 2021 the Year of Stefan Cardinal Wyszyński. In its resolution, Poland's lower house of parliament (the Sejm) paid tributes to the revered churchman: "In his priestly activity, the Primate of the Millennium paid attention to man's inherent dignity, the source of all his rights." The Polish senate (upper house) paid encomiums to Wyszyński and said of him: "One of the greatest Poles of the 20th century.... He watched over the fate of the Polish Church in the darkest years of Stalinism with exceptional care. For his steadfast attitude towards the communist authorities, for his opposition to the destruction of social and ecclesial life—expressed by the famous phrase 'Non possumus!'—he was imprisoned for several years." "*Non possumus!*" ("we cannot") is the title of the famous 1953 letter that the Polish episcopate, under the leadership of Cardinal Wyszyński, handed over to Bolesław Bierut, the Chair of the Central Committee of the Polish United Workers' Party and the *de facto* leader of the state. The letter unequivocally reiterated that the bishops were not going to allow the state to meddle in the administration of the Church in Poland, especially in the area of episcopal appointments. Basically, the Polish bishops were not ready to surrender God's altar to Caesar. Not surprisingly, *Soli Deo* ("To God Alone") was Cardinal Wyszyński's episcopal motto. As a result of the *Non possumus* letter, Wyszyński was arrested in September 1953. Interestingly, inspired by Wyszyński's *Non possumus* letter, Weronika and Kamil Kreczko have created a strategy game called "Non possumus."

Wyszyński was fondly known as the "Primate of the Millennium" because, as Primate of all Poland, he efficiently oversaw a nine-year program of preparation culminating in a nationwide celebration of the millennium of Poland's baptism in 1966. It was Primate Wyszyński who "helped to secure the approval of Karol Wojtyła as archbishop of Kraków in 1964, which ultimately led to Cardinal Wojtyła's election as Pope John Paul II in 1978" (Coppen, 2021). This explains why in an emotional and hearty letter to the people of his beloved Poland, just seven days after his election to the Petrine office, Pope John Paul II paid handsome tributes to Cardinal Wyszyński:

> Venerable and beloved Cardinal Primate, allow me to tell you just what I think. This Polish pope, who today, full of fear of God, but also of trust, is beginning a new pontificate, would not be on Peter's chair were it not for your faith which did not retreat before prison and suffering. Were it not for your heroic hope, your unlimited trust in the Mother of the Church! Were it not for Jasna Gora, and the whole period of the history of the Church in our country, together with your ministry as Bishop and Primate! (John Paul II, 1978).

Cardinal Wyszyński and Mother Elżbieta Róża Czacka (foundress of the Franciscan Sisters Servants of the Cross) were beatified at a Mass at the Temple of Divine Providence in Poland's capital, Warsaw, on September 12, 2021. Stefan Cardinal Wyszyński was an immense blessing to the Church in Poland and the universal Church.

Papal scholar John McDermott was spot-on when he ascertained, "Where the pacific Paul VI was inclined to compromise with the communist regimes of Eastern Europe, John Paul II had lived under their rule and had known their interior corruption." Cardinal Miloslav Vlk, who was compelled to work as a window washer to avoid arrest as a vagrant in communist Czechoslovakia, once noted that, unlike the new *Ostpolitik* of John Paul II, the old

Ostpolitik was designed and executed by men who did not understand communism because they had not lived it (Weigel, 2010:180). The pope knew communism very well and resisted it on all fronts. Seemingly, John Paul even resisted using the communist Russian language. Msgr. Fay made this observation:

> I am told that there are two Russian languages. And maybe it is in *Witness to Hope*. That there is one prior to the revolution and one after. Not that they are all different. But that there are certain words that were popular during the time of the Tsars and those words got transformed because of communism. They say John Paul would never use the communist words. The pre-revolutionary words he used. I could never imagine him using the word "communism" or "commune." I don't think you would ever find him quoting Lenin or Trotsky or anything like that. They say he was very strict about that. He could speak Russian like many Poles would do, but he could only do it without the communist overtones.

John Paul II held to a course of firm opposition and provided a beacon of moral uprightness and hope to millions of oppressed peoples around the world. Although John Paul II had a direct experience of communism, which is the distinguishing factor of his new *Ostpolitik*, his predecessors also had some deep knowledge of the totalitarian regimes in Eastern Europe. Indeed, most of them were seasoned diplomats of the Holy See before becoming pope. Casaroli served four popes as architect of their *Ostpolitik*. Achille Ratti (Pius XI) was apostolic delegate to Poland just two years before his papal election in 1922. Giovanni Battista Enrico Antonio Maria Montini (Paul VI) once served as apostolic nuncio to Poland.

According to international relations theorist Hedley Bull, one of the primary functions of representative diplomacy is the gathering of intelligence, communication, and negotiation (1985:171–72). The Vatican diplomatic service is one of the most informed, largest, and most efficient in the world. Indeed, when Vatican Secretary of State Domenico Tardini was reminded that the Holy See's diplomacy was the world's finest, his cheeky response was, "God bless whoever's number two" (Weigel, 2005:226). Eugene V. Rostow, American legal scholar, once noted, "... the Vatican has a well-deserved reputation for diplomatic expertise. It is, after all, the oldest continuing international organization in the world today. It possesses a knowledge of foreign countries and their governments which cannot be matched, in many respects, by any national state" (1970:20). In fact, the Church had the reputation as the listening post of Europe (Rychlak, 2000:267). The Catholic Church is a cosmopolitan bureaucracy with official and unofficial diplomats (Catholic Christians) in every corner of the planet. Indeed, Msgr. William Fay lauded the Holy See's prowess in information gathering, "We always had a sense that the Holy See knew very well what was going on in the world. Indeed, many countries rely on the Vatican to have information on the happenings around the world. In fact, there is no other president around who has so many people on the ground in the different countries. All bishops have a relationship with the nuncio, who has a relationship with the pope. So, the Holy See knows exactly what is going on around the world." Most of the Vatican representatives charged with the gathering of intelligence are *alumni* of the prestigious Pontifical College of Diplomacy in Rome. It was founded in 1701 by Pope Clement XI and is the elite school of diplomacy in Europe.

Unlike in Africa, where a majority of diplomats are political appointees, friends, and relatives of presidents and foreign secretaries, the Holy See has an outstanding number of career diplomats in its foreign service. In some quarters in Africa, it is not uncommon for persons with no knowledge of diplomacy to be appointed ambassadors and consuls for political rewards or retirement benefits and compensations. Regrettably, some political appointees have limited knowledge of issues relevant to the national interests of their sending states and are woefully uninformed about the country to which they are assigned. Some of these diplomats are not even cognizant of the art of raising wine glasses for diplomatic cheers and toasts. They spend their time in foreign lands playing lawn tennis and golf, instead of securing and bargaining the national interests of their sending governments. That notwithstanding, nominating ambassadors is a presidential prerogative and it is a common practice for presidents to nominate personal friends and significant contributors to their election campaigns to foreign missions. However, such political appointees normally constitute a minority in the foreign services of many Western nations. The Holy See invests in the training of her diplomats.

Unlike his predecessors, Wojtyła had an inside and direct knowledge of communism. In his homily during the beatification Mass of John Paul II, Pope Benedict XVI stated, "When Karol Wojtyła ascended to the throne of Peter, he brought with him a deep understanding of the difference between Marxism and Christianity, based on their respective visions of man" (2009). Knowledge is power. In the analysis of the great diplomatist Sir Ernest Manson Satow, the success of diplomacy depends on what might be called the "strategic outlook" of the policy-makers: their firm understanding of the nation's interests, their "knowledge of the past history of a question," and their "knowledge of men and how to deal with them" (Otte, 2001:139). John Paul II had the strategic outlook of communist Eastern Europe. Weigel concluded that, "Wojtyła became pope having accumulated a vast store of useful experience that could be brought to bear on the *Ostpolitik* of the Holy See" (1992:93). Under the motto *non possumus* (we are not allowed to place the things of God on the altar of Caesar), Wojtyła was part of the Church in Poland that put up a fight against the regime (1992:111).

Among the moral armamentarium Wojtyła had at his disposal were the popular piety and folk imagery of his homeland, which had been influential in his personal life. Poland is well-known for its robust Catholicism, with a legacy of deep religiosity. From some credible sources, about 95 percent of the Polish people are practicing Catholics, or baptized Catholics. As John Paul II would remind journalist André Frossard, Poland was referred to in the gazette of the Apostolic See as *antemurale christianitatis*, the "rampart of Christendom" (1982:23). The Great Novena in preparation for the millenary of the baptism of Poland in 966 A.D., which culminated in 1966, was a national renewal and a re-dedication of Poland to Mary, Queen of Poland. Polish religiosity is a national trait and is reflected in the political culture and life of the country. In diplomacy, national traits oftentimes find expression in the image of states' foreign policies.

From an official gazette of the Beijing government, China's first foreign policy principle is "Maintaining Independence, Self-Reliance, and National Sovereignty" (China, 1993:3). This Chinese first foreign principle is intricately linked to traits of her political culture and history, namely: Sinocentrism, insistent sovereignty, and a sense of being beset by foreign powers. The Chinese have a prickly insistence on self-reliance and sovereignty because of their Sinocentric notion, in which they see themselves as the political and cultural center of the world. Indeed, the Chinese word for country is *Zhong Guo*, which means "middle place" (Rouke, 1997:96).

Historically, the Chinese empire was built on its supposed cultural superiority over its neighbors. This explains why the Chinese state has never recognized a source of religious authority higher than itself and has easily controlled whatever priesthoods existed (Fukuyama, 2012:276). Writing to America's European NATO allies in the early 1960s, Henry Kissinger noted that nations are not abstract entities. A nation's aspirations (sense of identity and memories) are not merely a "morbid obsession with the past. They constitute the essence of nationhood" (Otte, 2001:184). In his study of the Vienna System, Henry Kissinger observed that "history is the memory of states." Poland's national traits also found expression in John Paul II's *Ostpolitik*.

Devotion to Mary was a major hallmark of Saint John Paul II's papacy. Marian piety had been influential in the life of Wojtyła, especially coupled with the fact that he was already motherless by the time he turned nine. After the death of his mother, Wojtyła and his father went on a pilgrimage to Our Lady of Calvary in the shrine of Kalwaria Zebrzydowska. At the shrine, Wojtyła's father reportedly told him, "You have lost your mother. But you will never lose this mother, for she will always be with you" (Emilewicz, 2018). Wojtyła treasured that counsel in his heart. When asked in the Sistine Chapel if he accepted his papal election, Wojtyła replied, "With obedience in faith to Christ, my Lord, and with trust in the Mother of Christ and the Church, in spite of great difficulties, I accept." It is not surprising that his first papal visit was to the Marian shrine Mentorella in Italy on October 29, 1978 (a week after his inaugural Mass as pope), and his last foreign visit was to the Marian Shrine in Lourdes. Because of his trust in the Blessed Virgin Mother, Wojtyła knew the communists would not have the last laugh when the history of Poland is written. During a visit to Boston, Massachusetts, USA, in 1976, Cardinal Karol Wojtyła confided in Msgr. William Manning Helmick, secretary to Cardinal Humberto Sousa Medeiros, "The communists do not dominate Poland. We know they have enormous power in industry, technology, and so forth. But they can only go so far. The real sovereign of Poland is the Blessed Mother, Our Lady of Czestochowa."

Political scientist Formicola Renée summarized the role of John Paul II's idiosyncratic variables in his diplomacy in the following words, "Everything in his life has been a prologue to his papacy, and everything about his papacy reflects the values of his family, his nationality, and his religion" (2002:13). The fact that he chose *Totus Tuus* ("All Yours") for his papal motto was not insignificant. John Paul II wrote, "On October 22, 1978, when I inherited the Ministry of Peter in Rome, more than anything else, it was this experience and devotion to Mary in my native land which I carried with me" (1994:220). Marian devotion and visiting Marian shrines became an integral part of his pilgrimages. On the evening of Monday, October 16, 1978, John Paul II told the anxious crowd in St. Peter's Square, "I was afraid of receiving this nomination, but I did it in a spirit of obedience in the Lord and trust in the Holy Madonna" (Oram, 1979:177).

Pope Saint John Paul II famously attributed to Mary his

survival of the attempt on his life by the Turkish terrorist Mehmet Agca on May 13, 1981, and placed the bullet on the statue of Mary in Fatima. Sr. Lucia, one of the seers of the vision of Fatima, made known that his survival was the third secret of Fatima in 1917, "The bishop of Rome, dressed in white, fell to the ground as though dead." John Paul II was an active member of the Living Rosary group in Poland under the guardianship of Jan Leopold Tyranowski. He was Karol Wojtyła's first spiritual director and would make a profound difference in his spiritual life. Jan Tyranowski was a tailor knowledgeable in the spirituality and mysticism of St. Teresa of Avila and St. John of the Cross. He introduced his young protégé to these Carmelite authors, setting him on a deeper spiritual path.

Idiosyncratically, Saint John Paul II never forgot the influence Tyranowski had on him; he had a small picture of him in his bedroom in the Apostolic Palace and credited him with bringing his vocation to fruition at a time when he wanted to be an actor. He would confide in André Frossard, "He (Tyranowski) was one of those unknown saints, hidden amid the others like a marvelous light at the bottom of life, at a depth where night usually reigns. He disclosed to me the riches of his inner life, of his mystical life. In his words, in his spirituality and in the example of a life given to God alone, he represented a new world that I did not yet know. I saw the beauty of a soul opened up by grace" (Frossard, 1982).

Weigel argued that John Paul II, "in his *Ostpolitik*, therefore could draw on a deep reservoir of popular piety and folk imagery, precisely because he did not dismiss these as pre-modern fantasies" (1992:99). In this regard, one can brand John Paul II a liberalist. The liberalist school of international relations and diplomacy, unlike its realist counterpart, argues that morality matters in diplomacy. Under John Paul II, the Vatican acted and the communists responded (post-Constantinian arrangement). Where Paul VI played diplomatic chess, John Paul II played diplomatic poker (Whale, 1982:252).

More still, John Paul II's public personality, and his having been an actor in the clandestine Rhapsodic Theatre, also shaped his *Ostpolitik*. His ability to pull huge crowds, as was seen during his first visit to Poland, was decisive. His gestures and use of theatrics were appealing to the media. The media coverage of his 1979 pilgrimage to Poland was magnanimous, since it was a Polish pope going to Poland. Indeed, one can presume, with the aid of a contrary-to-fact proposition, that if it were the Italian Pope John Paul I visiting Poland in 1979, the media attention would not have been so overwhelming. John Paul II was not a trained diplomat like his immediate predecessors, but his whole life, unique background, and experiences provided him with the necessary armory. Oftentimes, people's backgrounds account for the courses of their actions.

Polish poet and drama theoretician Boleslaw Taborski would write that John Paul II's experience and lessons in the Rhapsodic Theatre were instrumental in his *Ostpolitik* and the subsequent demise of communism. Boleslaw argued that, in the Rhapsodic Theatre, John Paul II learned the "living word," which is the ability to cut sharply and cleanly through the static of lies and propaganda (1987:1–16). Reflecting on the soft power of the "living word," Weigel asserted that John Paul II made use of it in his diplomacy against the Sandinista of Daniel Ortega in Managua, in Manila to challenge the dictatorship of Marcos Ferdinand, in Warsaw against the communist regime, and in the 1994 Cairo Conference on Population against the inclusion of the abortion bill of Bill Clinton (1996:87).

John Paul II's fearlessness was also a factor in his *Ostpolitik*. Journalist Peggy Noonan observes, "Be not afraid!" was the pope's first announcement to the people of Rome and of the world (Noonan, 2005:132). "Have no fear, open the doors to Christ. Start again from Christ. Open the borders of the country, the economic and political borders." He altered these words at his inaugural Mass as pope on October 22, 1978. Have no fear, *non abbiate paura, nolite timere, msiogope* in Italian, Latin, and Kiswahili translations respectively, was a regular theme in his pontificate. For instance, in his final blessing to the people of New York on Saturday, October 7, 1995, Pope John Paul II exhorted

New Yorkers, "Do not be afraid! I can see that Americans are not afraid. They are not afraid of the sun, they are not afraid of the wind, they are not afraid of 'today'" (Noonan, 2005:132). This fearlessness gave him the strength to challenge the communist regimes. After all, John Paul II came from a "fighting Church," as Camillo Cardinal Ruini once described the pope's background. His appeal to fearlessness also empowered the Polish people. It was the Yugoslav communist politician Milovan Djilas who famously said that he greatly admired John Paul II because of his Christian fearlessness. John Paul II ascended the papacy with a profound experience of the twentieth century as a century of fear and terror. He wanted to challenge the world to a new fearlessness (Anderson, 2018).

A few months after John Paul II's premier visit to Poland, the Solidarity Movement was formed in September 1980 by workers of the Gdańsk Shipyard ("Lenin Shipyard"), under the leadership of 37-year-old charismatic unemployed electrician Lech Walesa. This explains why in his analysis of the events in Poland leading to the *annus mirabilis* of 1989, Wojciech Witold Jaruzelski, Polish army general and premier, admitted that "John Paul II's return to Poland raised the level of consciousness of the Polish people, inspiring them with the sense of destiny and courage that gave rise to the Solidarity Movement" (McDermott, 1993:xi). Through his addresses during those nine consequential days in June 1979, Pope John Paul II created a revolution of conscience in his native Poland. He relentlessly reminded the Polish people that communists were deliberately attempting to alter their true identity. He told his fellow Poles, "If you take back the truth of your identity, you will find tools of resistance that totalitarianism cannot match" (Anderson, 2018). He reminded them that at the heart of the Polish person is the Catholic faith, since the Polish culture bears very clear Christian signs. He asked the people to remain faithful to their Christian heritage and to bequeath it to their children and grandchildren.

The Polish eyes were suddenly opened and their minds illumined. They began to see and to think. They started asking themselves: "Who am I?," "What am I doing here?," "What is the purpose of my life?," and "Can I truly resist this totalitarian system?" The pope gave them back their authentic history and identity, which the communists had attempted to alter. The people sang spontaneously, "We want God in our Polish books, we want God in our Polish schools." The status quo and the center could no longer hold. After being stung to life, the workers from the Gdańsk Shipyard and across Poland rose up and demanded that their human rights and dignity be respected and restored. They were no longer afraid. Strikes across Poland paralyzed the communist system. No communist regime had ever allowed the workers to demand and shape their own destiny and rights. However, this time around, they capitulated and acceded to the twenty-one demands by the workers. Thus, the Solidarity Movement was formed and Lech Walesa signed the agreement with a souvenir pen which bore the image of Pope John Paul II. That is how John Paul II sowed seeds for the eventual tumbling of communism in Poland and in the Soviet world. Hence, Pope John Paul inspired a revolution of conscience which inspired people to live outside the confines of the Soviet Union and communism.

According to American journalist Robert Blair Kaiser, Karol Wojtyła helped create the Solidarity Movement while he was a leader in Poland's underground Church, long before he became pope. As pope, John Paul II gave Solidarity millions of dollars—against the advice of his own Secretary of State, Agostino Casaroli, who would have preferred that the pope remain neutral (Kaiser, 2006:47). This independent labor union, whose principal instrument was the news-sheet "Solidarnosc," has been adorned with the legacy as the primary catalyst of the revolutions that swept Eastern Europe in 1980s and early 1990s.

The election of anti-communist leader Lech Walesa as president of Poland in December 1990 inspired a string of anti-communist revolutions in Eastern Europe: the Estonian Singing Revolution; revolutions in Lithuania, Latvia, and Belarus; and, subsequently, the collapse of communism in Eastern Europe and the Soviet Union. Analogously, the Solidarity Movement can be compared to the 2011 revolution in Tunisia, which rapidly inspired unprecedented strings of revolutions in the Arab world calling for reforms and the resignation of dictators like Mubarak of Egypt and Gadhafi of Libya, in what came to be known as the "Arab Spring" or "Arab Awakening." John Paul II's public and clandestine support of the Solidarity Movement via his meetings with the leadership was instrumental in the events leading to the collapse of communism in 1989.

Henry Campbell Black's legal maxim states that *causa causae est causa causati* ("the cause of a cause is the cause of the effect"). Stated in another way, *causa causantis causa est causati* ("the cause of the thing causing is the cause of the effect") (1891:1622). Logically inferring from the maxim, John Paul II caused the Solidarity Movement, which inspired a string of revolutions in Eastern Europe by 1989. The net effect of the revolutions in Eastern Europe was the collapse of Eastern European communism and the Soviet Union. Since the cause (John Paul II) of a cause (Solidarity Movement) is the cause of the effect (collapse of communism), *ipso facto*, John Paul II caused the demise of communism in Eastern Europe.

Saint John Paul II's diplomatic fearlessness and propensity to throw caution to the wind was also evident just three months after his election. Prior to his election, the last time the Holy See engaged in mediation was in 1885, when she successfully brokered peace between Spain and Germany in their dispute over the Caroline Islands. Pope Benedict XV tried unsuccessfully in his preventive diplomacy to mediate between the *Triple Entente* and *Triple Alliance* during World War I. His *Peace Note* of 1917 was the best that he could do. On December 23, 1978, John Paul II took his premier diplomatic initiative to mediate a solution to the "Beagle Channel boundary dispute" between Chile and Argentina. It was an act of Track Two diplomacy because he sent Antonio Cardinal Samorè on his behalf, and not on behalf of the Holy See which is an official Track One diplomatic entity. Against the fear and anxiety of some diplomats of the Holy See, John Paul II continued his personal diplomacy in that region until Argentina and Chile formally asked the Holy See to mediate on January 9, 1979 (Weigel, 1999:273).

According to the realist school of international relations, the efficiency of any foreign policy rests on the effectiveness of its instruments. From another perspective, the Machiavellian principle of the end justifying the means is what matters. One can logically infer that John Paul II's foreign policy towards the East was effective because the end result was the implosion of communism in 1989, and the subsequent disintegration of the Soviet Union in 1991. His primary instrument was his office as pope and status as the highest moral authority in the international community, which gave him leverage in his public diplomacy. Political scientist John Rourke defines public diplomacy as "a process of creating an overall international image that enhances a country's ability to achieve diplomatic success" (1997:296). The pope's status and his earlier diplomatic achievement in communist Eastern Europe in the 1980s enhanced his reputation as one to be heeded. That explains why American author and journalist Robert Blaire observed that since Rome has become the prime drawing room of international politics, "When a pope in Rome pushes a boulder into the sea, the waves roll up on every shore" (2006:xx).

John Paul II's public personality as portrayed by the media only added to the grandeur of his office. One of his closest colleagues revealed that when Wojtyła became pope, one of the first things he did was to ask for the file of Paul VI's *Ostpolitik*. His key appointments of Agostino Casaroli (Secretary of State) and Achille Cardinal Silvestrini (foreign minister of the Holy See) signaled the importance he gave to the Holy See's diplomacy in Eastern Europe. The name Casaroli is almost synonymous with *Ostpolitik* since he was the face of the *Ostpolitik* of four popes. Silvestrini had a comprehensive knowledge of the situation in Eastern Europe since he was a specialist on the history of Eastern Europe and the Middle East (Formicola, 2002:34).

The Cold War came to an unanticipated end in 1989 signified by the fall of the Berlin Wall. The Soviet Union disintegrated in 1991. There are myriad schools of thought accounting for the demise of communism. The *Standard Account* holds that Mikhail Gorbachev did it. In 1985, Gorbachev became the youngest leader of the Politburo since Stalin in 1922. His openness, brashness, and attempts to remodel or give communism a "human face" accidentally sowed seeds for its collapse. In his lecture in Kraków on June 2, 1990, Casaroli described Gorbachev as "someone who ran to the rescue to repair by democratic means the mortal wounds on the socio-political, moral, and economic levels inflicted on peoples during the long dictatorship" (1990:6–7). Gorbachev's rapport with John Paul II, which culminated in his historic visit to the Vatican on December 1, 1989, was a significant step in the realization of religious freedom in Eastern Europe. Gorbachev made history when he became the first communist chief to visit the Vatican since the meeting between Tsar Nicholas and Pope Gregory XVI in 1845. Idiosyncratically, Gorbachev, although not a practicing Christian at the time (1985–1991), was baptized in the Orthodox Church in Russia as a young boy. All his predecessors were professed atheists. Gorbachev once confessed to Casaroli that both he and his foreign minister, Eduard Shevardnadze, had been baptized, and that his parents had kept an icon behind the obligatory photo of Lenin in his childhood home (Weigel, 2010:177).

The *Realist Account* postulates that President Ronald Reagan of the United States was the main instigator. He is credited for containing the spread of communism. His propaganda to take the nuclear war to space at the expense of the Soviet Union, which had been stretched beyond capacity, his various disarmament efforts with Gorbachev, and the controversial well-regarded *Holy Alliance* make him a credible instigator of the revolution of 1989. The *Diplomatic Account* postulates that the *Helsinki Final Act* of August 1, 1975, did it. According to this school, the *Helsinki Accord* set the ball rolling for the death of the Yalta imperial system. Weigel argued that the famous "Basket Three" of the *Final Act* contained a set of human rights provisions which was a challenge to the communist rule in Eastern Europe. The *Marxist Account* argued that economics was the main instigator. The Soviet Union had to collapse because it had been stretched beyond capacity. The Soviet Union was already collapsing because of a lack of economic sustenance (1992:18–32).

One cannot talk of the demise of communism in 1989 without examining the role of Pope John Paul II. Papal diplomacy scholar Jada Patrisio, in an interview with this author, pointed out that, presumably, an Italian pope may not have gone the extra mile that Pope John Paul II did to see an end to communism. Commenting on John Paul II's pilgrimage to Poland in 1979, a Polish journalist from Kraków wrote, "If this were an Italian pope coming here, he might never act this way. He might wring his hands and be afraid of offending his hosts or saying the wrong thing. But this pope knows the government, knows himself, and knows the Poles" (Kwitny, 1997:478). Distinguished Yale professor John Lewis Gaddis described John Paul II's impactful epic visit to Poland in June 1979 in the following words, "When John Paul II kissed the ground at the Warsaw airport on June 2, 1979, he began the process by which communism in Poland—and ultimately everywhere—would come to an end" (2005:193).

In Gaddis' analysis of the unanticipated end of the Cold War, hard power, such as nuclear weapons, threats, propaganda, and military industrial complexes lost their potency towards the end of the Cold War. Soft power became more instrumental, as Gaddis wrote, "Real power rested, during the final decade of the Cold War, with leaders like John Paul II whose mastery of intangibles—such qualities as courage, eloquence, imagination, determination, and faith—allowed them to expose disparities between what people believed and the systems under which the Cold War obliged them to live" (2005:195–96).

After 1989, the French secular weekly L'Éxpress hailed on its cover page the fall of the Berlin Wall and dismantling of the communist empire as "the victory of the pope" (McDemott, 1993:xi). In 1992, President Mikhail Gorbachev submitted that everything that happened in Eastern Europe was thanks to the role of John Paul II, including his political role. In 2005, Henry Kissinger described John Paul II as the most influential political figure in the last quarter of the 20th century. German Chancellor Helmut Kohl confided in Italian politician Rocco Buttiglione that John Paul II "is the greatest man of the second half of the (20th) century, perhaps of the entire century. And you know, he even draws a bigger crowd than I do" (Weigel, 1999:795). Following his death in 2005, then-U.S. Secretary of State Condoleezza Rice paid handsome tributes to John Paul II, "At the time when communism was breaking down finally, and needed strong people who were prepared to push those boulders aside, and to make it possible for tyranny to end in Europe, the pope was one of the most important spokesmen for, and really one of the most important actors in, that great drama.... If you look at what happened in 1989 and 1990 and 1991, you cannot help but recognize the tremendous contribution of Pope John Paul II to those dramatic events and, therefore, to freedom." Msgr. William Fay, who met Pope John Paul II on multiple occasions, explained, "John Paul contributed to the collapse of Eastern European communism. Why? Because he showed the world the face of Christ and said this is your face. This is who you really are. And there is no way that you can look at the face of Christ and not love it. And people wanted to be who they were. And that is why what happened in Warsaw happened in Warsaw." John Paul II felt humbled with all the encomiums showered on him for his role in the demise of Eastern European communism.

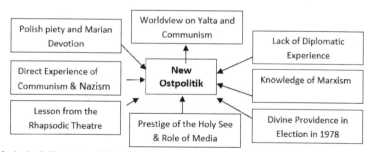

Fig. 1. Author's illustration of John Paul II's idiosyncratic variables which informed his *Ostpolitik*

CHAPTER SIX

DIPLOMATIC RELATIONS WITH THE STATE OF ISRAEL (DUAL DIPLOMACY)

After the destruction of the Temple of Jerusalem in 70 A.D., many Jewish people fled to different regions in despair. In the diaspora, the Jewish people were branded "Christ killers," treated with disdain, and systematically lynched. Traditional Catholic anti-Judaism was informed by accusations that the Jewish people crucified Jesus Christ (Deicide), drank the blood of Christians, poisoned wells, and exacted usury (especially from Christians who could not repay their loans). In modern times, the Jewish people were accused of championing modernity, Bolshevism, secularism, materialism, atheism, rationalism, liberalism, capitalism, and democracy (Marrus, 2002:44). It is a regrettable memory that the pre-*Nostra Aetate* Catholic Church was among the prime Jewish persecutors. Contextually, the word "memory" is different from Susan Zuccotti's definition of memory as that which is "personal, selective, imprecise, and arbitrary" (2002:205). Down through the ages, "the Jewish people" have been Christianity's most decisively disconfirming and, therefore, threatening "other" (Roth, 2002:242).

Some of the early Church Fathers did not only excel in orthodoxy, but were unwisely at the forefront of malevolent polemics against the Jewish people (*Adversos Judaeos*). Anti-Semitic declarations colored the beautiful discourses, sermons, treatises, apologies, and literature of Church Fathers like the lawyer Tertullianus, John Chrysostom, Hippolytus, Augustine of Hippo, and historian Eusebius of Caesarea. John Chrysostom ("golden mouth") is perhaps the greatest preacher of the Gospel the Church has ever known. However, the "golden mouth" simultaneously preached the Gospel and vomited venom against the Jewish people when he described them as no "better than pigs or goats, and they live by the rule of debauchery" (Cohn-Sherbok, 2006:152). In their Midrashic analyses, the Fathers of the Church saw the Esau-Jacob rivalry (Genesis 25:23–24) as a prefiguration of the Jewish-Catholic hatred. The "elder" refers to the Jewish people who will serve "the younger" (the Catholic Church).

Anti-Semitism was rife in the medieval period. Indeed, it was a pivotal moment in the history of anti-Semitism. In the medieval period, the Jewish people were called "slayers of the Lord," "murderers of the prophets," "adversaries of God," "haters of God," "men who show contempt for the law," "enemies of their father's faith," and "haters of righteousness," *inter alia* (Kedar, 1998:18). The Crusades, anti-Semitic decrees of ecumenical councils, and the Inquisition in medieval Europe changed the life of the Jewish people in Europe forever.

Crusades were commonplace in medieval Europe. The Crusades were military expeditions initiated and organized by western European Christians beginning in the late 11th century. The most famous of the Crusades were the eastern Mediterranean campaigns in the period between 1095 and 1271 that had the objective of re-conquering the Holy Land and checking the spread of Islam. The Crusades constitute a controversial chapter in the history of Christianity, and their regrettable excesses have been the subject of centuries of historiography. The First and Second Crusades (1095 and 1146) were certainly accompanied by anti-Jewish sentiments. Jewish people were tortured, forcefully converted, and slaughtered. In an attempt to stop the Muslims from seizing present-day Turkey, Albania, Bulgaria, and Palestine, Pope Urban II proclaimed the First Crusade at the Council of Clermont in November 1095. Even though there was no mention of vengeance in a letter Pope Urban II sent to the Crusaders at the beginning, some preachers of the Crusade mentioned violence and anti-Semitism in their sermons (Kedar, 1998:25). On their way to the Holy Land, crusaders slaughtered or forcibly converted the Jewish people. The massacres and depredations of the Jews were renewed at each Crusade (Kedar, 1998:14).

Inspired by the preaching of Peter the Hermit, in 1096 bands of peasants and knights, especially those under the leadership of the notorious Count Emicho, ferociously attacked Jewish communities in Speyer, Mainz, Worms, Cologne, Metz, Trier, Regensburg, and Prague. Jews were massacred, their property despoiled and destroyed. Faced with the choice of baptism or death, many Jews converted to Christianity. However, some Jewish people chose to take their own lives and those of their families and friends rather than converting or submitting to the execution of the crusaders. In his *Historia Hierosolymitana*, historian of the First Crusade Albert of Aachen vividly described the ordeal of some Jews during the massacre. "The Jews, seeing that their Christian enemies rose up against them and their children, and that they were sparing no age, attacked one another, brothers, children, wives and sisters, and they were killed at each other's hands. Mothers of nursing children, it is terrible to say, cut their throats with knives and stabbed others, preferring them to perish thus by their own hands rather than to be killed by the armies of the uncircumcised" (1879:293). In total about 25,000 Jews lost their lives during the First Crusade.

Different schools of thought postulate varied reasons for the massacre of 1096. French Jesuit Louis Maimbourg described the massacres as "barbarous, inhuman, deriving from a false zeal, perpetrated under the pretext of piety yet inspired, in truth, by sheer avarice" (1676:2). German historian Heinrich von Sybel pointed out that "the crusaders who attacked the Jews were stimulated by religious, avaricious or accidental motives" (Sybel, 1881:204). In *The First Crusade and the Idea of Crusading*, Crusade historian Jonathan Riley-Smith identified looting, forcible conversion, and vengeance as the reasons for the Jewish massacres of 1096 (1986:52). French philosopher Voltaire in his 1751 *Histoire des croisades* pointed out that "the Christians, believing to avenge God and to enrich themselves, laid violent hands on all these unfortunate people" (1751:17). Anglican historian Thomas Fuller in his

1693 book *Histoire of the Holy Warre* branded the Crusades as "a sinister design of the Romish Church" and denounced the knights as "wicked people who served the Devil while wearing Christ's livery" (1693:19).

It took two years for the crusaders to reach the Holy Land. Many of them died on the way because of the adverse conditions. In 1099, Jerusalem was conquered. In celebration of their victory, about 3,000 Jewish people were rounded up in all the main synagogues and burned, thereby destroying the Jewish population in Jerusalem. The First Crusade was the major watershed of Jewish history in medieval Europe for a plethora of reasons. The Crusades changed all of Jewish life in Europe. It changed the attitude of Christians towards Jews and Jews toward Christians and even Jews towards Jews (Riley-Smith, Jonathan, 1986:22). It was also the first time in Europe that there was a mass forcible conversion of Jews. This would also set the stage for the Spanish Inquisition.

In medieval Christendom, numerous pugnacious laws that curtailed the rights of the Jewish people were promulgated, especially in the *Codex Theodosianus* and the Justinian Code (Cohn-Sherbok, 2006:159). Pope Innocent III convoked the Fourth Lateran Council in the Lateran Palace beginning November 1215. The council was probably Pope Innocent III's greatest initiative (Tanner, 1990:227). It was the largest and most attended of the councils in the medieval epoch. The goals of the council were clearly spelled out by the pope himself: "to eradicate vices and to plant virtues, to correct faults and to reform morals, to remove heresies and to strengthen faith, to settle discords and to establish peace, to get rid of oppression and to foster liberty, to induce princes and Christian people to come to the aid and succor of the holy land" (Tanner, 1990:227).

Among others, the council issued seventy constitutions/canons and a decree, which had to do with the convocation for a new Crusade. Very unfortunately, the last four constitutions (67–70) and the additional decree were extremely anti-Semitic in nature and content. Canon 67 dealt with usury of Jews. The canon reads: "Wishing therefore to see that Christians are not savagely oppressed by Jews in this matter, we ordain by this synodal decree that if Jews in future, on any pretext, extort oppressive and excessive interest from Christians, then they are to be removed from contact with Christians until they have made adequate satisfaction for the immoderate burden" (Tanner, 1990:265). The same constitution also hinted that, if need be, Christians were to be compelled by ecclesiastical censure to abstain from commercial intercourse with the Jews.

Canon 68 stipulated that all Jews were to be publicly marked off through the character of their dress. The Jews were not to be seen in public on Palm Sunday and during the Easter Triduum, especially on Good Friday. A similar decree had previously been issued by the Synod of Macon in 581. Canon 69 prohibited Jews from holding public offices. The Council Fathers reasoned that Jews were blasphemers of Christ and as such it would be absurd for them to hold public offices. Such a prohibition had previously been issued by the Synod of Toledo in 589. Canon 70 prohibited Jews who had been baptized in the Catholic faith from retaining their old Jewish rite. *Inter alia*, it reads: "… we therefore decree that such people shall be wholly prevented by the prelates of churches from observing their old rite, so that those who freely offered themselves to the Christian religion may be kept to its observance by a salutary and necessary coercion" (Tanner, 1990:267).

The additional decree of the council forbade Jewish creditors from exacting interest on loans owed to them by Christians who took part in the Crusade to liberate the Holy Land. The council ordered that "Jews be compelled by the secular power to remit interest, and that until they do so all intercourse shall be denied them by all Christ's faithful under pain of excommunication. Secular princes shall provide a suitable deferral for those who cannot now pay their debts to Jews, so that after they have undertaken the journey, and until there is certain knowledge of their death or of their return, they shall not incur the inconvenience of paying interest" (Tanner, 1990:269).

In 1227, the Synod of Narbonne forbade the Jewish people from moving around on Sundays and other solemnities of the Church. They were also required to walk around with identifiable badges. Canon 3 of the Synod ruled: "That Jews may be distinguished from others, we decree and emphatically command that in the center of the breast (of their garments) they shall wear an oval badge, the measure of one finger in width and one half a palm in height. We forbid them moreover, to work publicly on Sundays and on festivals. And lest they scandalize Christians or be scandalized by Christians, we wish and ordain that during Holy Week they shall not leave their houses at all except in case of urgent necessity, and the prelates shall during that week especially have them guarded from vexation by the Christians."

The end result of a fiery public debate in Paris in 1240 was the burning of the Talmud, a Jewish holy book. The Talmud is a core text in Rabbinic Judaism and it basically refers to compiled commentaries on the Torah and Mishnah. It was compiled by Jewish scholars in Palestine and Babylonia in 200 CE and 500 CE. The Mishnah refers to a vast collection of centuries' worth of non-biblical laws/oral laws and customs.

The Jewish Virtual Library describes the Inquisition as "a Roman Catholic tribunal for discovery and punishment of heresy, which was marked by the severity of questioning and punishment and lack of rights afforded to the accused." Pope Gregory IX established the Inquisition in 1233 to combat heresies in Europe, especially Albigensianism, or Catharism, which was flourishing in Albi, a city in southern France at the time. The Albigenses taught that the universe was a battleground between good, which was spirit, and evil, which was matter. *Inter alia*, human beings were believed to be spirits trapped in physical bodies. Albigensianism was one of the major heresies the Inquisition courts sought to root out, since such dualism is against the teachings of the Church. Saint Dominic, who had been sent to preach to the Albigenses, formed the Order of Preachers (Dominicans) in the early 13th century in response to this particular heresy.

Even though the Spanish and Portuguese Inquisitions are much talked about, the Inquisition was also in full gear throughout central and western Europe with the exception of England and Scandinavia. In the beginning, the Inquisition dealt only with

Christian heretics, however, subsequently, Jews became the subjects of these tribunals. Inquisition tribunals under the control of the pope were established in the regions of Aragon and Castile, among others. That was not the case with the Spanish Inquisition, which started in 1481. Fear of Jewish influence led Queen Isabella and King Ferdinand of Spain to petition the pope for the commencement of the Inquisition in Spain. With the approval of Rome, Tomas de Torquemada was named Grand Inquisitor for most of Spain. Tribunals were set up in Seville, Aragon, Catalonia, and Valencia among others. The Jewish people suffered deplorably before the barbaric Inquisition tribunals.

During the Inquisition in Spain, the Jews were compelled to denounce Judaism and embrace Christianity or face death or expulsion. The "Edict of Grace," which lasted thirty days, obliged many Jewish people to apostasy and denounced all Judaizers. The story of the Jewish girl, Elvira del Campo, illustrates the cruelty of the Inquisition: "She was carried to the torture chamber and told to tell the truth when she said that she had nothing to say. She was ordered to be stripped and again admonished, but was silent. After being tortured severely, she said 'Senores, I have done all that is said of me and I bear false witness against myself, for I do not want to see myself in such trouble; Please God, I have done nothing'" (Cohn-Sherbok, 2006:168).

Many Jews who refused the coerced conversion to Christianity were killed. For fear of death, thousands of Jews accepted Christianity and they came to be known as *conversos* (Spanish for "converted" or "New Christians"). Some of the conversos still faced suspicion and prejudice. For the twelve years of the Spanish Inquisition 1481–1492, more than 13,000 *conversos* were put on trial. Some Jews professed the Catholic faith but still continued practicing Judaism in secret. They were known as *marranos*. Finally, in an attempt to eliminate ties between the Jewish community and *conversos*, Ferdinand and Isabella issued the Alhambra Decree on March 31, 1492, which led to the expulsion of 160,000 Jews from Spain. Many Jews expelled from Spain went to Portugal for refuge. Unfortunately, Pope Paul II agreed to institute the

Inquisition in Portugal in 1521. Many Jews were killed and tortured during the Inquisition in Portugal. Isaac de Castro Tartas, Antonio Serrao de Castro, and Antonio Jose da Silva were among the well-known Jews who lost their lives in the Inquisition (Kemen, 2014:41).

Journalist Jonathan Kwitny recorded that in 1555, Pope Paul IV banned Jewish people from doing business, tortured and humiliated them in public entertainment, reminiscent of the *Neronian* madness, and claimed the Jewish people had "fallen into eternal servitude by their own guilt in Jesus' death" (1997:318). Popes Paul IV and Pius V locked up the Jewish people of Rome in their ghetto. In 1556, over 20 Judaizers were burnt alive, about 26 condemned to the galleys, and many others set free only after paying hefty fines. Down through the ages, the Church was utterly anti-Semitic. Pope Pius IX reportedly kidnapped a Jewish boy and refused to return him to his parents despite an international outcry. The same pontiff also enacted an 1862 law prohibiting the Jewish people from testifying against Christians in civil or criminal proceedings, barring them from owning real estate, and forcing them to pay a tax for upkeep of a house of catechumens whose aim was to convert Jewish people. More still, Pius IX forbade Jewish people from leaving their quarter of the city after dark (Allen, 2002:52). This explains why the beatification of Pius IX on September 3, 2000, stunned and angered many Jewish groups.

In 1904, Theodor Herzl, the founder of the Jewish Zionist Movement, attempted to lure Pope Pius X to support Jewish reestablishment in the Holy Land. According to Herzl, the saintly pope responded, "The Jews have not recognized our Lord; therefore, we cannot recognize the Jewish people. Thus, while we cannot prevent the Jews from going to Jerusalem, we could never sanction it" (Metzger, 2005:13). Pius X's immediate successor, Benedict XV (1914–1922), also vehemently objected to Jewish resettlement in the Holy Land. In a speech delivered on March 10, 1919, when the Paris Peace Conference was in session, Benedict XV stated, "For surely it would be a terrible grief for us and for all the Christian faithful if infidels (Jewish people) were placed in a privileged and prominent position; much more if these most holy sanctuaries of the Christian religion were given into the charge of non-Christians" (*L'Osservatore Romano*, March 21, 1919).

No matter the credibility of Herzl's version of Pope Pius X's response to the question of Jewish re-settlement in the Holy Land in 1904, the Holy See did not support Jewish immigration to Palestine under the *Balfour Declaration* of 1918. Pietro Gasparri, Vatican's Secretary of State, wrote, "The danger we most fear is the establishment of a Jewish state in Palestine" (Minerbi, 1990:148). In another instance, Gasparri emphatically stated that the Holy See could not agree to "the Jews being given a privileged and preponderant position in Palestine vis-à-vis other confessions" (Minerbi, 1990:179). The Holy See did not recognize the State of Israel after the U.N. partitioned Palestine in 1948. In his book, *The Hidden Pope*, Darcy O'Brien enumerated a plethora of reasons and reservations informally cited by Vatican officials for her reluctance to recognize the State of Israel after the partition of 1948. First, the Holy See was concerned about Arab reprisals against hundreds of thousands of Christians living within the Holy Land. Second, the Holy See prioritized a resolution to the question of a homeland for displaced Palestinians. Third, recognition of the Jewish State would jeopardize the matter of guaranteed access for Christians to holy places. Israel's borders were not clearly defined.

Traditionally, until the promulgation of *Nostra Aetate* in 1965, the *Easter Triduum* was not a good period for the Jewish people. On Good Friday, the Church prayed for the conversion of the Jewish people. The Good Friday Prayer for the Jewish people labelled them "perfidious." The ancient meaning of the Latin word *perfidis* in that context was "unbelieving," yet the English cognate "perfidious" had, over the centuries, gradually acquired the meaning of "treacherous."

Despitet the horrors of anti-Semitism, Rabbi Dan Cohn-Sherbok controversially argued that anti-Semitism has been very paradoxical down through the ages. In his book, *The Paradox of*

Anti-Semitism, the distinguished rabbi illustrated the intrinsic inter-relationship between Jew-hatred and Jewish survival. "It is a paradox that Jews need enemies in order to survive" (2006:209). The State of Israel, in a way, is seen by Cohn-Sherbok as a paradoxical fruit (*felix culpa*) of anti-Semitism and a reminder of the survivability of the Jewish race, "The creation of a Jewish homeland was thus born out of Jew-hatred; without anti-Semitism, the State of Israel would not exist—this is the paradox of the Jewish history" (Cohn-Sherbok, 2006:190).

Even though two wrongs do not make a right, the Jewish people also exhibited some strong anti-Christian tendencies in the nascent epoch of Christianity. The Jewish people persecuted Christians, especially toward the end of the 1st century. There is a paucity of evidence for Jewish persecution of "heretics" in general, or Christians in particular, in the period between 70 and 135 A.D. Although its veracity is still questionable, it has been recorded in some accounts that anti-Christian prayer was a common part of the synagogue liturgy. Historians note that some Church Fathers recommended against synagogue attendance. That notwithstanding, Jewish Christians continued to worship in synagogues for centuries. In the first centuries, Christians were considered a group within Judaism and they enjoyed the same rights as other Jews.

But as Christians separated from Judaism, many Jews began to insist that Christians could no longer claim to be Jews. As a result, the Romans began persecuting Christians as a threat to the empire. Thus, the Jews are also indirectly responsible for the persecution of Christians within the Roman Empire until the promulgation of the Edict of Milan in 313 A.D. Many scholars believe that Jews began to view Christians as outsiders, at least partly because they felt betrayed by Jewish believers-in-Jesus who had left Jerusalem for the safer countryside during the rebellion of 66–70 A.D. that led to the destruction of the second Temple. Early Christians, influenced by the example of Jesus, believed in nonviolence and therefore refused to fight under any circumstances. The separation of Christianity from Judaism was not a single event but rather a painful process that took generations to complete. In the separation could be found the roots of the hostility between Jews and Christians and some aspects of anti-Semitism.

The fourteen-point *Fundamental Agreement* of December 30, 1993, which led to the Holy See's recognition of the Israeli state, marked a white page in the black book of Catholic-Jewish relations. The *Agreement* was signed by Msgr. Claudio Celli, Vatican assistant secretary of state and by Yossi Beilin, Israel's deputy minister of foreign affairs. The *Fundamental Agreement* extended the theological advances of *Nostra Aetate* into the political realm, creating in 1994, for the first time, formal diplomatic relations between the Holy See and the State of Israel. It addressed three spheres of relations: 1) political relations between Israel and the Holy See; 2) relations between the Jewish people and the Catholic Church; and 3) relations between the State of Israel and the Roman Catholic Church.

The *Agreement* was an apt example of open diplomacy because of the media coverage it received and by virtue of the fact that it was registered with the U.N. Secretariat. At the end of World War I, President Woodrow Wilson mentioned the danger of secret diplomacy as one of the remote causes of the War. That is why, as stipulated in Article 102 of the U.N. Charter, for any agreement between two Member States to be binding and invoked before any organ of the U.N., it must "as soon as possible be registered with the Secretariat and published by it" (1945). According to international relations scholar David Gibbs, secret diplomacy was dangerous because, more often than not, it was used by leaders to mislead the populations of their countries, rather than to keep information *incognito* from international opponents (1995:213).

Although open diplomacy has been lavishly hailed, British diplomat Harold Nicolson highlighted the danger of open diplomacy. "The endeavor to establish 'open diplomacy' has led delegates to make propaganda speeches in public and conduct serious negotiations in the privacy of hotel bedrooms—which leads to waste of time and farce" (2001:164). Secret diplomacy did not become obsolete after Wilson's Fourteen Points. Secret, backchannel negotiations and clandestine meetings were the hallmark of Henry Kissinger's diplomacy which, he argued, freed negotiators "from the necessity of living up to criteria set beforehand by media and critics" (1979:803).

Different schools of thought account for the positive change in Jewish-Catholic relations leading to the *Fundamental Agreement* of 1993. Achille Ratti (Pope Pius XI, 1922–1939), the more than three decades Ambrosian and Vatican librarian, was pro-Jewish. Pope Pius XI once said, "Spiritually, we are Semites." Thus, one cannot be a good Catholic until they have fallen in love with the religion and the people of Israel. Perhaps that is why Scott Hahn, the Protestant and Calvinist convert to Catholicism and Catholic Apologist, argued that anti-Semitism is spiritual stupidity (2003). Pope Pius XI passed away in his sleep on February 10, 1939. Due to the pope's pro-Jewish efforts, Bernard Joseph, on behalf of the Jewish Agency (the future Government of Israel) wrote:

> In common with the whole of civilized humanity, the Jewish people mourn the loss of one of the greatest exponents of the cause of international peace and goodwill…. More than once did we have occasion to be deeply grateful for the attitude which he took up against the persecution of racial minorities and, in particular, for the deep concern which he expressed for the fate of the persecuted Jews of Central Europe. His noble efforts on their behalf will ensure for him and for all time a warm place in the memories of the Jewish people wherever they live (Rychlak, 2000:106).

Perhaps unlike the "quiet diplomacy" of former U.N. Chief, Dag Hammarskjöld, the "silence" of Pius XII during the Holocaust has been unjustly and uninformedly criticized by some people. Recent scholarship, however, has certainly exonerated and vindicated the much-reviled Pope Pius XII on his role in the Holocaust. For decades, Pius XII was unfairly accused of anti-Semitism, being tolerant to the Nazi cause, silent in the face of persecution, and being under Hitler's influence. Five years after Pius' death, German playwright Rolf Hochhuth wrote *The Deputy* (*Der Stellvertreter*) in February 1963. The play grotesquely indicted the pope for his alleged inaction and indifference to the genocide against the Jewish people. To a large extent, *The Deputy*, a historical fiction, set the ball rolling for an "unshakable axiom of popular mythology that Pope Pius XII was, if not actually a crypto-Nazi, at least guilty of criminal cowardice and insensitivity in the face of the Holocaust" (Rychlak, 2020:250).

In 1999, British journalist John Cornwell's *Hitler's Pope: The Secret History of Pius XII* was published. Cornwell ridiculously concluded that Pope Pius XII "was the ideal Pope for Hitler's unspeakable plan. He was Hitler's pawn. He was Hitler's Pope" (1999:297). It has now been brought to light that even though the pope did not expressly call out Hitler during the Holocaust, he successfully worked indefatigably behind the scenes to save the lives of thousands of Jewish people. Although the villainous "silence" of Pope Pius XII has been alleged for decades now, there is much historical evidence to confirm that he was not really silent. He was not indifferent to the plight of European Jewry during the Holocaust (Dalin, 2020:2). He made pronouncements and sometimes thinly-veiled condemnation of Nazism and other evil regimes. "He spoke, and wrote, instead, in generic phrases, in allusions, with judgements marked by indirectness, naming no names and no country" (Graham, 2000:165). Pius XII's first encyclical, *Summi Pontificatus* ("Darkness over the Earth"), issued on October 20, 1939, was clearly a repudiation of Hitlerism. The pope condemned the "Godless State" and made reference to an "ever-increasing host of Christ's enemies" (par. 7). Heinrich Mueller, head of the Gestapo, said the encyclical "is directed exclusively against Germany, both in ideology and in regard to the German-Polish dispute ..." (Rychlak, 2000:125). The pope did not make any name-calling public denunciations because he knew that would only provoke and embolden Hitler to massacre the more. He was dissuaded from publicly calling out Hitler by many leaders including Jewish leaders, Polish Archbishop Adam Sapieha, German religious leaders, the International Red Cross, and several Jewish rescue organizations.

At the Nuremberg trials (between 1945 and 1949), German Field Marshal Albert Kesselring observed of the "silent" diplomacy of Pope Pius XII, "If [Pius XII] did not protest, he failed to do so because he told himself, quite rightly: If I protest, Hitler will be driven to madness; not only will that not help the Jews, but we must expect that they will then be killed all the more" (Rychlak, 2000:261). Pius XII was very aware of the possible fallouts from a public reprimand of Hitler, "No doubt a protest would have gained me the praise and respect of the civilized world, but it would have submitted the poor Jews to an even worse fate" (Rychlak, 2000:270).

In his well-researched book, *Hitler, the War, and the Pope*, Ronald Rychlak, American law professor, has painstakingly documented Pius XII's behind-the-scenes efforts to alleviate the sufferings of the Jewish people during the war. He also highlighted the accolades and encomiums the pope received from Jewish communities world-wide after the war. The pope was wholeheartedly against the massacre of the Jewish people. The 1943–1944 American Jewish Yearbook observed that Pius XII "took an unequivocal stand against the oppression of Jews throughout Europe." The pope used personal and pastoral means to help the persecuted Jewish people. This explains why Robert Leiber, the pope's private secretary and close advisor during the war years said, "The Pope sided very unequivocally with the Jews at the time. He spent his entire private fortune on their behalf.... Pius spent what he inherited himself, as a Pacelli, from his family" (Rychlak, 2000:253).

The pope received countless messages of appreciation from Jewish leaders for his manifold acts of charity after the war. Grand Rabbi Isaac Herzog of Jerusalem wrote, "I well know that His Holiness the Pope is opposed from the depths of his noble soul to all persecution and especially to the persecution ... which the Nazis inflict unremittingly on the Jewish people.... I take this opportunity to express ... my sincere thanks as well as my deep appreciation ... of the invaluable help given by the Catholic Church to the Jewish people in its affliction" (Rychlak, 2000:256).

It is now known that the pope was not a Nazi sympathizer. Neither was he indifferent to the genocide against the Jewish people. After the war, a group of Roman Jews came to thank the pope for having protected them from Nazi persecution. The pope remarked during their meeting, "For centuries, Jews have been unjustly treated and despised. It is time they were treated with justice and humanity. God wills it and the Church wills it. St. Paul tells us that the Jews are our brothers. They should also be welcomed as friends" (Rychlak, 2000:311). Raffael Cantoni, the head of Italian Jewry's wartime Jewish Assistance Committee reported, "The Church and the papacy have saved Jews as much and in as far as they could save Christians.... Six million of my coreligionists have been murdered by the Nazis, but there could have been many more victims, had it not been for the efficacious intervention of Pius XII" (Lapide, 1967:133). It was no exaggeration when American legal scholar Robert George wrote, "Indeed, it is almost certainly true that Pius XII saved the lives of more Jewish and non-Jewish victims of Hitler's madness than any other human being. In the estimate of Israeli diplomat Pinchas Lapide, the Vatican and other Catholic institutions, acting at the Pope's express direction, saved the lives of more than 800,000 European Jews" (Rychlak, 2000:311). Renowned Nobel Prize-winning physicist Albert Einstein, himself a Jewish refugee from Nazi Germany, paid hearty tribute to the moral "courage" of Pope Pius XII during the war:

> Being a lover of freedom, when the Nazi revolution came in Germany, I looked to the universities to defend it, knowing that they had always boasted of their devotion to the cause of truth; but, no, the universities immediately were silenced. Then I looked to the great editors of the newspapers, whose flaming editorials in days gone by had proclaimed their love of freedom: but

they, like the universities, were silenced in a few short weeks. Only the Catholic Church stood squarely across the path of Hitler's campaign for suppressing the truth. I never had any special interest in the Church before, but now I feel a great affection and admiration because the Church alone has had the courage and persistence to stand for intellectual truth and moral freedom. I am forced thus to confess that what I once despised, I now praise unreservedly (Dalin, 2000).

The Talmud, the great sixth century compendium of Jewish religious law and ethics, teaches Jews that "whosoever preserves one life, it is accounted to him by Scripture as if he had preserved a whole world." More than any 20th-century leader, Pius XII effectively fulfilled this Talmudic dictum when his direct efforts saved the lives of many Jews during the Holocaust. In his *Notes on the State of Virginia*, U.S. President Thomas Jefferson, wrote: "A patient pursuit of facts, and a cautious combination and comparison of them, is the drudgery to which man is subjected by his maker, if he wishes to attain sure knowledge." A patient pursuit of facts has certainly led many people of goodwill and reason to arrive at the denouement that Pope Pius XII was not silent and indifferent to the plight of the Jewish people during the war.

Pope Saint John XXIII is revered among various Jewish communities since he convened Vatican II (1962–1965), whose document, *Nostra Aetate*, drastically changed and improved the course of the Jewish-Catholic relationship. More still, the good Pope John XXIII once interrupted a Good Friday service and ordered the term "perfidious Jews" be removed from the prayer *Pro perfidis Judaeis* (for the faithless Jews). In 1960, he ordered it removed from all rituals for the reception of converts. The current prayer of the Roman Liturgy for Good Friday prays for "the Jewish people, first to hear the word of God, that they may continue to grow in the love of His name and in faithfulness to His covenant." Pope Saint John XXIII once stopped in his car to bless the Roman Jewish people leaving a synagogue after their Sabbath worship services.

Darcy O'Brien, American author of fiction and literary criticism, poetically and picturesquely captured that moment in his book, *The Hidden Pope:*

> On a Saturday early in his papacy, John XXIII was being driven northward along the River Tiber. When his car was slowed by traffic along the Lungotevere Cenci, he noticed a building that he didn't recognize. Its Assyrian-Babylonian architecture may have reminded him of places that he recalled from his days as nuncio in Istanbul. Soberly dressed people approached and passed between columns to enter it. As if marking an oasis, slender palms loomed from an adjacent courtyard, adding to the Levantine effect.
>
> "What is this palazzo?" Pope John asked.
>
> "That is the great temple of the Jews," his driver said. Pope John told him to stop. The familiar figure, large and round and with a face that radiated benevolence, emerged from the limousine. He stood there for a moment, alone in white on the busy boulevard, gazing at Hebrew characters chiseled on a gray granite slab affixed to the façade. Moving his upraised fingers, he silently blessed this place and its people. Then he sped away toward Vatican City, which lies less than a mile from the temple, across the Tiber.

It is no surprise then that on the night of Pope John XXIII's death, the Chief Rabbi of Rome and other leaders of the Jewish community gathered with hundreds of thousands of Catholics in Saint Peter's Square to mourn him and to pray that his benevolence had not died with him (O'Brien, 1998). The Council's document, *Nostra Aetate* ("In Our Time"), issued on October 28, 1965, seemingly got the ball rolling for the dialogue, since "perfidious" and other abusive language of the Church directed at the Jewish people were rescinded. *Nostra Aetate* stated that although the Jews present at Pilate's palace at the time of Jesus' trial called for his death, the Jewish race is not to be held responsible for his death. *Nostra Aetate* condemned anti-Semitism despite fierce opposition from some Council Fathers. Norman Tanner, S.J., a renowned expert in the ecumenical councils of the Church, in an interview with this author, indicated that Pope Paul VI's historic visit to the Holy Land in 1964 was a significant step in the Catholic-Jewish positive dialogue, although Pope Paul VI, the astute diplomat, intentionally did not mention the phrase "State of Israel" during that visit.

According to the Melady and Flynn's account, the U.S. pressured the Vatican to recognize the State of Israel. In his version of this account, Thomas Melady, one-time U.S. ambassador to the Holy See, reported that his instruction from Secretary of State James Baker, read, "You should also urge the Holy See to recognize the State of Israel" (1994:124). When did the Holy See start succumbing to such pressures? Some other accounts hold that the famous handshake between Palestinian leader Yasser Arafat and Israeli Prime Minister Yitzhak Rabin in Oslo, September 9, 1993, under the aegis of U.S. President Bill Clinton, hammered in the final nail to the establishment of the relations between the Holy See and the State of Israel.

George Weigel stated that "the Gulf War and the Madrid Peace Conference created conditions for accelerating a course on which the Holy See was already launched. They did not create the new course" (1999:712). In Kissingerian diplomacy and practical politics, every policy choice "is not an isolated act but an accumulation of previous decisions reflecting history or tradition and values as well as ... immediate pressures" (Otte, 2001:184). Accordingly, the Holy See's diplomatic relations with the State of Israel was not an isolated act. It was part of a process. Miracles happen only where conditions are possible, and all those initiatives and accounts, although not per se pivotal towards Holy See-Israeli diplomatic ties, played their remote roles. The above-mentioned accounts created the necessary conditions for the subsequent establishment of diplomatic ties in 1994, just as the speculations of the ancient thinkers of Ionia and Miletus set the ball rolling for the subsequent numerous philosophical schools of thought and debates. The *Wo-jtyłan factor* was pivotal in the establishment of diplomatic relations between the State of Israel and the Holy See.

The Wojtyłan Factor (John Paul II Difference)

According to Weigel, Bernstein, Politi, Darcy O'Brien, and David Dalin, the *John Paul II Difference* and the *Wojtyłan experiences* were the most decisive factors in the Holy See's realization of diplomatic ties with Israel in 1994. In his review, Weigel boldly stated, "The *Fundamental Agreement* was widely regarded as one of the diplomatic master strokes of Pope John Paul II's pontificate and a historic turning point in Jewish-Catholic relations" (1999:697). Weigel analogously compared the quote of the Duke of Wellington's stance on Waterloo as a "damn near-run thing" to the Holy See's establishment of diplomatic relations with Israel. It was via the initiative of Saint John Paul II, providential coincidences, and back-channel negotiation that brought the diplomatic ties to fruition (1999:697).

George Weigel also noted that only someone like Saint John Paul II, who had an intuition of the Jewish pain, could have sealed the historic *Fundamental Agreement* with the State of Israel. In Kissingerian diplomatic theory, intuitive understanding of a given situation and the forces at work within it is an important attribute of a good diplomat (1979:329). Wojtyła's idiosyncratic Jewish past (*the Wojtyłan experience*) was a major factor for his pro-Jewish outlook, which led to the relations in 1994. Karol Wojtyła (Saint John Paul II) was one of the drafters of *Nostra Aetate* in 1965, a document which was Jewish-friendly in content and decisive in the future Catholic-Jewish cordial relations.

The past experience of a leader is a major idiosyncratic variable in political science. Wojtyła was born in Wadowice in 1920. In his early childhood, 20 to 30 percent of the population in Wadowice was Jewish. Thursday was market day in the Rynek, the main square of Wadowice. The ordinary Polish peasants carried livestock and other produce to sell to the Jewish community. The

Jewish merchants were also in full gear on market days. Jerzy Kluger, a childhood friend of Karol Wojtyła, narrates some interesting market details, "The Jewish merchants had their own *stragan*, where they sold the foods prescribed by their Law. These included fish with fins and scales, unleavened bread and sweets for the *Shabbat*, and the meat of animals that chew their cud and have cloven hoofs.... Because pork is forbidden in the kosher diet (although pigs have cloven hoofs, they do not chew their cud), the Jewish merchants sold *koszerna kiełbasa*, a beef sausage that was not as flavorful as the pork variety, but was still highly prized" (Kluger, 2012:3).

During Wojtyła's childhood, 40 percent of the shops in Wadowice were owned by Jewish people (Yallop, 2007:235). Wojtyła interacted with the Jewish people on all fronts. His closest childhood friend was Jerzy Kluger, a Jew, and it is no surprise that Kluger was the first person to whom Pope John Paul II granted an audience after he became pope in 1978. The day after the audience, the headline in some leading newspapers around the globe read something to the effect of: "The Polish pope grants his first audience to a Jew."

During their childhood, Wojtyła visited Kluger's home almost every day and entered prep school with him. Jerzy Kluger's father, Wilhelm Kluger, was the president of the Jewish community in Wadowice and a defense attorney. Jerzy Kluger has personally and masterfully detailed his lifelong friendship with Pope John Paul II in his 2012 book, *The Pope and I*. This explains why papal biographer Tad Szulc stated that Wojtyła "had Jewish playmates and classmates with whom he enjoyed easy camaraderie" (1995:68).

From some accounts, Wojtyła's life in Wadowice was intricately intertwined with the Jewish people. The house within which Wojtyła was born belonged to a Jewish family. The landlord of the apartment that the Wojtyła family rented in Wadowice was Chaim Balamuth, a Jewish man. The Wojtyłas rented the second-floor apartment while the Balamuth family occupied the ground floor (Szulc, 1995:62). The apartment used to be called a "railway flat"—a small foyer, one large room, one small room, and a kitchen, with each room leading into the next. The toilet, shared with two other families was outside in the corridor; they bathed in a wooden tub in the kitchen.

Reminiscing in February 1994 about his childhood, the then-pontiff said, "The house where we lived was owned by a Jewish family. It is from there that I have this attitude of community, of communal feeling about the Jews ... it all comes from there" (Szulc, 1995:69). That confession of John Paul II is more than a biographical note. It espouses the heart, mind, and soul of Saint John Paul II. That is why in *His Holiness*, Carl Bernstein and Marco Politi stated strongly that "since the time of the Apostle Peter, no Roman pontiff has ever spent his childhood in such close contact with Jewish life" (1996:30).

In Marcin Wadowita school, soccer matches between the Jews against Catholics were common, especially in the springtime. Poldek Golberger was the goalie for the Jewish team. However, whenever he couldn't play, Lolek would take his place between the goalposts for the Jewish team (Kluger, 2012:24–25). Despite his ecumenical and determined sporting spirits, it is said that Golberger was a better goalkeeper. One of Wojtyła's former teammates in Wadowice said of him, "He was a great guy, but, confidentially, he was a lousy goalkeeper" (Szulc, 1995:68). Reflecting on Wojtyła's goalkeeping role for the Jewish team, Tad Szulc wrote, "In most places, this would have been insignificant, but in Poland it carried real meaning, defining Wojtyła's personality and attitudes for the future" (1995:68).

Wojtyła and Regina "Ginka" Beer, whom Kluger described as "a Jewish girl with stupendous dark eyes and jet-black hair, slender, a superb actress," were very good friends (Bernstein & Politi, 1996:36). In his book, *The Pope and I*, Kluger wrote, "She [Ginka] was very beautiful, and everyone at school was in love with her, including me" (2012:20). "Ginka had a special bond with Lolek, because they both loved the theatre and acted on stage together" (Kluger, 2012:21). The Beers were next-door neighbors of the Wojtyła family. According to American rabbi and historian David

Dalin, Karol Wojtyła's father offered his balcony to the Beer family for *Succoth* or *the Feast of Tabernacles* (2007:1). Enumerated in Leviticus 23 are feasts that the children of Israel were commanded to celebrate throughout their generations. One of these feasts is *Succoth*. Etymologically, the word *Succoth* means "tabernacles" or "booths," and refers to the temporary dwelling places of the children of Israel when they wandered through the desert after their departure from Egypt. Inferring from Tyranowski's conviction that "every moment had to be put to use," one can conclude that Wojtyła's early amiable acquaintances with the Jewish people must have been put to use in the events leading to the Holy See-Israeli diplomatic ties of 1994.

Jerzy Kluger wrote, "The people in the Vatican do not know Jews, and previous popes do not know Jews. But this pope is a friend of the Jewish people because he knows Jewish people. He grew up in Wadowice" (Goodstein, 1998). Addressing the Warsaw Jewish community on June 9, 1991, the pope said, "Man lives on the basis of his own experiences. I belong to the generation for which relationships with Jewish people was a daily occurrence" (Szulc, 1995:69). In the analysis of Bernstein and Politi, Saint John Paul II's early association with the Jewish people of Wadowice gave him an education that no Roman pontiff before him ever had (1996:54). In Cornwell's history, unlike Wojtyła, Pacelli (Pope Pius XII) had no camaraderie with the Jewish people in his childhood. "A groundswell of vicious antipathy toward Jews was promoted in the only circles to which Pacelli had access. This is in stark contrast to the experience of Pope John Paul II, who knew and had friendly relations with real Jews as a young man in Poland and who grew up in Cracow within an hour's drive from Oswiecim, or Auschwitz as we know it" (Rubenstein, 2002:183).

In the summer of 1938, Karol Wojtyła and his father left Wadowice and moved to Kraków, where he enrolled at the Jagiellonian University in the autumn semester. Wojtyła would then go on to live in Kraków for almost 40 years as a student, a laborer, a curate, a professor, an archbishop, and a cardinal. Thus, Wojtyła was a Cracovian *par excellence*. Idiosyncratically, Kraków's centuries-old and rich Jewish culture informed Saint John Paul II's pro-Jewish policies during his pontificate. The Jews arrived in Poland in the 10th century looking for new markets and greener pastures. Most of them had migrated from Germany and from the Saxon lands. Because of their industriousness and ingenuity, the Polish princes loved them and were kind to them. Actually in 1264, Prince Bolesław the Pious established a statute that protected Jewish property, synagogues, cemeteries, and guaranteed their right to practice any profession (Kluger, 2012:104). Prince Bolesław the Pious also warned that anyone who recklessly accused a Jew of practicing certain demonic rituals would be put to death. King Casimir III the Great (1333–1370) was a reliable protector of the Jews in Poland. On October 9, 1334, he confirmed the privileges granted to the Jews by Prince Bolesław the Pious in 1264. Death was the penalty for the kidnapping of Jewish children with the goal of enforced baptism during his reign. Legend has it that he had a Jewish mistress named Esterka, who bore him four children.

During the epoch when Europe was being ravaged by wars of religion (1618–1648), a unique tradition of religious tolerance and respect for the rights of conscience was the accepted public norm in Kraków and Poland in general (Kluger, 2012:105). As historian Norman Davies once put it, Poland was "a land without bonfires," while much of the rest of Europe self-destructed in the Thirty Years' War. There were no religious persecutions in reformation-era Kraków, no coerced conversions, no burning of heretics. In 1583, Poland's political leaders made a declaration of tolerance, the likes of which could be found nowhere else in Europe, "We who differ in matters of religion will keep the peace among ourselves, and neither shed blood on account of differences of Faith, or kinds of church, nor punish one another by confiscation of goods, deprivation of honor, imprisonment, or exile" (Weigel, Gress, and Weigel, 2015:4).

Even though Poland has a prestigious history of religious tolerance, Poles were considered inherently anti-Semitic in some circles. "There was a saying current among Jews of Polish origin, of whom Prime Minister Begin was one, that 'Poles drink anti-Semitism with their mothers' milk'" (O'Brien, 1998). A wave of the anti-Semitic virus swept across Eastern Europe following the end of World War 1. Poland was also infected. Some Polish peasants subscribed to the hearsay that "Jews stole and murdered Christian children to mix their blood with matzo meal for the Passover ritual meal" (Yallop, 2007:234). There were repugnant articles in Polish newspapers, *Orędownik* and *Polska Karta*, exclaiming "Na zidow!" (Kill the Jews!) (Kluger, 2012:15).

Unfortunately, some of the anti-Semitic rhetoric was done by top churchmen. In a public letter in the 1930s, Cardinal August Hlond, the then-head of the Polish Church, stated, "It is necessary to provide separate schools for Jews, so that our children will not be infected by their lower morality" (Yallop, 2007:237). Some of Cardinal Hlond's homilies were toxic and anti-Semitic. The churchman indefatigably urged the Catholic faithful to undermine and boycott Jewish businesses, because he believed they were after economic supremacy in Poland. His regrettable rallying call was *Bojkot owszem* (On with the boycott) (Klugger, 2012:15).

When anti-Semitism became rife and dangerous in Poland, some Jewish people migrated to Palestine. In 1938, Ginka Beer, Wojtyła's good friend and acting companion, and the entire Beer family began their journey to Palestine because some parts of Poland had become too unsafe for them. Unfortunately, "Ginka's parents never made it to Palestine. Her father was killed in the Soviet Union; her mother died in Auschwitz" (Yallop, 2007:238). Jerzy Kluger describes an emotional scene before Ginka's departure to Palestine:

> On the day of her departure, Ginka went to the Wojtyła home to say good-bye. Captain Wojtyła embraced her and tried to convince her that there were other Catholics in Poland like them, who were not hostile toward Jews. But Lolek said nothing. He was standing in the corner of the living room by the painting of the Black Madonna of Częstochowa. Ginka approached

him, and she must have been surprised that her friend wasn't saying a word, because she had become so accustomed to his grand speeches. She understood his silence when she touched his cheek. He was crying (2012:22).

Karol Wojtyła was never infected and remained immune to the anti-Semitic virus that was ravaging some parts of Poland in his childhood. This is evident in David Yallop's confession, "Karol senior, along with his son, would on occasions go to the local synagogue just as in turn Jurek Kluger, a particularly close Jewish school friend, would seek out Wojtyła in the local church where Karol was an altar boy. These attitudes and experiences were unusual in Poland at the time" (2007:236). Idiosyncratically, Wojtyła's Wadowice was comparatively less anti-Semitic. Yes, in Wojtyła's Wadowice, some Poles were hostile to the Jews. There were occasional tense moments in the Polish-Jewish relations in Wadowice. Jerzy Kluger who grew up in Wadowice explained:

> Mild insinuations were addressed, and every now and then occasional damage was done to Jewish shops and homes, as a feeble demonstration by some group of students from Kraków or by the processions making their way from the villages around Wadowice toward one of the shrines.... When the procession of the faithful heading to Kalwaria Zebrzydowska went through the city, a few stones were sometimes thrown at the half-closed windows and shuttered shops of Jews.... When they reached Wadowice, they took the route from Adama Mickiewicza Street to 3 Maja Street, crossing through the city, and then continued east for another nine miles, toward Klecza, finally reaching the shrine at the foot of Mount Zar (Kluger, 2012:17).

Anti-Semitism was uncommon in Wadowice when compared to the rest of Poland. This explains Kluger's assertion that a natural compromise between Jews and Catholics was part of everyday life in Wadowice (2012:17). Already as a young boy in middle school, the young Karol Wojtyła rejected all forms of discrimination against the Jewish people. Jerzy Kluger explains that Wojtyła used his knowledge of Polish history and literature to push back against pockets of anti-Semitic attitudes in his middle school. He knew that revered Polish writers always celebrated the two great traditions of Poland: Catholicism and Judaism. He often quoted Andrzej Towiański, a Lithuanian mystical thinker, who in his 1848 book, *Sktad Zasad* had called for respect for the Jews and famously referred to them as *starsi bracia* (older brothers), an expression the future pope would use in his 1986 visit to Grand Synagogue of Rome (Kluger, 2012:16). In his school days, Lolek, as the future pope was known, also quoted Adam Mickiewicz and his epic poem *Pan Tadeusz*, which featured a patriotic Jewish character named Jankiel. Lolek often said, "one of the people there spoke out and said that Jankiel was a kindhearted Jew, who loved his country like a true Pole" (Kluger, 2012:16). Barely twelve years old, Wojtyła had already memorized *Pan Tadeusz*, and would recite it from start to finish.

Prominent Jewish author David Dalin also maintained that Wojtyła's ecumenical personality was shaped by his early camaraderie with the Jewish people. As pope, John Paul II would say, "I remember the Jews who gathered every Saturday at the synagogue behind our school. Both religious groups, Catholics and Jews, were united ... by the awareness that they prayed to the same God" (2007). Karol Wojtyła personally witnessed the Holocaust, and not only did he lose some of his professors to concentration camps, but some of his Jewish friends as well. In 20th-century political lexicon, the term "Holocaust" refers to the Nazis attempt to terminate the Jewish population in Europe, as well as other minorities such as the gypsies and Romani people. Writing to his friend Jerzy Kluger in later years, Saint John Paul II mentioned, "Many of those who perished, your co-religionists and our fellow countrymen, were our colleagues in our elementary school and later, in the high school where we graduated together, fifty years ago" (Dalin, 2007).

George Weigel, papal biographer and perhaps the most authoritative interpreter of John Paul II in North America, noted that throughout his papacy, Saint John Paul II invested enormous energies towards the normalization and institutionalization of Catholic-Jewish relations. In Kissingerian diplomatic theory, "A true statesman is prepared to grapple with the circumstances, to wrench politics from the tight fist of the past, in order to reshape reality ..." (Otte, 2001:187). Pope John Paul II was a true statesman since he was prepared to grapple with the Catholic-Jewish age-old history of hatred.

As a young priest in Poland, Karol Wojtyła significantly rejected a request from two Catholic foster parents to baptize a young Jewish boy named Hiller into Catholicism. Hiller's parents had died in the Holocaust, and Fr. Wojtyła advised the foster parents (the Yachowitzes) to respect the wish of Hiller's deceased biological parents (Szulc, 1995:162). There are some parallels between the Hiller case and the Mortara case.

Pope Pius IX's (1846–1878) handling of the much-publicized Mortara case caused some international consternation and condemnation. Pius IX has been vilified for having "kidnapped" a Jewish boy named Edgardo Levi Mortara. Edgardo was born in Bologna in the year 1851. The said kidnapping happened in the Papal State of Bologna in 1858 when Pius IX was pope and sovereign of the Papal States. Against the civil laws in force in the Papal States, the Mortara family hired a young Christian woman named Anna Morisi for domestic services. When Edgardo was just a little over one year old, he was struck by a terrible disease and raging fevers to the point that the doctors had lost all hope of saving him (Messori, 2015:78). Aware of the teachings of the Catholic Church, Anna Morisi secretly baptized the sick child whose life was in great danger. However, Edgardo somewhat regained his health. As such, Anna Morisi found herself in a very disturbing situation after having baptized a Jewish boy without the consent of his parents. She lamentably kept the secret to herself for some five years. Anna Morisi was subsequently encouraged by her friends to confide in her confessor.

She did and the case was eventually brought to the attention of Pope Pius IX.

Through the archbishopric of Bologna, Pius IX communicated to Edgardo's parents that by virtue of the Sacrament of Baptism, Edgardo had been incorporated into Christ and his Church. As such, the Church had the duty and obligation to take charge of Edgardo's religious education (Messori, 2015:81). The pope argued, "A Christian boy could not be trusted to be brought up by Jewish parents" (Wills, 2000:40–41). Not surprisingly, Edgardo's parents vehemently opposed the idea of surrendering their son and his education to the Catholic Church. The case became internationalized and politicized and the Jewish community and papacy-haters rallied behind the Mortaras. However, much to the discomfort of the pope, on June 24, 1858, guards were sent to the Mortaras' house and the 6-year-old Edgardo was taken away.

In Rome, Edgardo was placed in the Institute for Neophytes, or new converts. Edgardo eventually became a Catholic priest and served as a missionary in Spain for many years. He was greatly loved by Pope Pius IX who considered him a dearest son. In his unpublished memoirs, Edgardo, who eventually took the name Pio Maria, described his case. "When I was adopted by Pius IX, the whole world shouted that I was a victim, a martyr of the Jesuits. But in spite of all this, I, most grateful to Divine Providence, which had led me to the true Family of Christ.... What is left of all that? Only the heroic *'non possumus'* of the great Pope of the Immaculate Conception" (Messori, 2015:1). Despite Edgardo's positive take of his adoption by the pope, Pope Pius IX has been harshly criticized for his action and many people are raising objections to his canonization because of the Mortara case. When faced with a similar situation, Karol Wojtyła handled it differently.

Saint John Paul II went the extra mile via his parallel personal diplomacy (PPD), whereby he sent persons on his behalf for informal talks with the Jewish people and not necessarily on behalf of the Holy See. Via his PPD, John Paul II sent his representatives on back-channel risky missions to war-torn areas. Cardinal Etchegaray described it as a "politics of presence" and in an interview, he stated that PPD was more effective in brokering peace than official Track One diplomacy (Weigel, 1999:506). Kluger, Etchegaray, and David Jaeger were key persons in John Paul II's personal diplomacy. Etchegaray was the embodiment of John Paul II's PPD. *Ingegnere* Jerzy Kluger, who played the role of "broker and host," later revealed that in 1981, the pope asked him to serve as informal intermediary between the Vatican and the State of Israel in the quest for possible diplomatic relations. Kluger played the role of broker and host, inviting Israeli and Vatican representatives to dine at his tennis club in Rome and playing bridge with key Vatican churchmen like Archbishop Andrzej Maria Deskur. Kluger made a couple of visits to Israel on behalf of the Holy See to facilitate the agreement leading to diplomatic ties between the two states. In his book, *The Pope and I*, Kluger reveals some interesting details of his January 1983 visit to Israel where he met with Israeli foreign minister Yitzhak Shamir. *Inter alia,* Shamir told him, "Oh, I am sure the important mediation you are carrying out with the Vatican will allow you to understand certain things…. You are working for the sake of Israel, and for this we are infinitely grateful" (Kluger, 2012:164–65). Saint John Paul II and President Shimon Perez exchanged personal diplomatic representatives after their meeting in 1992. Thus, the process leading to the establishment of diplomatic ties between the Holy See and Israel was Track One and a Half diplomacy, since unofficial and official agents of both parties played pivotal roles in the realization of the *Fundamental Agreement* in 1993.

The Jewish community had long been in Rome, even before the martyrdom of Saints Peter and Paul in Rome around 67 A.D. Judas Maccabee sent his emissaries to Rome hundreds of years before the apostles ever ventured there (Weigel, 1999:482). Rome's Grand Synagogue is just two miles away from Saint Peter's Square. Ironically, no Roman pontiff for two thousand years ever paid his Jewish neighbors a visit. Saint John Paul II changed that piece of history when on April 13, 1986, he became the first pope ever to visit Rome's chief Synagogue across the Tiber. David Dalin wrote, "In becoming the pope to go to the Great Synagogue of Rome to meet the Roman Jewish community at their own place of worship, John Paul II changed history" (2007). In his typical insightful fashion, André Frossard opined that the pope's crossing of the Tiber to the synagogue was a rarer event than crossing the Rubicon had been in an earlier day in Rome's long history (1990:97). *TIME* (1987) also captured the visit clearly when it stated that "the first known Pope to enter a Jewish house of worship since St. Peter." Ironically, during decades of persecution in Rome, the Jewish people expressed their hopelessness by a proverb: "The persecution will end when the Pope enters the synagogue." At last a pope entered the synagogue on April 13, 1986, even though the persecution had ended by 1870 when the Papal States were absorbed into the kingdom of Italy.

Significantly, John Paul II's visit was not just a pope visiting a synagogue, but a visible expression of *mea culpa* for the Church's culpability in the persecution of the Jewish people down through the ages. "For centuries the Jews of Rome, under papal rule, had suffered discrimination and humiliation, were confined to a ghetto and were forced to attend sermons urging them to convert" (*TIME* 1987). After a welcome address by Rabbi Eliot, John Paul II stated that the Church condemns anti-Semitism and apologized for the inhumane treatment of the Jewish people by the Church. In moving words, he addressed the Jewish people: "You are our beloved brothers, and in a certain way, our older brothers." Idiosyncratically, Adam Mickiewicz, one of John Paul II's favorite authors, had used that expression in his poem *Pan Tadeusz*.

In his very engaging book, *Lessons in Hope: My Unexpected Life with St. John Paul II* (2017), George Weigel confesses that he would have paid gold and frankincense to have known a major subplot in the events leading to John Paul II's historic visit to the Grand Synagogue when he was writing *Witness to Hope* (1999). Traditionally, the Jewish people do not like the sight of the Cross. The Cross has been a symbol of Jewish intolerance and hate against Jesus and the early Christians. It has also been a symbol of shame for the Jews for the role they played in the crucifixion of Jesus Christ. The Cross also evokes some painful memories for the Jewish people. Many think the symbol of the Cross was the remote cause of the Holocaust which, regrettably, led to the death of at least six million Jewish people. A rabbi famously said, "Every time I see a Cross it is a symbol of Hitler to me and every time I see a manger scene it is the birth of Hitler to me." Thus, some Jewish people consider the Cross a symbol of oppression and do not want the Cross displayed in their public spaces including Synagogues. The Great Synagogue of Rome has a strict rule against crosses in the sanctuary, to the point that ushers with batons forcefully rap the knees of anyone crossing their legs. In the run up to the pope's visit, some congregants of the Great Synagogue in Rome requested Rabbi Elio Toaff to ask John Paul II not to wear his pectoral cross in the synagogue during his visit. Rabbi Toaff communicated the request to the pope. In his typical way, the pope responded, "Look, if I were coming to your synagogue as a tourist I'd be happy to wear jeans. But I'm coming as the Bishop of Rome and the universal pastor of the Catholic Church, and to make that and all that it means unmistakable I have to dress the way I always do." Chief Rabbi Toaff went back to his congregation and announced that he and Pope John Paul were completely agreed: the pope *would* wear his pectoral cross (Weigel, 2017:241–42).

John Paul II once told French journalist André Frossard, "We must never separate ourselves from the Cross" (1990:111). Pope John Paul II refused to lay down the Cross during his visit to the Great Synagogue in 1986. However, when faced with a similar situation in 2016, Cardinal Reinhard Marx, archbishop of Munich and Freising, docilely succumbed and laid down the Cross. In October 2016, Cardinal Reinhard Marx and Bishop Heinrich Bedford-Strohm, the head of the Evangelical Church in Germany (EKD), together made an official visit to Israel. However, these two prominent leaders of German Christendom caused a big uproar in the Christian world when they hid their pectoral crosses while they visited the Jewish Wailing Wall, as well as the Muslim Dome of the Rock on the Temple Mount. Due to Jewish sensitivity to the Cross, these church leaders gave in to the demands of their Jewish and Muslim hosts to take off their pectoral crosses. They laid down the Cross, which is the most distinctive symbol and sign of Christianity. Writing for *Bild am Sonntag,* journalist Miriam Hollstein beautifully explained the implications of the action of Cardinal Marx and Bishop Heinrich Bedford-Strohm: "Jesus picked up His Cross 2,000 years ago in Jerusalem, the bishops now laid it down there. A symbolic gesture of infidelity or dishonorable obsequiousness." *Der Spiegel,* a secular German weekly news magazine, termed the action of the Church leaders "a denial of the faith." Indeed, it was a denial of the faith. Their action was contrary to Jesus' call for discipleship: "Then Jesus said to his disciples, 'if anyone wants to become my follower, he must deny himself, take up his cross, and follow me'" (Matthew 16:24). Instead, Cardinal Max and Bishop Bedford-Strohm put down their crosses in Jerusalem.

Saint John Paul II's visit to the synagogue in 1986 was idiosyncratic. The year 1986 was not Wojtyła's first entry into a synagogue. As a teenager, Karol Wojtyła was often taken to the synagogue in Wadowice by his father on the feast of *Yom Kippur* to listen to Moishe Savitski, a twenty-one-year-old youth with an angelic voice who sang the *Kol Nidre* (1996:31). As archbishop of Kraków, Wojtyła visited the synagogue in Kazimierz on February 28, 1969. His 1969 visit to the synagogue made the cover story of papers since there was no precedent of a cardinal visiting synagogues in Poland. During his 1986 visit, Chief Rabbi Elio Toaff asked Saint John Paul II to establish diplomatic relations with the State of Israel. It was Wojtyła's Jewish friend, Jerzy Kluger, who advised and actively encouraged him to make the historic visit to the Synagogue of Rome in 1986 and to establish diplomatic relations with the State of Israel. The visit, as Eugene Fisher has noted, "was not simply theoretical ... John Paul II lived under Nazism in Poland and experienced personally the malignancy of the ancient evil of Jew-hatred" (Dalin, 2007). Pope Benedict XVI became the second pope in history to visit a Synagogue when he entered the Grand Synagogue in Cologne in August 2005. Pope John Paul II was also the first pope to pray in a Lutheran Church and in a traditional African shrine.

Amidst all the historic personal diplomacy of Saint John Paul II to bridge the Catholic-Jewish rift, Goldhagen, the liberal papal critic, got it woefully wrong when he said, "Neither John Paul II nor any other pope has seen fit to make ... a direct and forceful public statement about Catholic culpability and the need for all the members of the Church who have sinned during the Holocaust to repent for their many different kinds of offenses and sins against the Jews" (Dalin, 2007). In line with the Latin adage, *argumenta non-numeranda sed ponderanda sunt*, Goldhagen's wordy critique does not imply veracity or soundness of argument. "Through visits, audiences, meetings, and public declarations, John Paul II began to build in earnest what some have called a 'spiritual bond' between the Catholic Church and Jews around the world" (Fisher & Klenicki, 1995). Saint John Paul II always had time for communities of different religions and denominations in all his pilgrimages. Among them were Jewish delegations. John Paul II made his boldest expression against anti-Semitism when he said, "Anti-Semitism is a great sin against humanity" (1994:97). In an International Catholic-Jewish Liaison Committee, the archbishop of Paris, André Vingt-Trois, sounded a similar sentiment. "Anti-Semitism must be unambiguously exposed as a sin against God and humanity ..." (Pepinster, 2011:2). David Dalin argued that the Holy See's establishment of diplomatic ties with the State of Israel was a brainchild of John Paul II, even against some resistance from some Curia bureaucrats.

On the occasion of the Jewish New Year (Rosh Hashanah) in October 1981, Pope John Paul II sent a papal telegram of good wishes to the president of Israel. "This holiday telegram was historically unprecedented: No such communication had ever previously been sent by a pope to an Israeli head of state" (Dalin, 2007). Eugene J. Fisher, an éminence grise of the Jewish-Christian relationship, described the *Fundamental Agreement* as more than a moment of international diplomacy when two Mediterranean states exchanged diplomats in 1994. John Paul II followed the signing of the *Fundamental Agreement* with his historic visit to the Holy Land in 2000, in the footsteps of the apostles. Haim Ramon, a senior officer of the government of Israel, said at a news conference in Rome on March 10, 2000, "This visit is the most significant event in the history of Israel."

There is the famous picture of Saint John Paul II at the Western Wall placing his own printed regrets for the Church's sins against the Jewish people. Especially moving during the visit was his impassioned emotional talk in the *Hall of Remembrance* at Israel's Holocaust memorial, Yad Vashem, where a flame is kept burning in remembrance of the victims of the Holocaust. In Yad Vashem, some of the death camp survivors wept in the presence of the pope. The pope apologized for the Church's sins of commission and omission against the Jewish people:

> As bishop of Rome and successor of the apostle Peter, I assure the Jewish people that the Catholic Church, motivated by the gospel law of truth, and love and by no political considerations, is deeply saddened by the hatred, acts of persecution, and displays of anti-Semitism directed against the Jews by Christians at any time and in any place. The Church rejects racism in any form as a denial of the image of the Creator inherent in every human being.

After his speech, Prime Minister Ehud Barak, whose maternal grandparents were killed by the Nazis at the Treblinka death camp, told the pope, "You have done more than anyone else to bring about the historic change in the attitude of the Church towards the Jewish people, and to dress the gaping wounds that festered over many bitter centuries" (Kaiser, 2006:56). Idiosyncratically, Weigel concluded that Saint John Paul II's intuition of the Jewish pain and theological commitment gave him the impetus and courage to make the basic decision to pursue diplomatic relations with the State of Israel (1999:712–13). He vicariously shared in the Jewish pain more than any pontiff in history did. He is the only pope to have had a death camp as part of his archdiocese before becoming pope, in his case, the infamously deadly Auschwitz Camp (Huntston, 1981:9).

In conclusion, the Catholic-Jewish relations is a black page in the Church's history. However, the Second Vatican Council, especially with the promulgation of the *Nostra Aetate* in 1965, set the ball rolling for a reversal of the Church's anti-Semitic attitudes over the centuries. With the election of Karol Wojtyła as pope in October 1978, and the signing of the *Fundamental Agreement* in 1993, there was a marked improvement in the relationship between the Jewish people and the Catholic Church. Pope John Paul II's idiosyncratic Jewish past and his intuition of the Jewish pain informed the Church's pro-Jewish leanings during his pontificate.

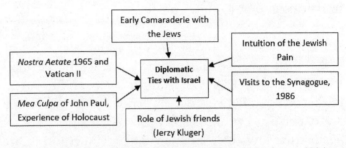

Fig. 2. Author's illustration of John Paul II's idiosyncratic variables and other factors which impacted on the Holy See's diplomatic ties with Israel in 1994.

CHAPTER SEVEN

POPE JOHN PAUL II'S DIPLOMACY IN AFRICA

Africa is blessed with immense natural, mineral, and human resources. It is a continent of diverse ethnicities, cultures, civilizations, landscapes, mountains, forests, languages, and philosophies. It is a continent of the Anglophones, Francophones, Lusophones, Hispanophones, Arabophones, and even Sinophones, especially with the recent conspicuous inroads made by the Chinese in Africa. The continent is home to some of the world's finest safari parks. Africa's glorious historical heritage is beyond all telling. Until its complete annihilation in 146 B.C., Carthage (modern day Tunis in North Africa) was a powerful military and diplomatic nerve center of the world. From biblical and historical accounts, the glories of ancient Egypt, especially under the Pharaohs, cannot be overemphasized. When death became an imminent possibility due to starvation and famine, ten of Joseph's brothers (sons of the patriarch Jacob) went down to buy an emergency supply of grain from Egypt (Genesis 42:2–3).

Egypt offered refuge for Jesus Christ (saviour of the world) and his parents during Herod's massacre of infants (Matthew 2:13). The Royal Library of Alexandria, Egypt was one of the largest learning centers in antiquity. The pyramids, constructed almost four thousand years before Christ, have continued to be a marvel of science and technology, and are still one of the great wonders of the world (Onaiyekan, 2016:199). To satisfy her curiosity, the Queen of Sheba (Ethiopia) went to Jerusalem to test King Solomon with subtle questions. After witnessing Solomon's great wisdom, she gave the king one hundred and twenty gold talents, a very large quantity of spices, and precious stones. The holy book records that "never again did anyone bring such an abundance of spices as the Queen of Sheba gave to King Solomon" (1 Kings 10:10).

Since ancient times, Africa has always had rich vibrant civilizations, empires, and kingdoms. Historians of the history of Africa such as P.L.O. Lumumba talk with nostalgia when they recount the glories of the Kingdom of Axum, the Buganda Kingdom, the Oyo Empire, the Songhai Empire, the Empire of Timbuktu, and the Sokoto Caliphate. Two millennia ago, the art of Egypt, the Sudan, and Ethiopia was well known to the rest of the world. Early European explorers to Africa came across a superior brand of red leather from Africa, which was termed "Moroccan leather." The leather was tanned and dyed by Hausa and Mandingo specialists in northern Nigeria and Mali (Rodney, 1973:66). As soon as the Portuguese reached the old kingdom of Kongo in 1483, they informed their homeland about the superb local cloths made from bark and palm fibre, having a finish comparable to velvet (Rodney, 1973:66).

Celebrated Guyanese intellectual Walter Rodney pointed out that by the 15th century, Africans had adapted to their ecological milieus. "By the 15th century, Africans everywhere had arrived at a considerable understanding of the total ecology—of the soils, climate, animals, plants, and their multiple interrelationships" (Rodney, 1973:62–63). The vibrancy, flourishing, and development of pre-European Africa is expertly narrated in Walter Rodney's *How Europe Underdeveloped Africa*. Indeed, Rodney concluded that Africa was developed until the Europeans came and its development became truncated (Rodney, 1973:).

The Trans-Atlantic, Trans-Saharan, Indian Ocean, and Red Sea slave trade took place between the 7th and 19th centuries. Africans were routinely rounded up, collected, and shipped under some grossly inhumane conditions to plantations in Europe and the Americas. Walter Rodney put the total number of slaves taken from present day Nigeria and Ghana at 2,021,859 and 1,614, 793, respectively, making them two of the most potent sources of slaves in Africa (Rodney, 1973:). Slavery and slave trade created a myriad of adverse effects on the development of the continent of Africa. The continent lost substantive manpower and skills which could have been used for her development, since a majority of the slaves were able-bodied men and women between the ages of 15–35, at a ratio of two men to one woman. American historian John Hope Franklin noted, "The captives who became slaves did not come to the New World empty handed—in language, music, graphic arts, sophisticated patterns of agriculture and other economic pursuits, and an understanding of the functions of government, they became a part of an evolving New World culture in the islands and the mainland (of the Americas)" (Davidson, 1984:148).

As a pupil in primary school, I was taught the history of slave trade in Africa. I was told Africans were inhumanely shipped off to work on plantations in Europe and the Americas. As a lecturer of international politics, I spent a couple of class sessions discussing the economy of slave trade in Africa with my students. However, it was only in 2010, when I traveled to offer humanitarian services in Haiti after the unfortunate earthquake, that the reality of slave trade really hit me hard. I found black-skinned persons like me on that small Caribbean island. Their ancestors had traveled to the Americas with their cultures, as John Hope Franklin observed. The cuisine of these islanders is similar to typical African cuisines. Voodoo temples are littered all over the country as is the case in some West African countries. Veteran photographer Lynne Warberg famously said, "Haitians are 70 percent Catholic, 30 percent Protestant, and 100 percent voodoo." It was very emotional for me when some of my Haitian friends kept telling me, "We want to go to Africa with you. Our great-grandparents came from Africa." Whenever I go to Zanzibar for a respite, I spend a considerable amount of time reflecting, mind wondering, and wiping my teary face in the Slave House where African captives were held before being taken to other continents. The effects of slavery are still very evident in the continent today. The unfortunate history of black Americans as descendants of slaves has informed the systemic racism in the United States of America. The painful lynching of George Floyd, which sparked a wave of protests across America and in the world in 2020, is a case in point. The Black Lives Matter movement has been born to raise awareness that blacks are sometimes racially killed, especially by the police in America.

To minimize conflicts among European colonial powers in Africa, Otto Von Bismarck, the German Chancellor at the time, convened the Berlin West African Conference (November 1884–February 1885). During the conference, the map of Africa was placed on a table in a hall in Berlin and partitioned like a baked cake among the prominent European colonial powers. The French were handed several territories in West and North Africa. The Portuguese were given portions of Southern Africa, and the Germans had territories in West, Central, Southern, and Eastern Africa. The British gained colonies in West, Central, Southern, and Eastern Africa. The whole of present-day Democratic Republic of Congo was given to King Leopold II of Belgium as his personal property. Historian Martin Meredith describes the savage partitioning of the continent, "When marking out the boundaries of their new territories, European negotiators frequently resorted to drawing straight lines, on the map, taking little or no account of the myriad of traditional monarchies, chiefdoms, and other African societies that existed on the ground. Nearly one half of the new frontiers imposed on Africa were geometric lines, lines of latitude and longitude, other straight lines, or arcs of circles" (2011:1).

The arbitrary slicing of Africa in a room in Berlin cut through some 190 culture groups. It is not uncommon today to see one ethnic group spread across different African countries. The Maasai people are in Kenya as well as in Tanzania. The Bakongo are in the Democratic Republic of Congo, Congo Brazzaville, and in Angola. The Cross-River States people are in Cameroon and Nigeria. There are now Kenyan Somalis and Somali Somalis, since Somaliland was carved up between Britain, Italy, and France. Another consequence of the Berlin West African Conference was the lumping together of some hostile, independent groups and nations with no common history, culture, language, and religions, *inter alia*. Present-day Nigeria is an amalgam of about 300 ethnic groups. The antagonistic kingdoms of Buganda and Bunyoro were merged in the same colony of Uganda (Meredith, 2011:2). Unending conflicts in some countries in Africa today are due to the lumping together of hostile groups in various African countries. John Cardinal Onaiyekan, Archbishop Emeritus of Abuja, expressed it succinctly. "Colonial boundaries have also brought together within a modern state peoples who had been at each other's throats and would never have come together as a nation" (2016:201).

Britain's premier, Lord Salisbury, described what happened in the halls of Berlin. "We have been giving away mountains and rivers and lakes to each other, only hindered by the small impediment that we never knew exactly where they were" (Meredith, 2011:2). The heartless partitioning of Africa without consideration of its impacts on the configurations of ethnic communities has been one of the reasons for unending bloody wars in the continent. In 1963 in Addis Ababa, the newly emerged African leaders, in their own wisdom, acknowledged the imperfect colonial boundaries, but agreed to make do with them as a lesser evil.

Economic motives underlined the scramble and partition of Africa. European powers colonized African territories to exploit raw materials for their industries at the height of the industrial revolution in the 19th century. Lord Frederick Lugard, the high priest of the British colonial policy of Indirect Rule, in his book, *The Dual Mandate of the British in Tropical Africa* (1956), stated, "The partition of Africa was, as we all recognize, due primarily to the economic necessity of increasing the supplies of raw materials and food to meet the needs of the industrialized nations of Europe" (1965:613). In another instance, Lugard confirmed that, "European brains, capital and energy have not been, and never will be, expended in developing the resources of Africa from motives of pure philanthropy" (Chiryankandath, 2007:7).

Despite her grandiose historical heritage and beauty, only a single story of Africa has been told repeatedly, especially by western literature. The single story of Africa has been one of oblivion, diseases, half-baked irrational humans, emptiness, and darkness. After having sailed to West Africa in 1561, a London merchant called John Lok penned the exploits of his voyage. Lok referred to Africans "as beasts who have no houses." "They are people without heads," he continued, "having their mouth and eyes in their breasts" (Chimamanda, 2009). This is what Nigerian novelist Chimamanda Ngozi Adichie makes of Lok's description of Africans: "Now, I've laughed every time I've read this. And one must admire the imagination of John Lok. But what is important about his writing is that it represents the beginning of a tradition of telling African stories in the West. A tradition of Sub-Saharan Africa as a place of negatives, of difference, of darkness, of people who, in the words of the wonderful poet, Rudyard Kipling, are 'half devil, half child'" (Chimamanda, 2009).

European powers like France argued that the need to expand their superior culture to the "dark primitive continent" (*terra incognita*) was a reason for the colonization of Africa. Africa has been derided as the "dark continent" by some bourgeois European historians, anthropologists, and philosophers. Some have excluded Africa south of the desert of Sahara from the rest of the world. German philosopher Georg Wilhelm Friedrich Hegel stated that "Africa proper, as far as History goes back, has remained—for all purposes of connection with the rest of the World—shut up; ... is enveloped in the dark mantle of Night" (1956:91). In *The Philosophy of History* (1956), Hegel stated, "At this point we leave Africa, not to mention it again. For it is no historical part of the world: it has no movement and development to exhibit" (1956:99). Hegel even expunged Egypt from the annals of Africa proper. In his dubious three-fold division of Africa, Hegel placed Egypt in the region of "European Africa." He branded the river district of the Nile as European Africa because this was a civilized and developed region since development, according to him, was alien to Africa. He wrote that the Nile river district was adapted to become a mighty centre of independent civilization, and therefore is as isolated and singular in Africa as

Africa itself appears in relation to the other parts of the world (Hegel, 1956:92).

Hegel went on to insinuate that rationality is to the white as emotionality is to the Africans. In other words, Africans do not even possess the rational faculty which sets human beings apart from animals of lower castes. Africans, therefore, according to him, should not be subjected to very rigorous intellectual activities because the African brain has no capacity to sustain those exercises. He and others insinuate that when the medulla oblongata (a long stem-like structure which makes up the lower part of the brainstem) of an African is exposed to rigorous scientific intellectual gymnastics, it gets tired and violence ensues. According to Hegel, the characteristic feature of the Negro is that their consciousness has not yet reached an awareness of any substantial objectivity. Africans, according to him, do not possess the rational faculty needed to abstract concepts such as God and law (Hegel, 1993:177).

Some racist European anthropologists went as far as placing Africans in the same class as orangutans and chimpanzees. Hegel boldly opined that "the Negro as already observed, exhibits the natural man in his completely wild and untamed state ... there is nothing harmonious with humanity to be found in this type of character" (1956:93). It is because of sentiments like those that, as recently as the 1950s, many European cities like Paris, Hamburg, Antwerp, Milan, London, Barcelona, and Warsaw were decorated with human zoos where Africans were brought in as zoo exhibits for passers-by at which to gawk. Africans were placed in zoos with primates because some racists did not think that blacks are human beings. An average of 200,000 to 300,000 visitors attended the exhibition in each city. Semi-naked or naked Africans were kept in those cages with primates such as monkeys as companions. In 1906, anthropologist Madison Grant, who was the head of the New York Zoological Society, put Congolese pygmy Ota Benga on display at the Bronx Zoo in New York City. The display was in the primate exhibit, and Ota was often made to carry around chimpanzees and other apes. These attitudes continue even today, when many African athletes are still racially abused with monkey chants and with bananas thrown at them during competitions. It is therefore not surprising that Hegel cannibalized the African black race, "But with the Negro this is not the case, and the devouring of human flesh is altogether consonant with the general principles of the African race.... At the death of a King hundreds are killed and eaten; prisoners are butchered and their flesh sold in the markets; the victor is accustomed to eat the heart of his slain foe" (Hegel, 1956:95). I wonder what came over the reputed philosopher to make such unfounded allegations against a whole race.

While urging the U.S. to take up the "burden" of a great empire, renowned British novelist and poet Rudyard Kipling in his February 1899 poem *The White Man's Burden*, writes of non-European races: "Your new-caught, sullen peoples, Half-devil and half-child" (Kipling, 1929). In 1963, Oxford historian Hugh Redwald Trevor-Roper, in an infamous speech at Oxford, repeated Hegel's sentiments, "Perhaps in the future, there will be some African history to teach. But at present there is none; there is only the history of the Europeans in Africa. The rest is darkness ... and darkness is not the subject of history." This is the repercussion of letting outsiders write your history, because they will write what they want to write and omit what they decide to omit. "European anthropologists who have studied African societies have done so mainly from a very prejudiced and racist position ..." (Rodney, 1973:58). This is the danger of a single story that the great Nigerian writer Chimamanda Ngozi Adichie talked about in her memorable 2009 TED talk, "The Danger of a Single Story." A dreadful single story of Africa has been told over and over again by western literature and media. This is the single story of Africa that is still oftentimes portrayed by some western media. Seldom does anything good come from Africa.

"How is a single story created? A single story is created by showing a people as one thing, as only one thing, over and over again, and that is what they become" (Chimamanda, 2009). What does the single story do? Adichie responded: "It robs people of

146

dignity. It makes our recognition of our equal humanity difficult. It emphasizes how we are different rather than how we are similar" (2009). The great Palestinian poet Mourid Barghouti was spot-on when he pointed out that if you want to dispossess a people, the simplest way to do it is to tell their story, and to start with, "secondly." The single story of Africa often begins with, "secondly." It often begins on the second line. The first line of the history of Africa has been omitted. The single story of Africa has enumerated the problems of Africa and intentionally omitted the genesis of many of Africa's problems. It has comfortably omitted history of slavery and slave trade in Africa, the European conquests of African territories, the scramble and partition of Africa, colonial powers in Africa, the creation of the colonial African state, post-colonialism, and the continuing Western-dominated international system and organizations.

The continent of Africa has largely been savagely treated and shortchanged by foreign powers. In *How Europe Underdeveloped Africa*, Walter Rodney recounts how the continent has been exploited. The tragedy of Africa did not end with the end of colonialism in Africa in the second half of the 20th century. On the eve of Ghana's independence in 1957, Kwame Nkrumah, Ghana's nationalist leader, expressed the independence optimism, "We shall achieve in a decade what it took others a century ... and we shall not rest content until we demolish these miserable colonial structures and erect in their place a veritable paradise" (Nkrumah, 1957:34). Upon independence, African nationalists like Jomo Kenyatta (Kenya), Jaramogi Oginga Odinga (Kenya), Julius Kambarage Nyerere (Tanzania), Ahmed Sékou Touré (Guinea), Kenneth David Buchizya Kaunda (Zambia), Félix Houphouët-Boigny (Ivory Coast), John Ngu Foncha (Cameroon), Ahmadou Babatoura Ahidjo (Cameroon), Nnamdi Azikiwe (Nigeria), Kwame Nkrumah (Ghana), and Léopold Sédar Senghor (Senegal) were hailed as heroes and saviours by their peoples. Many of these leaders were thinkers. They developed national developmental philosophies and ideologies for their nations. In 1960, Senegal's first president, Léopold Sédar Senghor, wrote the Senegalese national anthem,

"The Red Lion." Jomo Kenyatta popularized the notion of *Harambee* ("all pull together"). The effects of Mwalimu Nyerere's *Ujamaa* (brotherhood or community) is still felt in Tanzania today. Kaunda's African Socialism, Nkrumah's Consciencism, and Senghor's *Negritude* were all tried in their respective countries.

During the independence struggle in Africa, Ghanaian leader Kwame Nkrumah had a regular refrain for the people of Ghana and Africa, "Seek ye first the political kingdom and everything else will be added unto you." Sixty years down the line, attainment of political kingdoms across Africa have not occasioned food kingdoms, water kingdoms, economic kingdoms, religious kingdoms, and peace kingdoms on the continent. For many Africans, the paradise promised them by independence leaders turned out to be starvation, poverty, unemployment, and conflicts. Indeed, years later, many African countries became worse off than they were at independence. In 1968, Ghanaian scholar Ayi Kwei Armah published *The Beautyful Ones Are Not Yet Born* to describe the moral and economic decadence experienced in Ghana ten years after independence.

Tribalism, negative ethnicity, despotism, dictatorship, conflicts, diseases, and epidemics have been the order of the day in many parts of Africa since independence. The people of Africa have suffered the brunt of dictatorship from leaders like Mobutu Sese Seko Nkuku Ngbendu Wa Za Banga (meaning "The all-powerful warrior who, because of his endurance and inflexible will to win, goes from conquest to conquest, leaving fire in his wake"), Idi Amin dada (Uganda), Emperor Jean-Bédel Bokassa (the Central African Republic), Daniel Toroitich arap Moi (Kenya), Yuweri Kaguta Museveni (Uganda), Colonel Gadhafi (Libya), Hosni Mubarrak (Egypt), Sani Abacha (Nigeria), and Paul Biya (Cameroon), amongst others. The continent of Africa suffered during the Cold War and continues to suffer in the post-Cold War era. The Cold War protagonists did not directly engage in any overt conflict, but their proxies in Africa and other parts of the world did. Due to Cold War politics, the superpowers "went to bed" and "prostituted" with despots on the continent under the banner of "friendly tyrants." Some of the tyrants were aided by Western powers to remain in power and crush opposition movements in the various countries. During a state visit to the U.S. by Mobutu Sese Seko in 1983, President Ronald Reagan, without any shame, praised the Zairian strongman in broad daylight as "a voice of good sense and goodwill."

Many of the unborn in Africa are going to pay huge amounts of debts incurred by corrupt leaders during the Cold War. Mobutu Sese Seko used grants and loans given to the Democratic Republic of Congo for his personal aggrandizement by building villas in many European capitals. Upon the end of the Cold War, with the triumph of liberal capitalism over communism in 1989, Africa was no longer of interest to the superpowers since there was no need to court African states and leaders to subscribe to either of the Cold War ideologies. When President Mobutu was unceremoniously dumped by the U.S. and forced to adopt democracy in Zaire after the end of the Cold War, he bitterly remarked, "I am the latest victim of the Cold War, no longer needed by the US. The lesson is that my support for American policy counts for nothing" (Zagorin, 2001). In 1993, Mobutu was denied a visa by the U.S. State Department when he sought to visit Washington, D.C.

With the end of the Cold War, regional, ethnic, and intrastate animosities, and conflicts which had been held in check by the superpowers, overflowed across Africa. Longstanding wars and conflicts that had been off-limits for reasons of superpower geopolitics, especially in Angola, Mozambique, Rwanda, and Somalia, were dumped unceremoniously onto the United Nations' doorstep. With the fall of the Somali dictator Mohammed Siad Barre in 1991, the United States-led humanitarian and peacekeeping mission was deployed to Somalia in 1992. In the Battle of Mogadishu on October 3–4, 1993, 18 U.S. soldiers and hundreds of Somali militia fighters and civilians were killed. Justifiably, the footage of Somali warlord Mohammed Aideed's supporters dragging the body of U.S. Staff Sgt. William David Cleveland through the streets of Mogadishu caused a big public outcry and anger in the United States. Shortly after the incident in Mogadishu, President Bill Clinton withdrew all U.S. troops from Somalia. In March 1994, UN troops were also withdrawn from Somalia, thereby leaving the country at the mercy of warlords. Somalia imploded and was almost obliterated from the map of the world for almost twenty years. The world only remembered Somalia again after some young Somalis decided to venture into piracy decades later. Reflecting on the plight and predicament of Africa during and after the Cold War, conflict resolution guru John Paul Lederach said, "When two elephants [the Soviet Union and the United States] fight, it is the grass (Africa) that suffers and when two elephants make love, it is still the grass that suffers."

The United States and European powers played a semantic game with the word "genocide" on the floor of the United Nations Security Council as the fastest spree of human slaughtering continued in Rwanda in April 1994. Within a month, over 900,000 people had been brutally slaughtered in Rwanda. U.S. President Bill Clinton confessed in 1997 that had the U.S. intervened early enough and responded to pleas for more peacekeeping forces by General Roméo Antonius Dallaire when the genocide started in Rwanda, about half of the lives lost would have been saved. General Dallaire was the force commander of the United Nations Assistance Mission for Rwanda (UNAMIR) during the genocide.

African countries still remain in the periphery of the world's global capitalist economy, where their voices do not really matter in international affairs. Africans have not fully benefited from the globalization of the world. Many of the policies of the Bretton Woods institutions have not been favourable to Africa. The unfavourable position of Africa in the global economy has been clearly discussed by Joseph Stiglitz in his book *Globalization and its Discontents* and in Richard Peet's *Unholy Trinity: The IMF, World Bank and WTO*.

The concept and practice of life presidency is a staple in Africa. Many young Africans below the age of thirty have never known more than one president in their countries. Apart from a handful of exceptions, most African presidents and leaders will do all it takes to remain in power for life. The late President Omar Bongo, who ruled Gabon for 40 years, once said that it would be foolish for an incumbent African head of state to call for a presidential election, appoint the members of the electoral commission, and still lose the election. His son Ali Bongo succeeded him and, as of 2022, Ali Bongo is still the president of Gabon, even though he was incapacitated by a stroke that he suffered in 2019. Also, as of 2022, Paul Biya has been president of Cameroon for forty years. I have known no other president since Biya became the leader of Cameroon before I was born. Every year, Paul Biya spends at least six months in one of his villas in France or Switzerland. Cameroonians seldom know when their president is at home or abroad.

The response to the COVID-19 pandemic likewise highlights the problems of leadership in many African nations. On March 11, 2020, Tedros Adhanom Ghebreyesus, the WHO chief, characterized the coronavirus (COVID-19) a pandemic. The world was immediately thrown into pandemonium. At the height of this unprecedented global health crisis, world leaders were visibly leading from the front in the war against the coronavirus. Daily press briefings by heads of state were a staple on national televisions. U.S. President Trump standing next to Dr. Anthony Fauci and other members of the task force was an all-too-familiar sight. U.K. Prime Minister Boris Johnson spent some days in the ICU after contracting the virus from a robust leadership of his country during this pandemic. A couple of African leaders offered hope and encouragement to their people during this difficult time. They were procuring vaccines for their people. To encourage indoor exercise, 75-year-old President Museveni, who has ruled Uganda for 35 years, entertained Ugandans with an instructive workout video on April 9, 2020. President Museveni jogged for a few minutes and did 30 pushups from his house office.

Amid these fatalities and frenetic efforts by various countries, the situation in Cameroon is different. As of this writing, there have been thousands of confirmed cases of COVID-19 and deaths in Cameroon, making it one of the hardest-hit African countries.

The situation is worse in that robust testing has not been carried out in Cameroon. However, since the outbreak of the pandemic, President Paul Biya has seldom addressed the COVID-19 issue. Currently, Cameroonians do not know if the president is alive or dead. On April 3, 2020, the opposition leader gave a one-week ultimatum to President Paul Biya to show proof of being alive because the president had not been in public for five months.

Most leaders in Africa do not believe in the act of resigning or peaceful transfer of power. Customarily, they amend national constitutions by erasing references to presidential term limits. A couple of the leaders who had declared themselves presidents for life have had to be chased out, dead or alive. Many African leaders prefer to die while in power. When castigated by the media and other sectors of the society for corruption under his watch as the finance minister of Kenya, Amos Kimunya unequivocally stated in public that he would rather die than resign. On the contrary, barely hours after a majority of the people in the United Kingdom voted in favor to leave the European Union in a referendum on June 23, 2016, Prime Minister David Cameron, who led the *In Campaign,* announced his resignation. *Inter alia,* he said, "I will do everything I can as Prime Minister to steady the ship over the coming weeks and months, but I do not think it would be right for me to try to be the captain that steers our country to its next destination." I guess many African leaders sarcastically laughed at David Cameron for resigning and branded him a coward.

Fifty years since gaining independence, eating is still a luxury for many Africans today (Ayitteh, 1999:6). Scholars like Nobel Laureate Wole Soyinka, Kwesi Armah, George Ayittey, PLO Lumumba, and Stanley Chinedu Igwe attribute Africa's woes to poor leadership, governance, and corruption. Almost as a rejoinder to Walter Rodney's *How Europe Underdeveloped Africa,* Nigerian scholar Stanley Chinedu Igwe wrote *How Africa Underdeveloped Africa* in 2010. PLO Lumumba of Kenya often says that Africans are co-authors of their own misfortunes.

With the end of the Cold War, European powers dumped Africa. Africa became a liability. Bloodshed, carnage, hunger, and chaos became the order of the day. The Synod Fathers of 1994 acknowledged that Africa is a continent of bad news with many problems. They said, "One common situation, without any doubt, is that Africa is full of problems. In almost all our nations, there is abject poverty, tragic mismanagement of available scarce resources, political instability and social disorientation. The results stare us in the face: misery, wars, despair. In a world controlled by rich and powerful nations, Africa has practically become an irrelevant appendix, often forgotten and neglected" (E.A, 1995:32).

When the Cold War protagonists and the world at large abandoned Africa, one world leader did not. Pope John Paul II did not abandon Africa. He stood with Africa when others wandered. Papal historian George Weigel recorded that, "With the end of the Cold War, in which various of its countries had played proxy roles, Africa seemed ready to fall off the edge of history into an abyss of tribal brutality, rancid government, poverty, disease, and general chaos. Virtually alone among world leaders, John Paul II refused to write Africa off" (1999:372). He remained an ally of the continent. "The only world institution that insisted that a continent of 450 million people could not be allowed to fall off the edge of history was the Roman Catholic Church" (Weigel, 1999:372).

During the Synod of Africa in 1994, Archbishop Jean Zoa of the See of Yaoundé, Cameroon made a very poignant contribution. He analogously compared Africa to the man who went down from Jerusalem to Jericho; he fell among robbers who stripped him, beat him, and departed, leaving him half dead (Lk 10:30–37). The archbishop asked, "Who will stop to look after Africa in her present moment of distress? Who will take her for attention and care? Who will pour oil over her wounds?" (Onaiyekan, 2016:196). Pope John Paul captured the above image of Africa in the post-Synodal Apostolic Exhortation *Ecclesia in Africa*. Africa is a continent where countless human beings—men and women, children, and young people—are lying, as it were, on the edge of the road, sick, injured, disabled, marginalized, and abandoned. They are in dire need of Good Samaritans who will come to their aid. Pope John Paul II was the Good Samaritan who believed that Africa was not destined for death, but for life. John Paul II was the Samaritan traveller who came upon Africa and was moved with compassion at her sight. He approached Africa, poured oil over her wounds, and bandaged them. Then he lifted Africa on his own animal, took her to an inn, and cared for her. He returned to the inn on many occasions to check on her progress. Veteran American journalist Peggy Noonan captures John Paul II's concern for Africa, "Africa—the pope has a powerful sense of the tragedy of Africa as being forgotten in the modern world, that nobody cares about Africa" (Noonan: 2005:37).

Diplomatically, Pope John Paul II's concern for Africa was evident in his convocation of the Synod of Africa, his apologies to the continent for the Church's role in slavery and slave trade, his appointments of Africans to the Roman Curia, his establishment of Catholic universities and institutes in Africa, and his many visits to Africa, *inter alia*.

Pope John Paul II's visits to Africa

On July 31, 1969, Pope Paul VI became the first reigning pope to visit Africa when he landed in Kampala, Uganda for the inauguration of the Symposium of Episcopal Conferences of Africa and Madagascar (SECAM). It was during that historic visit that he made the famous declaration, "You can and you must have an African Christianity." After the brief reign of Paul VI's successor, Pope John Paul I, John Paul II became a regular visitor to the continent. There was a natural and flowing rapport between John Paul II and Africa. He was an "ally" and authoritative spokesman for Africa on the world's stage. In about 27 years, John Paul II made at least 104 journeys, visiting almost every country on the planet. A good number of those 104 journeys were to his beloved Africa. Barely nineteen months into his papacy, in May 1980, John Paul II visited six countries in Africa, namely Democratic Republic of Congo (former Zaire), Republic of the Congo, Ghana, Ivory Coast, Kenya, and Upper Volta (Burkina Faso). He made a total of 11 visits to Africa during his pontificate: 1980, 1982, 1985, 1988,

1989, 1990, 1992, 1993, 1995, 1998, and 2000. He visited at least 39 countries in Africa, some of them more than once. He never hesitated visiting trouble spots and pariah states in Africa.

Cardinal Stanislaw Dziwisz, Pope John Paul II's lifelong secretary, recorded that "… by means of the papal journeys, Pope John Paul II followed the shifting focus of evangelization from the global North (the First World) to the global South (the Third World)" (Dziwisz, 2008:195). In an interview with this author, papal biographer George Weigel noted that "… as to the place of Africa and Africans in John Paul's pontificate and diplomacy, I think the number of his pastoral pilgrimages to Africa speaks volumes about his determination to foster the New Evangelization in Africa." The new evangelization is the particular process by which baptized members of the Catholic Church express the general Christian call to evangelization.

Egypt was the last African country Pope John Paul II visited, which he did in 2000. His visit to Egypt was part of his preparations for the celebration of the Jubilee year and the 2,000[th] anniversary of the birth of Jesus Christ. In preparation for the Jubilee Year, the pope visited some of the places linked to the birth of Christ and salvation history. Amongst them were Egypt, Jordan, Israel, and Palestine. "Pope John Paul II's trip to the Middle East was a pilgrimage framed within the context of the 2000th anniversary of the birth of Jesus—the Great Jubilee. The sacred experience of a pilgrimage was of special significance to Pope John Paul II's spirituality" (Klenicki, 2006:6). In the presence of President Hosni Mubarak of Egypt, the pope said, "For many years I have been looking forward to celebrating the 2,000[th] anniversary of the birth of Jesus Christ by visiting and praying at the places specially linked to God's intervention in history…. Thank you, Mr. President, for making it possible for me to come here and go to where God revealed his name to Moses and gave his law as a sign of his great mercy and kindness to us, his creatures."

During his 1980 pilgrimage to Zaire, John Paul II took a swipe at critics of his globe-trotting apostolate. "Some people think that the pope should not travel so much. He should stay in Rome, as before. I often hear such advice, or read it in newspapers. But the local people say, 'Thank God you came here, for you can only learn about us by coming. How could you be our pastor without knowing us? Without knowing who we are, how we live, what is the historical moment we are going through?' This confirms me in the belief that it is time for the Bishops of Rome ... to become successors not only of Peter but also of St. Paul, who, as we know, could never sit still and was constantly on the move" (Sliwinski, 1982:166).

John Paul's visits gave him primary knowledge of the exploitation of African countries by foreign powers. He also saw the poverty and underdevelopment on the continent. Matthew Cassetta pointed out that of the many voyages that John Paul II made during his long pontificate, the most impressive were to Africa (2009:1). Although each pilgrimage had its own objective, the overriding aim of his visits was to offer hope to the people of Africa who had just gained political independence and were experiencing problems of corruption, tyrannies, diseases, and other societal ills. He visited Africa to build bridges and bring about reconciliation among different warring factions and to strengthen his brethren in the continent, which is his supreme Petrine mandate. After the convocation of the Synod for Africa, the theme of the Synod figured prominently in Saint John Paul II's apostolic visits. The pope's visits gave Africans, newcomers into Christianity, a sense of belonging in the Church. Africa had been consigned to the peripheries of the international system and the pope did not want such a predicament to befall Africa in the Church. This explains why Nigerian Cardinal Francis Arinze pointed out that John Paul's visits were to "help people understand that it's not when you become a Christian that counts; [what is important] is that all are in the Father's house" (Weigel, 1999:372).

Many African leaders saw any form of association with Pope John Paul II and the Holy See as a sign of legitimacy for their repressive regimes. They were willing to do whatever it took for a papal visit. They were willing to empty their national coffers to host the pope. Indeed, many African countries experienced financial crises after papal visits. A picture with the pope on a podium meant a lot for African leaders who oftentimes rigged their way to the presidency. Papal historian David Willey wrote, "In most African countries a papal visit is often a welcome political gift to the ruler and his local party machinery. The arrival of the pope presents a heaven-sent opportunity for an African head of state to reinforce his political authority in a society which may be lacerated by tribal, religious, and linguistic differences" (1992:152).

The Vatican often used those much anticipated and desired visits to make some human rights demands on countries. Before accepting an invitation to consecrate the Basilica of Our Lady of Peace in Yamoussoukro, John Paul II asked President Félix Houphouët-Boigny of Ivory Coast to build a health center within the premises of the basilica. The basilica is said to be the largest church in the world. Many people still find it difficult to comprehend why President Houphouët-Boigny would build such an expensive basilica in a place with an impressive Muslim population. Why would a poor African country spend exorbitant amounts of resources on such a project while most of her people are dying of hunger and tropical diseases?

On the eve of a visit by Pope John Paul II on May 1, 1980, President Mobutu Sese Seko of Zaire (D.R. Congo) married his mistress, Bobi Ladawa, so that she could greet pope with the status as the country's first lady. Interestingly, on trips across Zaire, Mobutu, the archetypal African dictator, often appropriated the *droit de cuissage* (right to deflower) as local chiefs offered him virgins; this practice was considered an honor for the virgin's family. That explains why he had a mistress to marry on the eve of the pope's visit. Mobutu Sese Seko was not the last African dictator who was customarily offered virgins during his visits. King Mswati III of Eswatini (Swaziland), as of 2018, had 15 wives and 23 children. His father had 125 wives and at least 210 children during his 83-year reign. The king customarily selects a virgin during the annual Umhlanga Reed festival. Sometimes during this annual rite, about 80,000 bare-breasted virgins would dance for the king and the king's mother. King Mswati would then inspect the virgins and choose the "lucky one." Some of the songs performed during the ritual read, "I am a virgin, please come and inspect whether I am still pure."

John Paul II was very aware that his visits to certain countries were used to gain political mileage by some African leaders. He used those visits to preach to political leaders on the need to respect human rights and dignity, and consistently asked for the release of political prisoners amongst others. In 1998, John Paul II visited Nigeria during the tyranny of General Sani Abacha. It was the pope's last visit to Africa south of the Sahara. Abacha was a merciless dictator who oversaw the systematic lynching, slaughtering, and incarceration of political opponents. At the time of the pope's visit, the popular Chief Moshood Abiola was still in prison and the hanging of Ken Saro Wiwa and other Ogboni leaders had led to the suspension of Nigeria from the Commonwealth.

Even though the pope's visit was primarily a religious and unofficial one for the beatification of Cyprian Michael Iwene Tansi, Sani Abacha saw it as a God-sent opportunity to reinforce his political authority and to redeem Nigeria's image abroad. Abacha played the role of the good host and was all smiles during the pope's three-day visit. He looked very serene and dignified in his white outfit and bore little semblance to the usual stoned-faced, no-nonsense dictator. The pope was introduced to Abacha's family and presented with a number of gifts, including a specially-crafted ebony and ivory walking stick. The pope asked President Abacha to respect human rights and to work toward national healing and reconciliation. He also called for the release of political prisoners and, before his departure, the pope handed Abacha an envelope which was later revealed to contain names of 60 political prisoners whom he wanted General Abacha to pardon.

Diplomatically and politically speaking, John Paul II regularly interacted with African countries with the hope that they would come to embody the social doctrine he laid out in his 1991 encyclical *Centesimus Annus*. There were some memorable moments of John Paul II's many visits to the continent of Africa. John Paul II's meeting with the anti-apartheid Nelson Mandela in South Africa in 1995 and talking to Muslim youth in Casablanca at the invitation of King Hassan in 1995 were among them.

Diplomatically, John Paul II's African trips forged a new, dynamic relationship between the Holy See and Africa. During the visits, African leaders often asked for diplomatic relations with the Holy See. John Paul II was open-minded, and, with respect and solidarity, was willing to establish diplomatic ties with newly independent developing nations such as Mozambique (1995), São Tomé and Principé (1984), Zimbabwe (1980), Eritrea (1995), and Seychelles (1985). Idiosyncratically, coming from a country which had been partitioned, repeatedly occupied, and victimized, John Paul II understood perfectly well the meaning of freedom, sovereignty, and international relations.

During his first visit to Africa in 1980, the pope made a brief stop in Burkina Faso, but that was enough for him to see with his own eyes the tragedy of a "country ravaged by drought." Shortly after that visit, he asked Cardinals Gantin, Thiandoum, and Zoungrana, and Archbishop Sangare to help him draft a statement. The pope then made his famous appeal: "I, John Paul II, Bishop of Rome and Successor of Peter, am here as the voice of the voiceless; the voice of the innocent who have died for lack of water and bread; the voice of the mothers and fathers who have watched their children die without understanding why" (Dziwisz, 2008:196). The result of the appeal was the establishment of the John Paul II Foundation for the Sahel. The Foundation is headquartered in Ouagadougou, Burkina Faso. The Foundation carries out some noble projects aimed at fighting droughts, desertification, and religious conflicts. The establishment and existence of this Foundation is a testament of Pope John Paul II's love for the poorest and least fortunate people in the world (Dicastery for Promoting Integral Human Development, 2020).

In his encyclical *Sollicitudo Rei Socialis*, John Paul II decried the widening gap between an ever richer First World and an ever poorer Third World. The pontiff also denounced the failure of Third World development projects and blatant exploitation of countries in the South. It was also the first encyclical to talk about the "structures of sin." During his visits to Africa, John Paul II interacted with some profound sons of Africa, and, later on, invited some of them to work with him at the Vatican.

Africans in the Roman Curia

The Roman Curia are the administrative institutions of the Holy See which aid the pope in exercising his Petrine office. Pope Pius XII started the process of universalizing and internationalizing what had traditionally been an Italian-dominated Roman Curia. Pope Paul VI made sure Africans were not left out of the process of globalizing the Roman Curia. Very notably, in 1971, he brought Archbishop Bernardin Gantin from the See of Cotonou, Benin Republic to Rome to serve as an adjunct Secretary of the Congregation for the Evangelization of Peoples. Gantin eventually became Secretary of the Congregation in 1973. In 1976, Pope Paul VI made him Pro-President of the Pontifical Justice and Peace Commission. On June 27, 1977, he was created a cardinal by Pope Paul VI.

Pope John Paul II took the process of internationalizing the Roman Curia a notch higher when, in 1984, he became the first pope to appoint a person from black Africa, Cardinal Bernardin Gantin from Benin, to head the Congregation of Bishops, one of the most influential Vatican Congregations. The Congregation of Bishops is the dicastery of the Roman Curia which oversees the selection of bishops in non-mission territories. In that same Curia shakeup, he also appointed Bishop Francis Arinze to head the Secretariat for Non-Christians. Francis Arinze was brought directly from the archdiocese of Onitsha, Nigeria. Francis Arinze eventually became the Prefect of the Congregation for Divine Worship and Discipline of the Sacraments (2002–2008). Cardinal Arinze is a credible voice for the Church in Africa and the universal Church.

John Paul II appointed many other Africans to work with him in the Vatican. In June 1993, Cardinal Gantin was elected and confirmed as Dean of the College of Cardinals, a post he held until his retirement in 2002. He was the first and only non-European to hold that position to date. The Dean of the College is the top cardinal since he serves as *primus inter pares* (first among equals). Very movingly, Pope Benedict XVI prayed before the tomb of the late Cardinal Gantin on November 19, 2011, during his visit to Benin. In his first address in Benin, Pope Benedict XVI said, "Cardinal Gantin won the respect and the affection of many. So, it seemed right that I should come to his country of origin, to pray before his tomb, and to thank Benin for having given the Church such a distinguished son." Joseph Ratzinger (Benedict XVI) and Bernardin Gantin were both created cardinals on the same day, June 27,1977, by Pope Paul VI. Pope John Paul II's appointment of these sons of Africa signaled the importance the pope gave to the black African Church.

Another significant African prelate that John Paul II brought to the Vatican is Cardinal Robert Sarah. In October 2001, the pope brought Archbishop Sarah from the See of Conakry, Guinea to the Vatican to serve as Secretary of the Congregation for the Evangelization of Peoples, a post he held until 2010. John Paul II had known and trusted this son of Africa for a long time, especially considering that he appointed him archbishop of Conakry in 1979 at the age of 34. In October 2010, Sarah was appointed president of the Pontifical Council *Cor Unum* by Pope Benedict XVI. In November that same year, Pope Benedict XVI elevated him to the College of Cardinals. In November 2014, Pope Francis appointed him Prefect of the Congregation for Divine Worship and Discipline of the Sacraments, a post he held until February 20, 2021, when Pope Francis accepted his resignation after he turned 75.

Cardinal Sarah is revered by many in the Christian world for his exceptionally fine intellect, deep spirituality, and piety. His writings, especially *The Power of Silence,* are widely quoted, even by non-Christians. In the aftermath of the controversial Amazonian Synod in 2019, Cardinal Sarah and Pope Benedict XVI co-authored *From the Depths of Our Hearts: Priesthood, Celibacy and the Crises of the Catholic Church.* This wonderful book explained the meaning and necessity of celibacy in the Church. During my time in the United States of America, I have been truly touched by the number of Americans and Europeans who talk very positively of Cardinal Sarah as soon as they learn that I am an African. It is fair to say that when he speaks, many Christians listen. Cardinal Sarah is an honorable ambassador of the Church in Africa.

Pope John Paul II was the first pope to appoint a person from Africa south of the Sahara to head an apostolic nunciature when he appointed Archbishop Augustine Kasujja as apostolic nuncio (the pope's ambassador) to Tunisia and Algeria in May 1998. A nuncio has a dual mandate. He represents the pope and the Holy See in a host state, and he also serves as a liaison between the Holy See and a particular local Church. Augustine Kasujja entered the Holy See's diplomatic service in 1979 and served at different nunciatures around the world, including Argentina, Haiti, Bangladesh, Portugal, and Peru, amongst others, before eventually becoming a nuncio in 1998. Since 1998, Archbishop Kasujja has held some significant postings, including serving as the nuncio to Nigeria (2010–2016). He was the apostolic nuncio to Belgium and Luxemburg from October 2016 – August 2021. He was the first non-European nuncio to Belgium. Today, a couple of Africans are serving the Church as apostolic nuncios in different parts of the world. Archbishop Jude Thaddeus Okolo from Nigeria is the current nuncio to Ireland. He is a seasoned Vatican diplomat and previously was the Holy See's nuncio to the Central African Republic and Chad. He has worked in different nunciatures around the world.

The Special Assembly for Africa of the Synod of Bishops (1994)

Pope John Paul II considered preparations for the Jubilee Year 2000 as one of the keys for interpreting his pontificate (E.A Par.18). Karol Wojtyła's lifelong interest in anniversaries and jubilee years derives from his conviction that God's action in history has sanctified time (*Tertio Millenio Adveniente*, 10). Stefan Wyszyński, Primate of Poland, told the pope upon his election that the Lord had called the new pontiff to lead the Church into the third millennium. The pope desperately desired to lead the Church into the third millennium and he confided this desire to his close friends and associates. Jerzy Kluger, the pope's long-time friend revealed, "Even though his body continued to deteriorate, he still had one last favour to ask from the Lord: to prolong his life and strength just a little while longer, so that he could lead his Church into the third millennium. I was touched by these words. For a long time, I had been able to see no other destiny for my friend than for him to love and serve God to the end, and he sincerely believed that the pope's mission was not quite finished yet. I approached my friend. 'You'll be the one to celebrate the holy year. You'll see, Lolek. The Lord will give you the strength'" (Kluger, 2012:210). Special Assemblies and General Assemblies were integral part of preparing for the Great Jubilee.

In 1994, Pope John Paul II convened the Special Assembly for Africa of the Synod of Bishops (April 10 – May 8). The Special Assembly of Africa was the first continental synod called by John Paul II to prepare the Church for the Great Jubilee of the Year 2000. He called a Synod for Africa with the intention of promoting "… in a particular way the proclamation of the gospel in Africa during these closing years of the twentieth century …" (Washington, 2015:206). The Synod of Bishops is a permanent institution established by Pope Paul VI in 1965 in response to the desire of the Council Fathers to keep alive the positive spirit of collegiality. Saint John Paul II noted that the Synod is "a particularly fruitful expression and instrument of the collegiality of bishops" (*L'Osservatore Romano*, May 1, 1983). A Synod of Bishops is a religious assembly at which bishops, gathered around and with the Holy Father, interact with each other and share information and experiences, in the common pursuit of pastoral solutions (Holy See Press Office, 2012). In his September 15, 1965, *motu proprio, Apostolica Sollicitudo*, Pope Paul VI outlined the nature, purposes, structure, functions, and definition of a Synod.

The theme of the Special Assembly for Africa was, "The Church in Africa and Her Evangelizing Mission Towards the Year 2000: 'You Shall Be My Witnesses'" (Acts 1:8). The Synod for Africa was a very poignant moment for the universal Church and the Church in Africa. Successors of the Apostles from Africa, the majority of whose parents and grandparents were witch doctors, atheists, traditionalists, *juju* practitioners, Voodooists, and recent converts to Christianity, congregated in Rome to evaluate the extent of evangelization on the continent of Africa. In his post-Synodal exhortation, John Paul II observed, "The Special Assembly for Africa of the Synod of Bishops was *an historic moment of grace*: the Lord visited his people in Africa. Indeed, this continent is today experiencing what we can call a *sign of the times, an acceptable time, a day of salvation*" (E.A. Par. 6). It showed that the local Churches in Africa hold a rightful place in the communion of the Church.

For about a month, the bishops of Africa discussed the prospects of the Church's evangelizing mission on the continent. The bishops talked at length about the challenges experienced in the Church's efforts to proclaim the Good News in Africa. Pope John Paul II sat through many of the deliberations by the bishops of the continent. He sat there patiently, listened attentively, took some notes, and occasionally dozed off with the rosary in his hands. Unfortunately, the opening of the Synod coincided with the beginning of the genocide in Rwanda. This senseless slaughter in one of the most Catholic countries on the continent put a question mark on the impact of the Christian faith in Africa. As is the custom, the pope made use of the deliberations and resolutions of the Synod to write his post-Synodal Apostolic Exhortation, *Ecclesia in Africa*.

Very symbolically and dramatically, instead of signing and releasing the document in the Vatican, the Holy Father took it personally to the people of Africa in the same fashion the missionaries took the Word of God to Africa. The document was then signed and given at Yaoundé, in Cameroon, on September 14, 1995, the Feast of the Triumph of the Cross. In Nairobi, Kenya, the pope symbolically placed the document into the hands of bishops, priests, catechists, and the laity and commissioned them to the take the Synod message to their small Christian communities. That Africa is the fastest-growing Catholic and Christian continent is a testament that the Synod message has been instrumental in evangelization. On November 13, 2004, Pope John Paul II announced the convocation of a second Special Assembly for Africa, which was later reconfirmed by his successor, Pope Benedict XVI, in the Weekly General Audience of June 22, 2005.

Debt Relief/Cancellation

As the Jubilee Year 2000 was approaching, Pope John Paul II put up a spirited campaign for debt relief for poorer countries of the world. He knew that, traditionally, the Jubilee Year was a year of debt cancellation as prescribed by the Book of Leviticus: "Thus, in the spirit of the Book of Leviticus (25:8–12), Christians will have to raise their voice on behalf of all the poor of the world, proposing the Jubilee as an appropriate time to give thought, among other things, to reducing substantially, if not cancelling outright, the international debt which seriously threatens the future of many nations" (T.M.A, no. 51).

Being a voice for the voiceless, the pope teamed up with international icons such as Mohammed Ali, Archbishop Desmond Tutu, President Benjamin Mkapa, and organizations such as "Jubilee for Africa's Debt Burden," and "Jubilee USA Network," to launch a vociferous campaign for the reduction or cancellation of unjust debts of poor African countries. He made pressing appeals to financial bodies like the International Monetary Fund and the wealthy industrialized countries to have mercy on these countries. He rallied episcopal conferences of wealthy Western countries to present the issue of international debt relief of poor countries to their home governments and Western financial donors. He repeatedly made the appeal in many forums and in his writings, especially *Ecclesia in Africa* and *Tertio Millenio Adveniente*. Through many forums, the pope also pleaded with leaders from the Third World to tame their appetite for loans. He wrote, "I particularly feel it is my duty to urge 'the Heads of State and their governments in Africa not to crush their peoples with internal and external debts'" (E.A, No. 120).

The Jubilee Campaign led to a series of commitments from the United States government, other G-8 nations, and international financial institutions to provide debt relief for some of the world's poorest nations. Since the creation of the IMF/World Bank Heavily Indebted Poor Countries Initiative (HIPC) in 1996, more than 30 nations have now received some form of debt relief. Twenty-two nations have reached "completion point" in the HIPC Initiative and have received 100% cancellation of eligible debt stock. The 22 countries which have reached the completion point, and thus have benefited from 100% debt stock cancellation of qualifying debts, are African countries: Benin, Bolivia, Burkina Faso, Cameroon, Ethiopia, Ghana, Guyana, Honduras, Madagascar, Malawi, Mali, Mauritania, Mozambique, Niger, Rwanda, São Tomé and Príncipe, Senegal, Sierra Leone, Tanzania, Uganda, and Zambia. More than ten countries have reached "decision point" in the HIPC Initiative and have begun to receive partial debt service relief. These countries include Afghanistan, Burundi, the Central African Republic, Chad, the Democratic Republic of the Congo, the Republic of Congo, the Gambia, Guinea, Guinea-Bissau, and Haiti (World Bank, "Debt Relief At A Glance," 2019).

In a letter to the Jubilee Debt Campaign in 2004, President Benjamin Mkapa of Tanzania outlined the impact of debt relief on his country:

> When I became President of Tanzania in 1995, our country was witnessing a serious deterioration of basic services, and a high and unsustainable debt burden. One of my first priorities was to reverse these trends by increasing government revenue and seeking debt relief.... In 2001, Tanzania was granted significant debt relief. As promised, this was directed to the priority sectors of education, health, water, rural roads and HIV/AIDS, enabling us to increase resources for poverty reduction by 130 per cent. 8 IDA and IMF 2006, p. 64. 3 We have already witnessed tremendous successes. The primary school population has increased by 66 per cent—the

greater part of an extra two million children—and the shortfall in the enrolment of girls has been eliminated. We have built 45,000 classrooms, 1,925 new primary schools and over 7,500 homes for teachers in partnership with their communities; between 2000 and 2004, we recruited 37,261 new teachers, and retrained another 14,852. The pass rate in the Leaving Examination doubled in two years.

Catholic Universities and Institutions in Africa

During his pontificate, Pope John Paul II pushed for the establishment of Catholic universities and institutes of higher learning in Africa. Catholic universities had already been created on other continents. For instance, Pope Leo XIII established the Catholic University of America (CUA) in 1887. Africa and Pope John Paul fully understood the importance of Catholic tertiary institutions in the development of a people. During his pontificate, the Congregation of Catholic Education accorded regional episcopal conferences in Africa the right to establish regional Catholic universities and colleges. The Catholic University of Eastern Africa (CUEA), initially named the Catholic Higher Institute of Eastern Africa, was established in 1984. Hekima College, a Jesuit School of Theology and International Relations in Nairobi, Kenya, opened in 1984. The Catholic University of Central Africa, in Yaoundé, Cameroon, was created in 1991.

Pope John Paul II outlined the mission and purpose of Catholic universities in Africa in par. 103 of *Ecclesia in Africa*:

> The Catholic Universities and Higher Institutes in Africa have a prominent role to play in the proclamation of the salvific Word of God. They are a sign of the growth of the Church insofar as their research integrates the truths and experiences of the faith and helps to internalize them. They serve the Church by providing trained personnel, by studying important theological and social

questions for the benefit of the Church, by developing an African theology, by promoting the work of inculturation especially in liturgical celebration, by publishing books and publicizing Catholic truth, by undertaking assignments given by the Bishops and by contributing to a scientific study of cultures.

Idiosyncratically, the pope's experience of university life in Poland informed his zeal for the establishment of Catholic universities in Africa. Pope John Paul II taught in universities in Poland, even after his appointment as auxiliary bishop. In his Apostolic Constitution on Catholic universities, *Ex Corde Ecclesiae*, the pope underscored the importance of his time as a university professor when he wrote, "For many years I myself was deeply enriched by the beneficial experience of university life: the ardent search for truth and its unselfish transmission to youth and to all those learning to think rigorously, so as to act rightly and to serve humanity better" (John Paul II, 2005:57).

Idiosyncratically, the pope's profound meetings with members of different Catholic universities over the years gave him a personal appreciation of the importance of Catholic institutions and propelled him to create Catholic universities in Africa. The pope acknowledged this when he said, "In a particular way, I wish to manifest my joy at the numerous meetings which the Lord has permitted me to have in the course of my apostolic journeys with the Catholic University communities of various continents. They are for me a lively and promising sign of the fecundity of the Christian mind in the heart of every culture. They give me a well-founded hope for a new flowering of Christian culture in the rich and varied context of our changing times, which certainly face serious challenges but which also bear so much promise under the action of the Spirit of truth and of love" (John Paul II, 2005:57).

The pope knew the importance of Catholic institutions, especially in a continent of first-generation believers, "Through the encounter which it establishes between the unfathomable richness of the salvific message of the Gospel and the variety and immensity of the fields of knowledge in which that richness is incarnated by it, a Catholic university enables the Church to institute an incomparably fertile dialogue with people of every culture" (John Paul II, 2005:59). In another instance, John Paul II underscored the importance of Catholic universities. "Together with all my brother Bishops who share pastoral responsibility with me, I would like to manifest my deep conviction that a Catholic University is without any doubt one of the best instruments that the Church offers to our age which is searching for certainty and wisdom" (John Paul II, 2005:61).

How Idiosyncratic Was John Paul II's Diplomatic Rapport with Africa?

As the senior-cardinal deacon, Pericle Felici was tasked with the responsibility of announcing to the world the election of Karol Wojtyła as pope on October 16, 1978. It is said that when Cardinal Felici pronounced the surname of the newly elected pope "Woitiwa," many at the esplanade of St. Peter's Basilica started asking each other, "*E un Africano?*" "Is he is an African?" (Onaiyekan, 2016:313). Perhaps they were right in their wonderment. Karol Wojtyła was Polish by birth, but an African at heart and in spirit. George Weigel authoritatively stated that, "No world leader in the last two decades of the twentieth century paid such sustained attention to Africa as John Paul II" (Weigel, 1999:372). When I asked George Weigel to substantiate his bold assertion, his response was, "I think it's the simple truth, on the numbers. Did any UN secretary-general, any US president, any British prime minister, or any president of the World Council of Churches spend as much time in Africa as John Paul II? I doubt it." John Paul II knew that Africa was the least developed continent with many problems and, as such, he dedicated more time to this continent. "Africa—the pope [John Paul II] has a powerful sense of the tragedy of Africa as being forgotten in the modern world, that nobody cares about Africa" (Noonan, 2005:37).

From October 1978 when he was elected supreme pontiff, John Paul II's eyes were fixed on Africa. He boldly called himself an ally and spokesperson for Africa. He appealed on many occasions that Africa should not be forgotten. As already highlighted, during his pontificate, John Paul II made a series of pilgrimages to Africa; the Holy See established diplomatic relations with a good number of African states; he became the first pope to appoint a person from black Africa to head a Curia Congregation and invited many Africans to work with him in the Vatican; he convened the Synod for Africa; he established the John Paul II Foundation for the Sahel; he vociferously campaigned for the reduction or cancellation of debts of Third World countries; he emotionally apologized to the continent for the tragedy of slavery and slave trade; and he was a passionate voice for Africa in the international scene.

Pope John Paul II's sustained attention to Africa was not only informed by the demands of his office as head of the Catholic Church. It was idiosyncratic. John Paul II's many voyages to Africa were a continuation of a precedent set by his predecessor, Pope Paul VI, who had already visited the continent in 1969. Wojtyła was fifty-eight years old when elected pope in 1978. He was the youngest to be elected pope in 125 years. John Paul II's comparative youthfulness, and his being a fit athlete accustomed to hiking, swimming, skiing, and kayaking, made it easier for him to visit Africa many times. Before assuming the Petrine office, the pope already had a foretaste of international visits. That experience propelled him as pope to undertake many pilgrimages to Africa. In an interview with French journalist André Frossard, the pope noted, "The experience which I acquired in Cracow has taught me that it is important to visit the communities personally, starting with the parishes. Of course, this is not an exclusive duty, but I consider it of the first importance" (1982:28).

In my interview with George Weigel, he pointed out that John Paul II made numerous trips to Africa to encourage African Catholics and to inspire less fervent Catholics with Africans' faith by bringing African Catholicism to the attention of the World

Church. The pope was more successful in encouraging African Catholics to live the New Evangelization than he was with his European brethren. In a sense, he wanted European Catholics to look to African Catholicism for inspiration. There was an immediate rapport between John Paul II and Africa following his election in 1978. A very plausible explanation for the rapport was the similar backgrounds in terms of national and personal histories. The Poles and Africans are a people stung by history. Birds of a same feather flock together says the old adage. John Paul II's Poland and Africa each have a long history of foreign rule, occupation, and partition. The Poles and Africans both lost their sovereignties to foreign powers. The Poles and Africans had been enslaved and oppressed by occupation forces. Poland has been repeatedly occupied by foreign powers and at one point did not even feature on the map of the world due to territorial occupation. In October 1795, Poland was partitioned among her neighbours Germany, Austria, and Russia. The great Polish historian and nobleman Adam Zamoyski emotionally captured the Polish pain:

> As a Pole you were born into a bankrupt business, you weren't like other people. Every Pole has to confront— why have we made such a mess? Three hundred years ago we were a great power and a normal country. Then we'd become a pathetic country whose history no one knew. Every Pole has a question mark somewhere. For the Pope, for all of us growing up after the war, anybody going through the war, even people born in Poland after the war were born into its arguments. We are a people stung by history (Barnes, 1999).

Poland's repeated humiliation and devouring by her neighbours was a constant bitter memory for the Poles, especially considering that in the 16th century, Poland was the largest country in Europe. Very shamefully, what was the largest country in Europe in the 16th century ceased to exist on the European map in the 18th century. The loss of her geography did not erase the nation in the memory of her people, "The Polish nation has often only existed in the Polish mind. Having no geography, the Poles feel history must take its place. They gave the oaks of their forests the names of lost kings. They bury and rebury their beloved leaders" (Barnes, 1999). Inevitably, Poland developed an inferiority complex toward other nations because of her unfortunate history. "Poland's pain lies behind every tree, every mound" is Jane Barnes' summary of the awareness and ubiquity of the nation's pain. John Paul II grew up in a Nazi-occupied Poland, and he at one point worked in a quarry to avoid deportation to a concentration camp by the Nazis. Poland was also unfortunately occupied by the communists after World War II. Likewise, Africa suffered an unfortunate history, as explained previously. Apart from Ethiopia and Liberia, all other African countries were partitioned and colonized by different European powers. During the Berlin West African Conference of 1884, Africa was arbitrarily partitioned among European colonial powers. As late as the 1970s and 80s, some Southern African countries were still under colonial rule. Africa lost many of her able sons and daughters to the evil of slavery and slave trade.

Based on the similar histories of Poland and Africa, the pope perfectly understood the plight of the African people. He was sympathetic to the continent. He therefore vicariously identified with the people of Africa and understood full well the importance of freedom, birth of a nation, and sovereignty. During his visit to Zaire in 1980, John Paul II, remarked to Polish missionaries in Zaire that he found the process of a new nation's "sense of a beginning" to be "most fascinating" (Weigel, 1998:374). As a result, the pope did not hesitate to establish diplomatic relations with many African countries such as Zimbabwe (1980), São Tomé and Principé (1984), Seychelles (1985), Eritrea (1995), and Mozambique (1995). Buoyed by his appreciation of internal self-rule and his knowledge of the challenges of nation building, the pope was oftentimes en route to Africa to offer hope and encouragement to these newly independent states.

John Paul II's most trusted ally, Monsignor Dziwisz, pointed out that the pope lived in Poland under very authoritarian regimes like the dictatorships and authoritarianism characteristic of many countries in Africa (Dziwisz, 2008:193). Idiosyncratically, the pope's affection for Africa could be explained by the history of Poland, his native country. John Paul II was a student of history. Remarkably similar to the history of Africa, Poland has a long history of suffering, oppression, repression, annihilation, and humiliation. Poland has suffered the brunt of totalitarian atheistic regimes—Nazism and communism. The pope lived through these regimes, which grossly curtailed basic human freedoms. Cambridge University professor Eamon Duffy describes the powerful ways suffering connected Poland to Pope Saint John Paul II's papacy:

> Suffering is crucial for understanding John Paul, at a personal level, and at a racial, ethnic, historical, and theological level. His personal life is one of enormous personal deprivation: the loss of his mother when he was very young; the loss of his brother who was perhaps the person he was closest to in the world; then when he was a very young man, and before he'd really shaped his own life choices, the loss of his father, whose piety had been crucial in shaping his own religion.... But the Polish people for 200 years have been a victim-people, partitioned between Germany and Russia, religiously oppressed, enslaved, abandoned by the world at the beginning of the Second World War. And that experience of desolation for him is part and parcel of the religious desolation for the East, a church which is the Church of Silence, which was cut off from the West.... He feels he has given the churches of the East a special vision, a special access to the Gospel of the Crucified.... Personal suffering for him chimed in perfectly and became an image of this greater vocation to the suffering of the church of the East (Barnes & Whitney, 1995–2014).

Wojtyła was a clandestine member of the Rhapsodic theatre and a clandestine seminarian because those freedoms were outlawed in Nazi Poland. The young people under Fr. Karol Wojtyła's tutelage called him "Wujek" to conceal his real identity and to prevent him from getting into trouble with the repressive communist regime. Pope John Paul II had first-hand knowledge of how the communists designed all sorts of plans to curtail religious freedoms in Poland. Karl Marx, the father of communism, taught that "religion is the opium of the people." Primate Stefan Wyszyński battled with the communists to safeguard the Church's autonomy in Poland. That led to his incarceration and house arrests on a number of occasions. In many instances, the communist regime would not allow Cardinal Wyszyński to leave the country.

In 1981, General Wojciech Jaruzelski imposed martial law in Poland. John Paul was not happy with the martial law and petitioned President Leonid Brezhnev on many occasions to rescind it. The communist government was always tapping people's conversations in Poland. John Paul II once opted for a hallway conversation with Lech Walesa because he knew the Polish secret service was spying on them. Due to religious oppression in the Soviet Union, Pope John Paul II strongly warned the communists during his June 1979 visit to Poland that one could not do away with God in any geographical longitude or latitude. The suspension of constitutions and imposition of martial law is a common practice in Africa. The military had come to power in many parts of Africa through military coups.

Poland and Pope John Paul II's history of oppression and repression is in congruence with that of African countries. Repressive colonial regimes did not consider Africans as human beings. The freedoms of the people in the colonies were greatly curtailed. Africans were forced out of their lands by the white colonialists. Africans were impelled to walk around with identity tags around their necks in their own home countries. Africans were killed and incarcerated for loitering around white neighbourhoods. Africans were routinely jailed without trial and could not be served in restaurants and hotels reserved for the white settlers. The barbarity of the apartheid regime in South Africa needs no substantiation. I develop goose pimples whenever I listen to Nelson Mandela's speech at the Rivonia Trial in 1964, before his 27 years of imprisonment for challenging the grave injustice of the white minority rule in South Africa:

> During my lifetime I have dedicated myself to this struggle of the African people. I have fought against white domination, and I have fought against black domination. I have cherished the ideal of a democratic and free society in which all persons live together in harmony and with equal opportunities. It is an ideal which I hope to live for and to achieve. But if needs be, it is an ideal for which I am prepared to die.

Africans continued to suffer the brunt of authoritarianism and dictatorial regimes even after attaining internal self-rule. Many post-independent regimes infringed on almost all the rights of people, especially in countries led by the military who were always very quick to seize power from civilian leaderships through military coups. Freedom of speech and assembly was and is not tolerated in many African states. When it became clear that President Jomo Kenyatta's presidency was coming to an end due to poor health and advanced age, Charles Njonjo, Kenya's attorney general at the time, warned the politicians and Kenyans that contemplating/thinking about the death of the president is tantamount to treason. Arbitrary detention without trial and torture and assassination was the order of the day in many of these states. In Kenya, the Nyayo Chamber was the center for torturing political opponents like Raila Odinga and Kenneth Matiba.

During his 1992 visit to Angola, which was still under a Marxist-style dictatorship, John Paul II drew a personal parallel between Angola and communist Poland. Speaking to the bishops, the pope said, "The same process is at work. The geography is different, but it's the same system and the same program of ideological atheism.

On the other side is the Church which does not peddle some program, but which follows the Word of God and the promises of Christ" (Dziwisz, 2008:193–94). On May 5, 1980, John Paul visited Brazzaville, the capital of Congo. At that time, Congo was under a Marxist government. There were pockets of socialist and Marxist governments in Africa in the 20th century. Some leaders tried their hands at socialist and Marxist forms of political organization, especially during the Cold War. In Zambia, Kenneth Kaunda was figuring out his African Socialism. In Tanzania, Mwalimu Julius Nyerere tried his hand at socialism—*Ujamaa* and Ujamaa villages.

John Paul II perfectly understood the plight of the African people and that is why he did not shy away from calling on the leaders on the continent to respect the human rights of their citizens. He encouraged bishops and episcopal conferences to speak out against dictatorships and authoritarianism. He also knew that his presence, like his voice from Rome, protected local churches against authoritarian rulers. The pope knew that he had to encourage the leadership of the Church in Africa to speak out for the rights of their peoples. In a continent where the opposition was systematically squashed by dictatorial regimes, the Church was, perhaps, the last bastion of hope for the people. Interestingly, many dictators in Africa had great respect for the leadership of the Church on the continent. President Mwai Kibaki of Kenya always pleaded with the bishops of the country to speak out and he called them "the conscience of the nation." He implored church leaders to always call out the government whenever it fails in her responsibilities.

The efforts of John Paul II were mirrored in the work and bravery of church leaders in the continent. The role played by Church men and women in Africa for the expansion of democratic space and respect for human rights on the continent cannot be overemphasized. The efforts of people like the Rev. Timothy of Njoya of Kenya, Bishop Alexander Muge of Kenya, Catholic Archbishop Ndingi Mwana Nzinki of Kenya, Anglican Archbishop Desmond Tutu of South Africa, and Christian Cardinal Tumi of Cameroon are well documented. In their struggles for the respect of human rights and political pluralism, some of these churchmen were publicly battered or mysteriously killed. Kenyans of a certain age will remember the horrible sight of Archbishop Timothy Njoya being battered on the side of the road by the Kenyan police in 1990. George Weigel noted in an interview with this author that "in both Poland and Africa in the twentieth century, Catholicism was experienced as a force for human liberation. That sense may be fading in Poland, but it still seems strong in Africa."

The Catholic Church has a preferential option for the poor. The preferential option for the poor is "... a special form of primacy in the exercise of Christian charity, to which the whole Tradition of the Church bears witness ..." (par. 43). The preferential option for the poor is based on Jesus' preference for the extremely poor and downtrodden in society. Jesus Christ ministered to the poor and did well to reintegrate many in society by healing and speaking out in their favor. He praised the widow who placed her last coin in the offertory basket (Mark 12:41–4). He restored Bartimaeus' sight (Mark 10:46–52). Some of his parables did not depict the rich in favorable light, such as the parable of Lazarus and the rich man (Luke 16:19–31) and the parable of the rich fool (Luke 12:16–21). Informed by the Catholic social teaching, the Church's vast outreach to the poor in the world is perhaps unrivaled by any existing institution.

John Paul II hailed from Poland, which, at the time, was a relatively poor country. In Alfred Sauvy's classification, Poland was a Second World country since all the Eastern communist nations were so categorized. The pope's poverty-stricken background found resonance with the realities in Africa. He was born in a humble apartment which his family rented from a Jewish family. Before her death, his mother took on sewing to augment the family's meagre finances. After the death of his mother and brother, Karol Wojtyła lived with his father in a very humble way. Neighbors and friends were very generous to the young Karol Wojtyła, especially after the death of his father. During the Nazi occupation of Poland, the young Karol Wojtyła worked in a quarry to avoid deportation. During his time in the quarry, he traded his extra rations and vodka coupons in the black market for meat and other necessities that he needed. The pope's poverty-stricken history in a way informed his love for Africa. That explains why Cardinal John Onaiyekan of Nigeria once said that "only John Paul II understood us [Africans] when we said we were hungry." When once asked by a German theologian what Africans thought of Pope John Paul II, Cardinal John Onaiyekan of Abuja archdiocese responded, "The problem we have in Africa is about survival, of war and peace, of hunger and disease. In these matters that touch our daily lives, nobody is doing anything sufficient in our favour more than this pope. He continues to shout and ask the world not to forget us. So, I told him that we love our pope because he is our advocate" (2016:322). The pope's humble and frugal background aided him to understand the pangs of poverty in Africa. That is why he always challenged the leadership in Africa to make policies aimed at improving the lives of their people. When invited to bless the basilica in Yamoussoukro, constructed by President Félix Houphouët-Boigny, John Paul bargained with the country's leadership to attach a medical facility in that huge complex that would serve the poor in that country.

His appeal for debt cancellation on behalf of the poor countries, especially in Africa, was idiosyncratic. Being a person who hailed from a poor country and who had a very humble upbringing, the pontiff had a good understanding of poverty and the burden of debts. He knew how the yoke/burden of debt was strangling the aspirations of many people in Africa. Africa's debt burden was rendering many of its economies dysfunctional because its governments were using their limited resources to service external debts at the expense of the provision of basic services, such as education and health care. It is therefore not surprising that the Polish pope had a great sensitivity for the downtrodden people of Africa, the dark and forgotten continent. The pope felt the world was "callous" toward the continent of Africa (Noonan: 2005:37). He vicariously understood the predicament of the people of Africa. At least from pictorial representation, John Paul II felt very much at home in Africa. During his visits, he interacted freely with ordinary people, ate with them, and even went as far as taking a photo with practitioners of the African Traditional Religion in Africa, amidst many criticisms.

Pope John Paul II "was convinced that only Christ and his liberating Gospel could heal the wounds of history, restore to the African people a sense of dignity, identity and a healthy pride in their culture. He wanted Africa to regain its rightful place in the human family. 'After the fall of the Berlin Wall, the pope seems determined to tear down another wall, the wall of silence and oblivion … the wall that separates Africa from the rest of the world, the indifference of the Western World towards its part in the destruction of an entire continent' …" (Shonecke, 1995). Pope John Paul II, as he noted in *Sollicitudo Rei Socialis*, did not want any part of the world written out of the script of history, as some in the West wanted to do with the post-colonial Third World, and Africa in particular.

Pope John Paul II knew that, in spite of a history of oppression and exploitation at the hands of a Christian West, the seeds of the Gospel had fallen on fertile ground in Africa. He was convinced that the African Church, with its vitality and dynamism, could make a major contribution to the mission of the Church. Due to that conviction, he convoked the Synod for Africa. Idiosyncratically, Pope John Paul II was aware of the past glorious splendour of Africa's Christianity. That is why he recalled the ancient glories of Christian Africa in *Ecclesia in Africa*:

> We think of the Christian Churches of Africa whose origins go back to the times of the Apostles and are traditionally associated with the name and teaching of Mark the Evangelist. We think of their countless Saints, Martyrs, Confessors and Virgins, and recall the fact that from the second to the fourth centuries, Christian life in the North of Africa was most vigorous and had a leading place in theological study and literary production. The names of the great doctors and writers come to mind, men like Origen, Saint Athanasius, and Saint Cyril, leaders of the

Alexandrian School, and at the other end of the North African coastline, Tertullian, Saint Cyprian and above all Saint Augustine, one of the most brilliant lights of the Christian world. We shall mention the great Saints of the desert, Paul, Anthony, and Pachomius, the first founders of the monastic life, which later spread through their example in both the East and the West. And among many others we want also to mention Saint Frumentius, known by the name of Abba Salama, who was consecrated Bishop by Saint Athanasius and became the first Apostle of Ethiopia. During these first centuries of the Church in Africa, certain women also bore their own witness to Christ. Among them Saints Perpetua and Felicitas, Saint Monica, and Saint Thecla are particularly deserving of mention (E.A. par. 31).

While emphasizing the early roots of the Church in Africa, in *Ecclesia in Africa*, the pope also recalled the role of great figures in the Church in later ages. He recalled the great missionary endeavours of Nzinga-a-Nkuwu, the great King of Congo, who asked for missionaries to proclaim the Gospel in his kingdom in the 15th century. The pope paid tribute to the martyrs of Uganda, who were bold enough to sacrifice their lives for the sake of their newly acquired faith. Martyrs such as Kizito were still catechumens at the time of their death. Mathias Mulumba was a local chief in Uganda and had four wives. Because of the teachings of the Church against polygamy, he let go of three of his wives. The pope recalled the list of saints Africa bequeathed to the Church in the 20th century: Blessed Clementine Anwarite (Virgin and Martyr of Zaire), Blessed Victoria Rasoamanarivo of Madagascar, Saint Josephine Bakhita of the Sudan, and Blessed Isidore Bakanja, Martyr of Zaire, amongst others.

Pope John Paul II was acutely aware of many positive values of cultures in Africa which could enrich the Christian faith. In *Ecclesia in Africa*, he states, "The sons and daughters of Africa love life" (E.A. 43). Africans pay attention to the veneration of their ancestors. Africans offer libation to their ancestors before drinking. Africans believe intuitively that the dead continue to live and remain in communion with them. Is this not in some way a preparation for belief in the Communion of the Saints (E.A. par. 43). Africans show their respect for human life until its natural end and keep elderly parents and relatives within the family. Africans have a communal philosophy, "I think, therefore we are, and, since we are, therefore, I am." The importance of belonging to a community is expressed in various African developmental philosophies: *Ubuntu, Ujamaa,* African socialism and *Harambee*— to pull together. John Paul II had respect for the African Church because of her great values. It is for that reason he allowed and encouraged the African Church to develop its own liturgical rite (the Zairean Rite) and its worship forms.

"Although Africa is very rich in natural resources, it remains economically poor. At the same time, it is endowed with a wealth of cultural values and priceless human qualities which it can offer to the Churches and to humanity as a whole" (E.A. par. 42). John Paul II knew that Africans are notoriously religious, as James Mbithi had postulated. Africans have a sense of the deity and the supernatural. Africans celebrate life during birth and death. Africans dance with their waist and life is centred around the waist of a human being. According to the pope, "Africans have a profound religious sense, a sense of the sacred, of the existence of God the Creator and of a spiritual world. The reality of sin in its individual and social forms is very much present in the consciousness of these peoples, as is also the need for rites of purification and expiation" (E.A. par. 42).

In his homily at the closing liturgy of the Special Assembly for Africa of the Synod of Bishops (May 8, 1994), Pope John Paul II repeated the words of his predecessor Pope Paul VI that Africa is "… a new homeland for Christ," a land loved by the Eternal Father. Paul VI made the remark in his homily at the canonization of Blessed Charles Lwanga and companion martyrs on October 18, 1964. The pope was prophetic to believe that the Church in Africa was going to play a huge role in 21st-century Christianity. The pope knew that Africa was destined to become the seat of Catholicism in the very near future. Investing in Africa was going to yield dividends in the near future. In an interview with this author, George Weigel noted that John Paul II paid particular attention to Africa because he knew that Africa was where the demographic center of world Catholicism was shifting. Africa was the next big market for Catholicism. Africa is now the most Christian continent in the world and will shortly become the most Catholic continent.

At the beginning of the twentieth century, Hillaire Belloc, the great Catholic writer, wrote, "Europe is the faith and the faith is Europe" (Noonan, 196–97). From colonial times in the 19th century, thousands of missionaries from Europe boarded boats and ships carrying the Word of God to evangelize the people of Africa. I always get emotional when I read the experiences of the early missionaries to Africa. In exceedingly difficult and harsh conditions, these missionaries introduced to Africans the God of Abraham, Isaac, and Jacob—the God who became a human being in the fullness of time. Some of these missionaries lost their lives within a few weeks in Africa due to tropical diseases (malaria, cholera, and typhoid). I remember with gratitude the great Mill Hill Missionaries with whom I interacted in my native Cameroon, Kenya, and Uganda: Frs. Anthony Murphy (Ireland), Bill Tolan (Scotland), Maurice McGill (England), Fons Eppink (Holland), Dermott Byrne (England), James Nielen (Holland), John Kelder (Holland), Peter Droog (Holland), Jan Lion (Holland), Hans Smiths (Holland), Peter Major (U.S.A), Gerry Doyle (Ireland), Harry Peters (Holland), Brendan Jordan (Ireland), John Sweeney (Scotland), Brother Duncan (England), Fr. James Fanning (England), Fr. Kees Groenewoud (Holland), Colin Davies (Bishop/Spain), Joseph Willigers (Bishop/Holland) and Adolf Poll (Tyrol).

On May 24, 2021, I was moved to tears when I saw Fr. Adolf Poll's farewell photos in Witu, Kenya. Fr. Adolf, popularly known as "Fr. Alleluia," was leaving Kenya after 53 years of great missionary work in many parts of Kenya. He is fondly called Fr. Alleluia because, when he first arrived at Kisii, in the Western part of Kenya, as a young missionary in 1968, he did not know any word in the local dialect. So, when the first local people encountered him, he kept on shouting "Alleluia," "Alleluia." So, the name "Fr. Alleluia" was born. As a young missionary student, I worked with Fr. Alleluia for two years (2006–2008). Very moving to me was the sight of Fr. Alleluia leaving Kenya with only two small bags after 53 years of great missionary service in Africa. All of his possessions amounted to two small bags. A big lesson to us all in these times of consumerism and infatuation with material possessions. The stories of great missionary service in Africa are inexhaustible and inspiring.

History is full of ironies. The evangelized are now evangelizing the evangelizers. The trend has now been reversed. In the 21st century, Africa is now sending many missionaries to Europe and North America for the re-evangelization of the West. Indeed, it is not hyperbolic to say that African priests are the future of the Church in the West. The excruciatingly dwindling number of vocations to the priesthood and religious life in many traditional Catholic countries in the West is worrying. In the year 2020–2021, some dioceses in the Western world were without any seminarians for the priesthood. In the 18th and 19th centuries, the island of Ireland sent out thousands of Catholic missionaries to Africa. However, in the year 2020, there were at most two persons ordained to the priesthood in Ireland. Ironically, there were more episcopal than presbyterial ordinations in Ireland in 2020. "You can walk the streets of Dublin—Dublin!—on a Sunday morning and see more people at brunch than in church" (Noonan, 2005:197).

The opposite is true in Africa, especially south of the Sahara. Seminaries and religious houses in Africa are flooded with men and women preparing for the priesthood and the religious life. In the academic year 2019–2020, Bigard Memorial Seminary, Enugu, Nigeria, which is one of just seven seminaries in Nigeria, had a total enrollment of 855 seminarians. Some bishops in Africa go for years without accepting candidates for the priesthood because they have more than enough priests already for their various dioceses. A good number of seminarians and priests from Africa are now being exported to the Churches in Europe and

America. Mindful of the high number of priests being shipped out to the Western world, some seminaries in Africa are already training and preparing seminarians for missions in foreign lands.

In his insightful presentation during the celebration of the 95th anniversary of Bigard Memorial Seminary in November 2019, renowned biblical scholar and the seminary's former rector, the Rev. Peter Damian Akpunonu, argued that the seminary's formation of seminarians should also be geared towards future ministry in foreign lands. In addition to Greek, Latin, and Hebrew, he advised that seminarians should also acquire proficiency in the use of other foreign languages. In 1969, Pope Paul VI visited Kampala, Uganda for the inauguration of the Symposium of Episcopal Conferences of Africa and Madagascar (SECAM). On that occasion, the pope asked the Church in Africa to be missionary to herself. Looking down from his Father's house, Saint Pope Paul VI must be very pleased to see that the Church in Africa today is not only missionary to herself, but missionary to the rest of the world, *ad gentes*. John Paul II saw this happening within a short time. Commenting on John Paul II's main legacy for Africa, George Weigel noted, "John Paul II challenged Africa to live a Christ-centered faith, and the tremendous growth of the Church in Africa testifies to the success of that kind of Christocentric evangelization." It is therefore of no surprise that in his homily during the eucharistic celebration for the opening of the second Special Assembly for Africa on October 4, 2009, Pope Benedict XVI, amongst others, said, "Africa constitutes an immense spiritual 'lung' for a humanity that appears to be in a crisis of faith and hope."

Pope John Paul II's visits to Africa were the most impressive. He thoroughly enjoyed himself in Africa and was fascinated by the Christian spontaneity of the recent converts to Catholicism and Christianity. "He had enjoyed himself enormously in Africa and was moved and invigorated by the unselfconscious joy of these new Christians" (Weigel, 1998:376). He loved the very lively enculturated Eucharistic celebrations animated with singing and dancing. The Eucharistic celebrations were often far longer than those to which Western journalists and Curia members who accompanied John Paul II were accustomed. Some of the celebrations lasted five hours in scorching tropical temperatures. While his collaborators were often very exhausted, John Paul looked fresh and focused. In Africa, in 1980, John Paul teased a very exhausted German TV crew, "How about you guys, are you still alive?" (Weigel, 1998:376). John Paul often returned to the Vatican rejuvenated and happy. Cardinal Francis Arinze summed up the political impacts of the pope's many visits to Africa, "Many countries in Africa are still dealing with the problem of national unity and harmony between people of varying backgrounds. People who were put together by colonial masters. The pope's visits to many countries in Africa have been moments of grace. When people of varying political parties are together as they have never been before, they felt as one. They felt challenged to face a common necessity to build up their countries" (Hallet, 2002).

The great Jesuit liturgist John Baldovin, S.J., my former liturgy professor, never stops talking about a forty-five-minute offertory procession during a Eucharistic celebration over which he presided in South Africa some years ago. A white American woman, Marita Beagan, once visited her son Jessie Beagan on a Peace Corps service trip in Cameroon and she had this to say about offertory processions in Cameroon. "You people are crazy over there. Everyone is dressed in their beautiful Sunday regalia. They dance up to the altar with yams or coins. When they reach the altar, they place their coin and then go back and join the line and the procession continues."

As George Weigel pointed out in *Witness to Hope*, John Paul II's appointment of African churchmen like Bernadin Gantin and Francis Arinze sent shockwaves among traditional associates of the pope. It was unprecedented and some of them found it difficult to come out of the shock. Those appointments were significant. Idiosyncratically, George Weigel, in an interview with this author, pointed out that John Paul II invited these sons of Africa to serve in high offices in the Vatican because he was deeply impressed by the African bishops he met at Vatican II. Weigel observed that John Paul II's experience of African churchmen at

Vatican II was the key to his interest in Africa. Weigel noted, "At Vatican II, Karol Wojtyła was deeply impressed by the vitality and freshness of the faith of African bishops, about whom he wrote one memorable poem. I think it seemed to him, as it did later to scholars like Philip Jenkins, that Christians in Africa were living a New Testament-type experience of Christ and the Church. So, he wanted to make the world Church aware of that, both to support what was underway in Africa, and to inspire a similar evangelical fervour in older local Churches."

John Paul II trusted the African churchmen, with whom he shared a Vatican II-inspired vision of the Church of the future, the Church of the New Evangelization. Pope John Paul II's trust and openness to Africans was in full view in 1982, when he appointed a young African priest, Emery Kabongo Kanundowi, originally from Zaire (the Democratic Republic of the Congo), as his personal secretary. For five years, Fr. Kabongo (1982–1987) faithfully served the Holy Father, and was always by his side both in the Vatican and abroad. Kabongo attested to John Paul's trust in the ability of an African when he writes, "My first memory of John Paul II was when he appointed me as his personal secretary, so that I could help his first secretary, Stanislaw Dziwisz. I didn't write a letter or ask for an appointment. That's why I thank him for his Catholic mentality and for thinking that an African would be a good secretary" (Wlodzimierz, 2014).

Before becoming the pope's personal secretary, Msgr. Emery Kabongo was working with the Vatican secretariat of state and had served in nunciatures in Korea and Brazil. On December 10, 1987, Pope John Paul appointed him as the bishop of the diocese of Luebo in former Zaire. Monsignor Kabongo was consecrated bishop by the pope himself on January 6, 1988. On January 7, 1988, the day after his episcopal ordination, Pope John Paul II offered hearty encomiums and encouragement to Bishop Kabongo: "Do I need to tell you that it was a joy for me to celebrate this ordination, to confer on Monsignor Kabongo the fullness of the priesthood! I remembered his long intellectual and spiritual preparation for pastoral service, his experience in the representations of the Holy See in Asia and South America, and, of course, the six years in which I have continuously enjoyed his careful collaboration" (John Paul II's Address, January 7, 1988). Archbishop Kabongo was bishop of Luebo from 1988–2003. Since 2003, he has been a canon of Chapter of St. Peter's Basilica. Very tellingly, the pope's most authoritative biographer and interpreter in the anglophone world poignantly observed that John Paul II's appointment of these great sons of Africa was informed by his curiosity and inquisitiveness. Weigel noted, "As for personal characteristics, he was the most relentlessly curious man I've ever met; he always wanted to know more, and that included knowing more about Africa and Africans." John Paul II wanted to know more and understand the Church in Africa through those he invited to work with him in the Vatican.

The Jubilee Year 2000 also saw an event with more lasting significance, a public apology by the pope for the past errors of the Church. It was a stunning break from a tradition of never admitting mistakes. The apology was expressed in a 1999 document, *Memory and Reconciliation: The Church and The Faults of The Past*. It was an exercise aimed at purifying the memory of the Church from all forms of counter-witness and scandal which have occurred in her history, especially in the past millennium. Among others, the document states: "The Church is invited to become more fully conscious of the sinfulness of her children." She "acknowledges as her own her sinful sons and daughters" and encourages them "to purify themselves, through repentance, of past errors and instances of infidelity" (no. 21). On the first Sunday of Lent, March 12, 2000, Pope John Paul led the Church in a ceremony dubbed "Day of Forgiveness."

The Church apologized for specific sins she has committed over the years. Top Curia cardinals read out the different *mea culpa* of the Church. At his Angelus address later that same day, Pope John Paul II said, "The Holy Year is a time of purification: the Church is Holy because Christ is her Head and Spouse, the Spirit is her vivifying soul, and the Blessed Virgin and the saints are her most authentic expression. However, the children of the Church know the reality of sin, whose shadows are reflected in her, darkening her beauty.

Because of this, the Church does not cease to implore God's forgiveness for the sins of her members." The Vatican and Pope John Paul II were criticized for not having apologized to the African people for the role of the Church in the slave trade and slavery in the continent of Africa, especially considering that Cardinals Gantin and Arinze (from Africa) were among the prelates who read out the specific apologies. However, standing in the ancient slave center on Gorée Island during his visit to Senegal in 1992, John Paul II asked for forgiveness for the enslavement of the African people:

> For a whole period in the history of the African continent, black men, women and children were brought to this narrow ground, uprooted from their land, separated from their relatives, to be sold there like commodities. They came from all countries and, chained, leaving for other skies, they kept as the last image of their native Africa the mass of the basaltic rock of Gorée.... This sin of man against man, this sin of man against God, must be confessed in all truth and humility.... From this African sanctuary of black pain, we implore forgiveness from heaven (John Paul II, 1992).

Pope John Paul II stood with the people of Africa in words and actions. He identified with the people of Africa and spent quality time with them. He repeatedly championed the cause of the African people. He was a caring father to the African people. His Polish background and experiences made it easier for him to relate to the plight of the people of the continent of Africa and the pope attested to this during a visit to Africa. "Because I used to live in a land which had to fight for its independence and freedom, a land that was subject to the aggression of its neighbors, I can relate to the suffering of the Third World countries, which are also subjected to a kind of dependence. Another kind, the economical dependence. I have experienced what exploitation means and I have uncompromisingly taken the side of the poor, the disinherited, the oppressed, the segregated and the defenceless."

John Paul stood with Africa, the richest of the continents in terms of natural resources, but the poorest in terms of economic development and opportunities. Even before becoming pope, Karol Wojtyła loved the people of Africa, identified with them, and wrote a memorable poem for them.

The Negro*

My dear brother, it's you, an immense land I feel
where rivers dry up suddenly—and the sun
burns the body as the foundry burns ore.
I feel your thoughts like mine;
if they diverge the balance is the same:
in the scales truth and error.
There is joy in weighing thoughts on the same scales,
thoughts that differently flicker in your eyes and mine
though their substance is the same (Peterkiewicz, 1982:103).

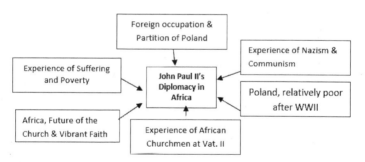

Fig. 3. Author's illustration of John Paul II's idiosyncratic variables and other factors which impacted his diplomacy in Africa.

CHAPTER EIGHT
GLOBE-TROTTING DIPLOMACY
(GLOBALIZATION OF THE PAPACY)

Vaticanologists and Church historians would definitely reckon that voluntary and involuntary papal itinerancy is not a novel phenomenon. The slogan "woe to me should I fail to preach the Gospel" carried St. Paul from Jerusalem to Antioch and culminated in Rome where he faced death in Nero's circus around 64–67 A.D. Former British politician Norman St. John-Stevas recorded that in the 6th and 7th centuries, Constantinople was a familiar destination for pontiffs on voluntary and involuntary bases. Pope John I voluntarily visited Constantinople, while Martin I reached Constantinople because he was abducted and eventually died in Crimea (1982:25). Clement V (1305–1314) transferred the papacy from Rome to Avignon because of turbulence in the former. That was the commencement of the *Babylonian Captivity,* or the Great Schism. Pius VI and Pius VII traveled extensively during the Napoleonic era. Tales of the travelling papacy prior to 1870 are unending.

Due to the Italian reunification, the expropriation of the Papal States by King Victor Emmanuel II in 1871, and the bombardment of Rome by General Giuseppe Garibaldi and Camillo Benso (Count of Cavour), Pius IX's journey through Rome to St. John Lateran on September 19, 1870, was the last public act of a pope in papal Rome, according to St. John-Stevas' accounts. Pius IX famously called himself "a prisoner of the Vatican" ("*prigioniero del Vaticano*") and did not venture out of Rome, nor did his immediate successors (self-imprisonment of the Roman pontiffs). Until 1964, no pope ventured out of Rome. Pius XII (1939–1958) went to St. Lorenzo and the

Quirinale. John XXIII (1958–1963) went by train to the Marian shrines in Assisi and Loreto in 1962 before the opening session of Vatican II. His plans to visit the Holy Land did not come to pass since he died in 1963. Paul VI held the international media hostage in 1964 with his unprecedented visit to the Holy Land.

Papal international visits became a hallmark of Saint John Paul II's diplomacy. He made them into his typical papal apostolate. They gave a new public picture and image to the papacy. In about 27 years, John Paul II made at least 104 journeys to almost every country on the planet. For instance, he made a total of 11 visits to Africa during his pontificate. He visited at least 39 countries in Africa, some of them more than once. He was in Cameroon in 1985 and 1995 when he combined his visit with the promulgation of the post-Synodal exhortation, *Ecclesia in Africa,* in Yaoundé.

Pope John Paul II sought a geopolitical presence since *de facto,* popes are transnational and supranational actors. One of his aides said, "It is as though he is always travelling in spirit: even when he is here in Rome, he is thinking of his next journey" (Whale, 1980:250). In his article, "Papal Foreign Policy," Bryan Hehir, philosopher and theologian, branded John Paul II a political "revisionist." Pius XII was pro-Western. John XXIII had an Eastern European outreach, and Paul VI was preoccupied with developments in the developing world. John Paul II examined all the orientations of his predecessors and sought a combination, which inevitably left him with a global approach to international politics (Formicola, 2002:3).

In distance travelled, Pope Saint John Paul II circumnavigated the world at least 30 times, or more than 2.8 times the distance between the earth and the moon (Weigel, 1999:844). Papal itinerancy became a novel way of managing the Catholic Church and an inseparable part of his papal Magisterium. A joke by some critics of John Paul II's globalization of the papacy goes, "The pope really should add to his full agenda of international pilgrimages, a short halt at the Vatican" (Woodrow, 1998:84). In the prologue of *The End and the Beginning* (sequel to *Witness to Hope: The Biography of Pope John Paul II*), George Weigel stated, "John Paul II had given new meaning to the papal title 'Universal Pastor of the Church,' bringing the ministry of the bishop of Rome to the Church in a series of papal pilgrimages inside Italy and around the globe that was unprecedented in history" (2010:2).

Unlike the *ad limina Apostolorum* ("to the threshold of the apostles"), the oldest expression of collegiality, whereby bishops undertake pilgrimages to Rome, the pope's visits to the people of God has been termed *ad limina Ecclesiae,* or *un movimento inverso e complementare* (a visit by the pope to the people of God) (Borgomeo, 1988). The *ad limina* and *ad limina Ecclesiae* visits are analogous to a particular distinction between religion and revelation. In this context, religion is seen as humankind's attempt to reach God (*ad limina*), while revelation is God's deliberate effort to reach humankind (a pope's visits). The *ad limina* visits come from the custom of praying at the tombs of the apostles Peter and Paul, who were martyred in Rome. John Paul II's international papal debut came three months after his election when, in January 1979, he made a series of stops in Latin America and the Caribbean on his way to Mexico to address the Latin American Bishops' meeting at Puebla.

In his interview with this author, papal diplomacy scholar Jada Patrisio argued that most of John Paul's journeys were to developing countries since he vicariously identified with the poor, owing to his humble background and the Church's preferential option for the poor. His first foreign papal international visit in January 1979 was to Latin America and the Caribbean, a developing continent, where he made a couple of stops in countries such as the Dominican Republic. His second papal visit was to Poland in June 1979, and in the "Three Worlds" classification of countries by demographer Alfred Sauvy during the Cold War era, Poland, just like all the other Eastern communist countries, was considered a Second World country. His third visit was to Ireland, at the time a relatively poor country in Western Europe. Ireland is one of the four European countries to have accepted a rescue package from the European Community and the International Monetary Fund (IMF). The others are Portugal, Hungary, and

Greece. On June 30, 2015, Greece became the first developed nation to default on its debts to the IMF. Greece already holds the record for the biggest default ever by a country from 2012 when it went into technical default and had to restructure about $138 billion of its debt. Back then, Greece was quickly bailed out by some European countries.

Nineteen months after his election, in May 1980, John Paul II visited six countries in Africa, namely Zaire (Democratic Republic of Congo), Republic of the Congo, Ghana, Ivory Coast, Kenya, and Upper Volta (Burkina Faso). John Paul II's famous nine-day visit to his native Poland in June 1979, which, according to many pundits, shook the Soviet Union at its very foundation, set the tone for his later visits. His journeys were principally pilgrimages, pastoral in nature, although in some instances they had political consequences and undertones as politicians tried to make use of his pilgrimages for political maneuvers, leverage, and legitimacy. At the airport in the Philippines in 1981, John Paul II said, "I come to you in the name of Jesus Christ. And I come on a visit of a religious and pastoral nature to proclaim His gospel, to proclaim salvation in His name" (John-Stevas, 1982:72). Ideas are consequential. The pope's ideas, outlined during his pilgrimages, had political consequences, thereby orchestrating the overthrow and collapse of some dictatorial and atheistic regimes.

Commenting on the impact of John Paul II's visits, papal historian Jonathan Kwitny wrote, "But it was politicians who thrust him into the priesthood, politicians who pushed him into high church office, and most of it all, it would be politicians who would reel from the impact of his papacy" (1997:76). Examples abound. Ferdinand Marcos of the Philippines, Pinochet of Chile, Jean-Claude Duvalier (Baby Doc) of Haiti—whose father, Francois Duvalier (Papa Doc), was a dictator *par excellence* and had the Lord's Prayer "Our Father" translated and substituting his name, are a few political careers cut short after John Paul II's pilgrimages. The Duvalierist variant of the Lord's Prayer reads as follows: "Our Doc, who art in the National Palace for life, hallowed be Thy name by present and future generations. They will be done in

Port-au-Prince as it is in the provinces. Give us this day our new Haiti and forgive not the trespasses of those anti-patriots who daily spit upon our country...." (Abbott, 1988:133). His journeys called forth statements of position and could be termed religious-political diplomacy. According to André Frossard, "Each of his (John Paul II's) speeches caused Christianity to spurt up like a gusher of crude oil, where it was generally thought that there was nothing" (1982:203). John Paul II's international visits constituted an essential part of his diplomacy. The essence of papal diplomacy is the promotion and upholding of the absolute values, namely human rights and dignity, love, freedom, a culture of life, and respect for minority groups, among others. John Paul II travelled to every corner of the world to preach his vision of man, and to defend human rights before every type of dehumanizing oppression. The pope of human rights was indefatigable in calling for respect of the absolute values.

Legendary French historian and diplomat François-René de Chateaubriand said, "In every age, the mission of the popes has been to maintain or vindicate the rights of man" (Frossard, 1982:208). John Paul II's visits attracted enormous crowds and he used every meeting and occasion to speak out against abuse of fundamental human rights. Some of the largest human gatherings in history have been crowds attracted by John Paul II. For instance, in 1995, during the closing Mass of the World Youth Day in Manila, it is estimated that there were about 5 million people in that square, the largest recorded human gathering in the history of the world—a record only surpassed when 6 million attended a Mass celebrated by Pope Francis in the Philippines 20 years later in 2015.

Although mainly pilgrimages, John Paul II's international visits could be pastoral or state visits. Pastoral visits refer to those visits of a pope at the invitation of episcopal conferences and not necessarily the state. For instance, John Paul II's visit to the United Kingdom in 1982 was a pastoral visit because it was not at the invitation of the Queen of England, but rather a visit to the Catholic Church, since Cardinal Hume and Archbishop Worlock issued the invitation. It was an act of unofficial diplomacy since the Church is an agent of Track Two diplomacy.

Pope Benedict XVI's much-hyped visit to the United Kingdom in 2010 was a state visit because there was an official invitation from the Queen of England, endorsed by the British Parliament. It was an apt example of Track One and a Half diplomacy because he went at the invitation of the state and the episcopal conference of England and Wales. Dual diplomacy is a combination of official and unofficial diplomacy. In some instances, because of ecumenical sensitivities, Pope John Paul II turned down invitations from heads of state. After his historic December 1989 visit to the Vatican, President Mikhail Gorbachev reciprocated by inviting John Paul II to visit Russia. However, that did not happen because Alexis II, the Orthodox Patriarch of Moscow, did not consent.

Cuban strongman Fidel Castro was desperate for a papal visit for diplomatic implications. Castro's sister got her heart's desire in the papal hug and many political prisoners were freed before the pope's historic visit to Cuba in January 1998. Hard-core dictators in Africa, such as Mobutu Sese Seko Nkuku Ngbendu wa za Banga of former Zaire and Daniel arap Moi of Kenya saw the pope's visits as support for their dictatorial regimes which had lost legitimacy. Jonathan Kwitny recorded that "right-wing dictators try to demonstrate how popular they are with the Holy Father by joining him on his cavalcades and taking communion from him, but then six months later are either toppled or suffer serious reverses" (1997:580). In an interview with this author, Archbishop Maurice Muhatia opined that some political careers prematurely ended after John Paul II's visits because he carried the message of truth in his journeys. Since truth is liberating (*veritas liberavit vos*), people had no fear after knowing the Truth, and could stand up against false propagandists and bloodthirsty despots, leading to political obituaries. In his typical comic fashion, Cardinal Seán O'Malley of Boston often says that Pope John Paul II went around giving out "Last Rites" to dictators. Indeed, it is alleged that whenever Pope John Paul II met with a Catholic head of state or head of government, he would ask, "When was the last time you went to confession?"

Pope Saint John Paul II's presence in most countries was joyous. His electrifying personality captured the attention of the media. The poor felt consoled that their human dignity was for once honored because of the papal visits. However, as recounted by Saint Paul, pilgrimages are not without dark sides. Oftentimes, Saint Paul went without food, was imprisoned on several occasions and subjected to 39 lashes of the cane. At the *Areopagus*, the philosophers sarcastically made Saint Paul a laughingstock and asked him to pay them another visit with his news of a certain risen Christ. He was also shipwrecked a couple of times. Likewise, John Paul II's pilgrimages were not without challenges and drama. His visit to Turkey in 1979 was not a memorable one. For diplomatic reasons, the crowd was deliberately ushered away and silence befell Turkey during those days. Several times, he found himself in the midst of a state of siege: Argentina (1982), El Salvador (1983), Guatemala (1983), Timor (1989), Sarajevo, and Beirut (1997) (Accatoli, 1998:111). In Sandinista Nicaragua (1983), the picture of Christ was placed adjacent to that of the revolutionary leader, Che Guevara, and protests abounded. It was utterly despicable that a section of the crowd stationed just next to the altar indulged in revolutionary chants during the Mass in Managua and the pope shouted repeatedly "Silencio!" so that his homily could be heard. Still, in Nicaragua John Paul II admonished Fr. Ernesto Cardenal and asked him to regularize his situation with the Church.

Ernesto Cardenal was a Nicaraguan Roman Catholic priest, ordained in 1965. Contrary to the teachings of the Church, Cardenal played an active role in the Sandinista Revolution that overthrew the government of President Anastasio Somoza Debayle in July 1979. Cardenal was then appointed the minister of culture in the new government. Since Roman Catholic priests are not to be actively involved in politics, the Vatican advised Cardenal and other priests, including his brother Fernando Cardenal, S.J. to resign from the pro-Marxist Sandinista government. Possibly the most famous image of Ernesto Cardenal came in 1983, during John Paul's visit to Nicaragua. Cardenal knelt on the tarmac and attempted to kiss the pope's ring. Instead, the pope dramatically wagged his finger at him and admonished him, *"Usted tiene que arreglar sus asuntos con la Iglesia"* ("You must fix your affairs with the Church"). In 1984, after failing to get Cardenal and the other priests to resign their positions in Daniel Ortega's government, Pope John Paul II suspended their priestly faculties. In 2019, Pope Francis lifted the canonical sanctions against Cardenal after thirty-five years. Fr. Ernesto Cardenal, who is considered the second most important Nicaraguan poet, after Félix Rubén García Sarmiento, died on March 1, 2020, in Managua.

During a Mass in Santiago, Chile in 1987, there was a disturbance in which tear gas fumes and a large cloud of acrid smoke from burning tires reached the altar. During a flight from Botswana to Lesotho, Africa, the papal plane was forced to land at Johannesburg, and the pope then traveled 4 hours across the savanna by car. In 1984, a snowstorm in Canada prevented a landing at Fort Simpson (located near the Arctic Circle), where the pope was scheduled to meet with Eskimos (Accatoli, 1998:111). Once, during a visit to Saint Benedict's Parish in Rome, an altar boy named Alessandro Monno asked the pope, "Why do you always travel around the world?" The pope replied, "Because the whole world is not here! Have you read what Jesus said? 'Go and evangelize the whole world.' And so I go to the whole world."

How idiosyncratic were Pope John Paul II's international visits? British journalist and biographer Peter Hebblethwaite called Paul VI "the first modern pope," since he officially began the tradition of the itinerant papacy in recent history. Because of continuity (albeit diversity) in the running of the papal office, Norman St. John-Stevas rightly concluded that "John Paul II's travels are a continuation, a confirmation, and an intensification of those of his predecessor, Paul VI" (1982:22). One can argue that it is the prerogative of the pope to go out and preach the Good News in accordance with the apostolic mandate, "Therefore go and make disciples of all nations, baptizing them in the name of the Father and of the Son and of the Holy Spirit" (Matthew 28:19). On June 12, 2003, John Paul II explained to a group from Alitalia, the Italian airline:

> Right from the day I was elected as bishop of Rome, October 16, 1978, with special intensity and urgency I heard the echo of Jesus' command: "Go into all the world and preach the gospel to all of creation"—to tell everyone that the Church loves them, that the pope loves them, and likewise to receive from them the encouragement and example of their goodness, of their faith.

John Paul II personally took part in the Second Vatican Council and contributed in drafting *Gaudium et spes* (Pastoral Constitution on the Church in the Modern World). *Lumen Gentium* (Dogmatic Constitution on the Church) defined the Church as the people of God. John Paul II's pilgrimages were a meeting of the pontiff (Vicar of Christ) and the people of God. Paul VI's pilgrimages were, to some extent, of religious and political symbolism (Bernstein & Politi, 1996:396). Paul VI was in Bombay in 1964 for the Eucharistic Congress, although he did bless the sick and ordinary people. His visit to Jerusalem in 1964 was overshadowed by ecumenical repairs after he embraced the Orthodox Patriarch, Athenagoras, and the 1054 A.D. mutual excommunication of the pope and patriarch was repealed. Pope Paul travelled to New York in 1965 to address the U.N. General Assembly. In 1969, the pope made a historic visit to Uganda for the symposium of the episcopal conferences on the continent after the canonization of the Martyrs of Uganda in 1964.

John Paul II personalized his pilgrimages. Kissing tarmacs at airports became the spiritual hallmark of his journeys. Kissing babies, and meeting the young and people of all categories were idiosyncratic of his visits. The Council document *Inter Mirifica* invited the Church to utilize whatever means of communication are available for evangelization. John Paul II understood clearly that his international visits provided a wonderful opportunity for a more public character of the Church and he took it closer to the people. Reflecting on his travels, John Paul II said, "The Council demands it." He also said that "the Second Vatican Council opened up a new way of performing my pastoral mission. This was not a tactical or strategic opening, but a form of dialogue" (John-Stevas, 1982:ix). Thus, the implementation of the Council was a major objective of his visits. American scholar and researcher Margaret Melady asserted that John Paul II intentionally used his overseas visits as a communication strategy, which she terms the *rhetorical papacy*. The rhetorical papacy relies on persuasive discourse to lead the Church (1999:17).

In international diplomacy, age, good health, and physical fitness are significant idiosyncratic variables. Old age is associated with maintenance of the status quo (incremental politics). Old leaders are prone to consulting old files on how things have traditionally been done and handled. How was this problem solved ten years ago? In his post-Synodal Apostolic Exhortation, *Africae Munus*, Pope Benedict XVI, while referring to the elderly, wrote, "Old age is also a time of wisdom, since length of years teaches one the grandeur and the fragility of life" (2011:43). Youthfulness is associated with risk-taking, adventures, and revolutions. The Latin adage reads *facilis est lapsus juventutis* ("easy is the slipup of youth.").

In his usual insightful reflections, Dutch poet and philosopher Hans Burgman argued, "It is not as if young people are by definition progressive: when youthful persons discover something, it is not something new but something old. Young people begin to talk about old commonplaces in a new way" (2010:51). Karol Wojtyła was fifty-eight years old when elected pope in 1978. He was the youngest to be elected pope in 125 years. The youngest pope elected in the last two centuries was Pius IX in 1846 at the age of 54. Seven of John Paul II's immediate predecessors died as octogenarians, and the nonagenarian Pope Leo XIII died in 1903 at the ripe old age of ninety-four (94). John XXIII was elected to the papacy in 1958 at the age of 76. Benedict XVI was elected the 265th pope at the age of 78.

John Paul II's comparative youthfulness, and his being a fit athlete accustomed to hiking, skiing, and kayaking, made it easier for his world-wide travels. Commenting on the pope's youthfulness at the time of his election, *The Wall Street Journal* columnist Peggy Noonan pointed out, "He looked Slavic. He looked young. He was a fit fifty-eight years old, the youngest pope in a century, and looked younger than his age—a solid build, straight posture, five feet eleven, and 170 pounds. Steely gray hair, deep blue eyes. He looked robust" (2005:21). Regarding the age factor in his international journeys, John Paul II said, "How could a relatively young pope who in general enjoyed good health not have taken over this duty and followed the example of an octogenarian pope and Paul VI of advanced years and delicate health?" (Frossard, 1982:197).

A popular joke goes, "The more John Paul II stayed in Rome, the older he became and the younger he looked in his journeys." Paul VI made nine international journeys within the first seven years of his pontificate, when he was still relatively young and enjoying good health. He was elected in 1963 at the age of 67. This explains why Norman St. John-Stevas would argue that age and ill-health prevented Paul VI from travelling after 1970 (1982:22). Paul VI's visits were systematically and logically planned and programmed. John Paul II embarked on his first foreign journey just three months after his election.

Youthful adventures could in a way explain John Paul II's papal travels. In an interview with journalist David Willey, John Paul II confessed that he never had a clear idea of what he was trying to achieve via his journeys. The obligation to pray (remaining in a relation with God) is prior to the desire to pray, said Basil Cardinal Hume in one of his conferences as Abbot of Ampleforth Abbey. Hume taught, "It is not because we are drawn to prayer (desire) that we first begin to pray; more often we have to begin prayer (relation with God), and then the taste and desire for it comes" (1976:118). In line with Hume's theology of prayer, John Paul II must have taken the journeys as an obligation. He later explained, "With the passing of time I found these travels more and more useful in developing policies. My presence in a particular country added a direct witness, something that was immediately understandable" (1992:ix).

Risk-taking was obviously part of John Paul II's travels, especially after the attempt on his life in 1981. Amidst extraordinary security and diplomatic concerns, he went to Turkey in 1979. In 1993, he still opted for a short stop in Khartoum, even though the Muslim fundamentalists threatened to kill him. Idiosyncratically, John Paul II was pushed by that typical Polish fearlessness. "Do not be afraid" is part of the Christian vocation. John Paul II's fearlessness, which found expression in his journeys, was certainly unique. Prominent Yugoslav dissident and politician Milovan Djilas famously said that he greatly admired John Paul II because of his Christian fearlessness. "Do not be afraid" was a frequent refrain from John Paul II during his papacy. Cardinal Wyszyński had warned the Polish bishops, including Wojtyła, that "the greatest weakness in an apostle is fear ... use fear to enforce silence" (John, 2002:190). In the book *Do Not Be Afraid* by André Frossard, John Paul II confessed that not even he had fully understood the deepest meaning of the phrase "do not be afraid" by 1978, and to where that call was to lead him.

For more than 30 years as priest, bishop, and cardinal in Poland, John Paul II had a foretaste of international visits. As archbishop of Kraków (a "mini-papacy" in the words of Tad Szulc), Wojtyła did numerous pastoral visits to various parishes of his diocese. Logically, one can infer that John Paul II translated his parochial and episcopal visits into papal pilgrimages. In an interview with veteran French journalist André Frossard, John Paul II acknowledged the consistency of his fundamental views and actions when he said, "The experience which I acquired in Cracow has taught me that it is important to visit the communities personally, starting with the parishes. Of course, this is not an exclusive duty, but I consider it of the first importance" (1982:28).

Pope Saint John Paul II interpreted his international pilgrimages as visits to parishes since he was *de facto* a universal pastor.

Perhaps not without hyperbole, Polish researcher Radoslaw Malinowski, commenting on the pope's pilgrimages in an interview with the author, said, "John Paul II was more of a priest and bishop than pope." Asked why he was travelling to Australia in 1994, the pope responded, "... because I am the parish priest of the whole world and a parish has many outstations...." Kissing the tarmac was the trademark of John Paul II's international pilgrimages. Traditionally, it was a practice he began more than twenty-five years before becoming pope. His first priestly pastoral appointment was to Niegowić in 1948. On reaching the parish, Karol Wojtyła knelt down and kissed the ground. He had learned this gesture from his readings of the Curé of Ars, Saint John Mary Vianney (Weigel, 1999:92).

Moses took off his sandals when he learned that he was standing on a holy ground near the burning bush. The pope kissed the tarmac of every country because those countries were the "sanctuaries of Christ" where the people of God dwelt. Peggy Noonan beautifully captured the essence of the pope's habit of kissing the earth whenever he arrived in a new country: "We could sense that by kissing the earth he was kissing Creation, the God-rich, God-inhabited, God-made place around us. By kissing the earth he was also kissing a singular and specific place, a patch of ground inhabited by a particular people with a particular culture, history, and tradition" (Noonan, 2005:123).

The first time that John Paul II failed to kiss the tarmac upon alighting from an airbus in a foreign country was in Zagreb, Croatia in 2004. Due to his deteriorated health, two young Croatians instead presented the pope some soil in a wooden bowl. Bernstein and Politi remarked that the pope kissed the soil with a sad expression (2006:502).

In a concise way, John Paul II's early life experience, which is an idiosyncratic variable, was a preparation for his Petrine office since most of those experiences and orientations were relived in his papacy. John Paul II concurred when he told Frossard, "Finding after Paul VI this policy of travelling well established, I continued to follow it because it fitted in with the ideas which I had formed during the preceding stage of my life. The notions of the episcopal service put into effect at Cracow were just as valid in Rome for the pontifical ministry" (1982:198–9). In 1969, Wojtyła travelled extensively in the United States and Canada. During those 37 days in North America, he preached in Ottawa, Winnipeg, Toronto, Hamilton, Philadelphia, Boston, and Washington, among others. In 1973, he represented the Polish Church at the International Eucharistic Congress in Melbourne. In Australia, Wojtyła visited Papua New Guinea, where he got a foretaste of Pidgin English. As pope, Wojtyła visited Papua New Guinea in 1984 and preached in fine Pidgin English.

In 1974, Cardinal Wojtyła visited Czechoslovakia for the funeral of Stefan Cardinal Trochta. It was during this visit that the communist secret police barred Cardinal Karol Wojtyła and Cardinal Franz König from concelebrating the funeral Mass. Wojtyła sat in the pews with the rest of the congregation. The culmination of his pre-papal pilgrimages came in 1976 when Paul VI invited him to preach the Lenten retreat to the curialists in Italian and not Latin. Cardinal Wojtyła preached his now famous "Sign of Contradiction" Lenten meditations to the pope and curialists. It would be illogical not to think of these pre-papal visits of John Paul II as a prefiguration of his papal pilgrimages. How could John Paul II spend almost two years of his pontificate out of Rome if his pre-papal visits had not made an impression on him with decipherable efficacy? Certain patterns of John Paul II's pre-papal visits were incorporated in his apostolic pilgrimages. It was a common practice for Cardinal Karol Wojtyła to visit Polish communities on a regular basis. In Canada in 1969 and in Papua New Guinea in 1973, he visited many Polish communities. There was a popular joke that John Paul II was "a full-time Pole and a part time pope," because of the Polish influence of his entourage led by Monsignor Dziwisz, his secretary, close friend, and confidant for more than forty years.

Stanislaw Dziwisz was ordained a priest on June 23, 1963, by Karol Wojtyła, then-Auxiliary Bishop of Kraków. In 1966, Archbishop Wojtyła of Kraków appointed him as his chaplain and secretary. When Cardinal Wojtyła was elected pope in October 1978, he appointed Dziwisz as his personal secretary; a post he held until the pope's death in 2005. In 1998, Monsignor Dziwisz was appointed titular Bishop of San Leone and Adjunct Prefect of the Pontifical Household. He was ordained bishop by Pope John Paul II on the Feast of St. Joseph on March 19, 1998. On September 29, 2003, the pope elevated him to the dignity of archbishop.

Pope Benedict XVI appointed him to succeed Cardinal Macharski as archbishop of Kraków on June 3, 2005. His appointment as archbishop of Kraków was poignant and significant, considering that Kraków was the See of Dziwisz's mentor and friend Cardinal Wojtyła before he became pope in 1978. More still, in 1981, Monsignor Dziwisz earned a Doctor of Sacred Theology degree from the Faculty of Theology of Kraków with a dissertation entitled, "The Cult of Saint Stanislaus, Bishop of Kraków, until the Council of Trent." Archbishop Dziwisz was created and proclaimed cardinal by Pope Benedict XVI in the consistory of March 24, 2006. On December 8, 2016, Pope Francis accepted his resignation as archbishop of Kraków on having reached the retirement age. Dziwisz is only one of two persons Pope John Paul II mentioned in his will: "… and I thank him [Dziwisz] for his help and collaboration, so understanding for so many years" (Testament of the Holy Father John Paul II, 2021). (The other person mentioned in his will was the former chief rabbi of Rome, Elio Toaff, who had welcomed John Paul II to the Great Synagogue of Rome in 1986.) Renowned French journalist André Frossard, after many interactions with secretary Dziwisz, described him as follows, "His hardworking Polish secretary Don Stanislas Dziwisz, a young man with a calm demeanor and a brilliant, slightly ironic mind, is by nature a quiet person; but he knows all the right things to say and all the right times to say them, and he is always on his toes, ready for anything, like a cat about to jump out of a basket" (1990:31).

During his visits, Wojtyła delivered numerous speeches which left a lasting impression on his hearers. No pope in the last century came to the Petrine office with a wider pastoral experience than Wojtyła. He visited the parishes in Rome more often than previous popes did. His extroverted personality, and his being an actor who was rejuvenated by a crowd, gave him the impetus for international visits. Victorio Messori, who, in the view of Vaticanist Sandro Magister, is "the most translated Catholic writer in the world," sees John Paul II's *Slavonic Spirituality* as an idiosyncratic factor for his globetrotting diplomacy (2004). Veteran Italian journalist Messori, who was John Paul II's interlocutor in *Crossing the Threshold of Hope* (1994), in an interview pointed out, "I think that impulse, that typical *Slavonic Spirituality* acts in him and leads him to the eschatological horizon.... I think behind his efforts as a tireless traveler is an attempt to hasten what theology calls *Parousia* (a return of Christ). Preaching the Gospel to the farthest corners of the earth is according to Christ a condition for his return" (Zavattaro, 1999). That was part of the Polish Messianism and piety. Papal pilgrimages were an integral part of John Paul II's diplomacy and his governance of the Roman Catholic Church.

Fig. 4. Author's graphic summary of John Paul II's idiosyncratic variables, which informed his international visits

CHAPTER NINE

THE WRITINGS OF JOHN PAUL II:

ENCYCLICALS (TRACK SEVEN DIPLOMACY)

In Multi-Track diplomatic theory, public letters issued by Catholic bishops or leaders of other religions to guide their congregants is a visible element of Track Seven diplomacy, or peacemaking through faith action (Diamond & McDonald, 1996). Thus, the writings of Saint John Paul II constitute Track Seven diplomacy, since they aimed at guiding Catholics and other Christians on a wide range of issues. Theologian and historian George Huntston Williams records that "no pope before John Paul II has produced such a cascade of documents, from addresses ... to encyclicals, almost all drafted ... by him" (Kwitny, 1997:344).

Within twenty-six and a half years in the Petrine office, Pope John Paul II's written Magisterium included 14 encyclicals, numerous apostolic exhortations, and close to a thousand *ad limina* addresses. By 1999, the *Insegnamenti di Giovanna Paoli II* (a printed record of his teaching), covered ten linear feet of shelf space in libraries (Weigel, 1999:844). Writing for the Catholic News Agency, journalist John Thavis pointed out that, "Papal speeches are important to Vatican diplomacy" (June 17, 2011). The writings of John Paul II constituted one of the cultural instruments of his foreign policy and diplomacy. The old legal maxim states that *scribere est agere* ("to write is to act").

Archbishop Maurice Muhatia of the archdiocese of Kisumu, Kenya, opined that one of the salient aspects of John Paul II's personality was his intelligence and learnedness. He had two Ph.Ds., was indiscriminately well-read before becoming pope, and was a scholar of great philosophical and theological culture. His friend and former classmate Zbigniew Silkowski said of him, "From the intellectual point of view, Karol was by far superior to all of us. He absorbed knowledge almost without having to study. On the other hand, his interests were much more numerous than those of any of us" (Nemec, 1979:40). In his celebrated *A Guide to Diplomatic Practice*, 19th-century English diplomat Sir Ernest Satow defined diplomacy as "the application of intelligence and tact to the conduct of official relations between the governments of independent states" (1917:1).

John Paul II was a poet with an encyclopedic knowledge of almost every subject. To be a poet and pope sounds oxymoronic. However, Pope Leo XIII (1876–1903), wrote a good number of poems. British journalist and essayist, Walter Bagehot noted that poetry is "… a deep thing, a teaching thing, the most surely and wisely elevating of human things...." British politician Norman St. John-Stevas opined that poetry is a holy thing with a consecrating power (1982:141). At a time when the country is very divided following the hotly contested presidential election, it was no surprise that the young black woman, Amanda Gorman, and her powerful poem, "The Hill We Climb," stole the show at U.S. President Joe Biden's inauguration on January 20, 2021. Twenty-two-year-old Amanda Gorman, the first US National Youth Poet Laureate and Harvard graduate, has become the youngest-ever poet to recite at a presidential inauguration in the United States.

Poetry was always part and parcel of the life of Karol Wojtyła. As a student, he read many of the great Polish poets. The young Wojtyła knew the poems by heart and recited them without any hesitation. For instance, he took to memory the national epic poem, *Pan Tadeusz: The Last Foray in Lithuania*, written in 1834 by Adam Mickiewicz, the main figure in Polish literature. As a student, a worker, a priest, a university professor, a bishop, and a cardinal, Wojtyła expressed his concerns and happenings in his life in poems/verse. That is why he wrote numerous poems on a wide range of topics, including motherhood, the quarry, confessors, the Church, Easter, Poland, and death. In communist and Nazi Poland, some of the future pope's verse were published under pseudonyms. It was only after his election as Pope John Paul II in 1978, that Wojtyła was identified as a poet and much of his poetry was published. Authorized by the Vatican in 1982, all the poems written by the pope between 1939 and 1978 were collected and published in a book called *The Place Within*. Upon its publication in 1982, the *Catholic Herald* said: "These poems are astonishing for their luminous imagery, their rhythmic range and, above all, for their penetrating imagination." As pope, John Paul still found time to write poetry. In March 2003, "Roman Triptych: Meditations," became the only poem John Paul II published during his pontificate. Idiosyncratically, the themes in Wojtyła's poetry form an interface with the ideas expressed by the pope in his encyclicals and other writings, but because they are in poetic form, their impact is both more powerful and more universal (John-Stevas, 1982:143). The poems are a perfect introduction to the thought and inspirations that have formed and guided Pope John Paul II (Peterkiewicz, 1982). They provide a window and introduction to understanding the words, actions, inspirations, thought, and diplomacy of John Paul II. In a foreword to an anthology of poetry written by priests and published in 1971, *Words in the Wilderness*, Cardinal Wojtyła pointed out, "Poetry has its own significance, its own aesthetic value and criteria of appreciation which belong to its proper order."

An encyclical is the most important papal document. It is a reflection and meditation on some topic of high importance. Etymologically, the word is derived from the Greek *kyklos*, which means circle, and hence an encyclical is a letter meant to circulate widely in the Church (Allen, 2002:25). Writing and publishing was an essential part of Wojtyła's pre-papal life. "Thinking and writing—and thinking through writing—had been essential parts of Karol Wojtyła, the man, since the Second World War; thinking and writing—and thinking through writing—remained an essential facet of the life of Karol Wojtyła the pope" (Weigel, 2010:467). Hence, the papal intellectual project of John Paul II is visibly traced from his pre-papal intellectual formation.

In March 2006, an international conference on "Karol Wojtyła's Notion of the Irreducible in Man and the Quest for a Just World Order" was organized by Saint Joseph College, West Hartford,

Connecticut, U.S.A. Professor Hans Köchler delivered the keynote speech on *Karol Wojtyła's Philosophical Legacy.* John Paul II was an enthusiastic philosopher and taught philosophy in his native Poland. Hans Köchler started analyzing the philosophical and phenomenological approach of Karol Wojtyła long before Wojtyła became pope. His interest in the philosophical conception of Wojtyła predates the latter's election as pope.

Köchler and Wojtyła were active members of the World Phenomenology Institute headed and founded by Professor Anna-Teresa Tymieniecka, a Polish-born American philosopher. Hans Köchler and Karol Wojtyła worked together on a couple of philosophical treatises before the assumption of his high office in 1978. Thus, Köchler was very familiar with the philosophy of the pope. In his keynote address during the said conference under the auspices of Saint Joseph College, Hans Köchler focused on how the philosophical convictions of Saint John Paul II eventually redefined the papal office and the traditional teachings of the Church—particularly as regards the general policies and positions of the Holy See. Köchler found elements of Wojtyła's phenomenological orientation in his pontifical writings and pronouncements:

> I identified, however, a persistence of his original phenomenological approach—namely a consistent emphasis on the *irreducible* element in the human subject—in many pronouncements he made as head of the Roman Catholic Church, particularly those dealing with social responsibility, and in what I would like to call his "cosmopolitan reinterpretation" of the papal mission.

Some of the pope's writings were his personal testimonies. In the words of George Weigel, "the pope's personality—his theological and philosophical personality, and his pastoral personality—shone readily through his apostolic letters" (2005:30). In the same line, Gerald McCool, S.J., held that Wojtyła, in his early years as a factory worker and underground seminarian, had already understood that a coherent philosophy of being had to be informed by a unity of intellectual framework and personal life experiences. The goal of John Paul II's philosophy was to make sense out of his own experience and to guide his human actions (1993:32). The Holy See does not represent a nation but rather a world of values. The axis of Pope Saint John Paul II's thinking was the human person. Prominent Catholic priest Richard John Neuhaus underscores the importance of the human person in John Paul II's thinking, "He's a humanist through and through.... If you look at his writings ... he has two phrases, number one, 'Man is the only creature that God has made for Himself,' and then the other, and perhaps the more important, that the revelation of Jesus Christ is not only the revelation of God to man but of man to himself. The Christian Gospel is the revelation of man to himself ..." (Noonan, 2005:126). It was no coincidence, therefore, that the pope's first encyclical was *Redemptor Hominis* ("The Redeemer of Man") (1979). Inevitably, the human person became the axis of his international diplomacy.

John Paul II's first social encyclical was *Laborem Exercens* ("On Human Work"), 1981. It was the first time a pontiff devoted an entire encyclical to the topic of labor. In his encyclical *Rerum Novarum* (1891), Leo XIII discussed the condition of workers in the world. *Laborem Exercens* was more than a discourse on the situation of workers in the world. John Paul II had the legacy of a worker-pope. He worked as a stonebreaker in Solvay's Zakrzowek quarry and in the factory at Borek Falecki during the Nazi occupation of Poland. One of his supervisors remembers him as a starveling student, "just bones and yellow skin," whose job it was to pack holes drilled in the rock with explosives—dangerous, physically exhausting work in a world of wheelbarrows, dust, rock, and dynamite. As pope, John Paul II told Polish writer Antoni Gronowicz how his fellow workers had helped him. "I will always remember with gratitude the simple people who supervised me, knowing I was a twenty-one-year-old student.... When I received orders to work the second or third shifts without rest, the old workers came to me with a piece of bread and said, 'eat, brainy fellow, you should not go hungry, you should survive. For your bright future is coming.'... They were simple workers who behaved as children of God." In Borek Falecki, Karol Wojtyła was able to exchange on the black market the extra rations and the monthly vodka coupons he received from the plant for meat, eggs or other rare provisions (Yallop, 2007:246).

In the analysis of Bernstein and Politi, "a philosopher-pope was born amid the pipes and boilers of Solvay" (1996:65). Thinking of his time in the quarry as a *felix culpa* ("happy fault"), John Paul II told journalist André Frossard, "The experience that I acquired in that period of my life was priceless. I have often said that I considered it possibly more valuable than a doctorate" (1982:15). In Africa in 1982, the pope said, "A great grace of my life is to have worked in a quarry and in a factory. This experience of working life, with all its positive aspects and its miseries ... has profoundly marked my existence" (Bernstein & Politi, 1996:55).

During one of his vacations as a student in the Belgian College in Rome in September 1947, Wojtyła took charge of the Polish Catholic Mission where he worked among the miners in Charleroi, Belgium. In *Gift and Mystery*, the pope acknowledged the importance of his time among the miners in Charleroi: "This was my first visit to a coal mine and I was able personally to witness the hard work done by miners" (1996:69). Thus, Wojtyła ascended the papacy with a whole history of labor with him. His experience as a worker in the quarry and the factory gave him an important education that none of his predecessors ever had (Bernstein & Politi, 1996:54). As the pope later expressed, "Having worked with my hands, I knew quite well the meaning of physical labor. I came to know their living situations, their families, their interests, their human worth and their dignity" (Bernstein & Politi, 1996:35). His experience as a worker in the Solvay chemical plant gave him a firsthand lesson on the condition of workers in the world and shaped his social teachings as pope. That explains why Tanzanian scholar Aquiline Tarimo, S.J., in an interview with this author, argued that Saint John Paul II's writings were an extension of his personality. Wojtyła had been a worker, and that explains why he vicariously identified with the ordinary workers of the world during his pontificate. As pope, he visited the steel mills of Terni in Italy and the workers put a helmet on him as if he was one of them.

In memory of his experience as a worker in the quarry and one of his deceased worker friends, Wojtyła wrote a poem entitled *The Quarry* in 1956. *The Quarry* is reflected in *Laborem Exercens*. At the age of fifteen, Wojtyła took part in a recitation contest when Polish actress Kazimiera Rychter visited Wadowice. Wojtyła opted for the difficult poem *Promethidion* of Cyprian Norwid, a 19th-century poet-philosopher. It was a poem on human work. Author and political economist Samuel Gregg convincingly argued in his book, *Challenging the Modern World: John Paul II/Karol Wojtyła and the Development of Catholic Social Teaching* that Wojtyła's pre-pontifical texts had an influence particularly on the social encyclicals promulgated by him as a pope. The encyclical *Laborem Exercens* is a case in point. Hans Köchler pointed out that the distinction introduced in "Work and Man," the second chapter of *Laborem Exercens,* between work in the *objective* and *subjective* sense, resembles very much the distinction made in Wojtyła's phenomenological writings between the human being in the objective and subjective dimension. Köchler went on to conclude that *Laborem Exercens* is perfectly in tune with his earlier phenomenological approach:

> By describing the person as "a subjective being capable of acting in a planned and rational way ... and with a tendency to self-realization and emphasizing the 'preeminence of the subjective meaning of work over the objective one'" (Art. 6: *Work in the Subjective Sense: Man as the Subject of Work*), the encyclical resembles in its conceptual approach the phenomenological description of man in *The Acting Person* and in Wojtyła's contributions to the phenomenological conferences (Köchler, 2006:12).

The encyclical's critique of capitalism and its phraseology relate to the personalistic philosophy of the pope's pre-pontifical writings. According to Bernstein and Politi, Cyprain Norwid was one of those influences on Wojtyła as pope, and his encyclical, *Laborem Exercens,* reflected some of the ideas in the *Promethidion* (Bernstein & Politi, 1996:39). Perhaps this explains why former United States Secretary of State Henry Kissinger, in one of his memoirs, stated that the pre-office convictions of politicians "are the intellectual capital they will consume as long as they continue in office" (1979:54). John Paul II's labor past gave him the armory to devote an entire encyclical on the subject of human labor.

In a papal audience on December 9, 1978, with some 2,500 workers from various countries, the then newly elected pope underscored the importance of his pre-papal experience as a worker: "For a short period of my life, during the last World War, I also experienced directly working in a factory. Hence, I know what the daily exertion of working at the dependence of others means; I know the hardship and the monotony, I know the needs of the workers, their just exigencies, and their legitimate aspirations. And I know how important it is that work should never alienate nor frustrate, but correspond always to the superior, the spiritual dignity of man."

Pope Saint John Paul II definitely consumed his pre-papal intellectual capital in his writings as pontiff. A couple of months after his premier visit to Poland in June 1979, the Solidarity Movement by workers in Poland was formed. Solidarity became his trademark word in the early years of his pontificate and meant a great deal to the pope. It is for this reason that the word solidarity is littered all over *Laborem Exercens.* In a U.N. Conference in Geneva, he could not stop uttering the word solidarity: "There is one characteristic that is a requirement, solidarity.... Today, a new solidarity must be forged ... an open and dynamic solidarity" (Kwitny, 1997:443). "Solidarity" was an important word that Wojtyła carried with him to the Vatican. It meant a lot to him. The word "Solidarity" was the title of the concluding sections of Wojtyła's 1969 philosophical master piece, *Person and Act,* where he defined "solidarity"—a condition in which personal freedom serves the common good and the community supports individuals as they grow into true maturity—as the most humanistically authentic attitude toward society (Weigel, 2010:119). Commenting on John Paul II's idiosyncratic influence on *Laborem Exercens*, the first encyclical in the tradition of papal social teaching to reflect its author's own experiences, Weigel wrote, "Together, the pope's experiences and the poet's reflections led to a rich portrait of the working person ..." (2005:28).

Veritatis Splendor ("The Splendor of Truth"), 1993, was one of Saint John Paul II's famous encyclicals. It was very phenomenological in orientation, and the actions of the human person were discussed by the pontiff. According to some historians and experts of Wojtyła's papacy, *Veritatis Splendor*, although primarily situated within a theological context, was like a confirmation of an earlier work of Wojtyła and Anna-Teresa Tymieniecka entitled, *The Acting Person*. Commenting on *Veritatis Splendor*, George Huntston Williams observed: "It is part of the relationship. He cannot be understood, even as pontiff, without this encyclical; he couldn't have done what he's done without that relationship (with Tymieniecka). It cannot be wiped out of the biographical, intellectual account" (Bernstein & Politi, 1996:132).

Although Tymieniecka fell out with the Vatican because of copyright complexities, her contribution in the *Acting Person*, reflected in *The Splendor of Truth*, cannot be forgotten. John Paul II was a philosopher and Tymieniecka was one of the important philosophical influences in Wojtyła's life. One of Wojtyła's protégés, Rocco Buttiglione, called Tymieniecka a "partner in a philosophical dialogue" in the *Acting Person* ("*Osoba i Czyn*"), and acknowledged that she must have helped Wojtyła reach a more intimate contact between phenomenology and Thomism (Bernstein & Politi, 1996:132).

Archbishop Muhatia, in an interview with this author, stated that John Paul II, via his *Acting Person*, had a proper understanding of the human person and understood what the human body can do. He had reached a certain level of respect for the human body and that is why he put it to use in his diplomacy by putting his body at the disposal of people in his pilgrimages. He knew how to talk, greet, and listen to people. Reflecting on the frescoes in the Sistine Chapel, John Paul II talked of "the sanctuary of the theology of the human body." In the analysis of Archbishop Muhatia, John Paul II's philosophical and Christian anthropological background played a role in his gestures. In the same line, while commenting on the idiosyncratic antecedents and foundation of Saint John Paul II's spirituality, John Sheets, S.J., wrote, "Everything in Pope John Paul II's personality, life experience, grace turned him to man. His esteem of man is in sharp contrast to his experience of man's inhumanity to man during the whole of his life, especially his youth.... The horrors of Auschwitz took place within a day's journey from his home" (1993:113).

On June 2, 1985, John Paul II issued *Slovarum in Apostoli* ("Apostles to the Slavs"), dedicated to Saints Cyril and Methodius (creators of the alphabet used in eastern Slavic languages). The encyclical was a commemoration of the eleven-hundredth anniversary of the work of evangelization carried out by Saints Cyril and Methodius. Prior to 1985, John Paul II, intensively aware of his Slavic roots and history, declared Saints Cyril and Methodius co-patrons (with Benedict) of Europe. In the encyclical, informed by his pan-European view of Europe's cultural history, John Paul II called the continent "a body that breathes with two lungs"— Catholicism and Orthodoxy (Weigel, 2010:176). Idiosyncratically, John Paul II was the first-ever pope from the mixed realm of two distinctive forms of Christian spirituality: Catholic and Orthodox. The schism of 1054 between the east and the west was felt on daily basis by Karol Wojtyła in his native Poland and Eastern Europe in general. The schism between the East and West was for John Paul II an integral part of his daily awareness as the Supreme Pastor of the Church of Christ, which he knew included the imperiled Orthodox churches (Huntston, 1981:10). John Paul II's Slavic roots and comprehensive knowledge of the history of the Slavic people must have been instrumental in his writing of the encyclical, *Slovarum in Apostoli*. Could an Italian pope have declared two Slavs co-patrons of Europe? Could an Italian pope have devoted a whole encyclical to the Apostles to the Slavs?

John Paul II stressed the importance of his Eastern European roots while presenting the encyclical in the following words, "You will all understand how cordially this anniversary is shared by the first son of the Slav family summoned after nearly two thousand years to the apostolic capital of St. Peter in Rome" (Szulc, 1995:402). Stressing the importance of John Paul II's Slavic roots in some of his actions, General Jaruzelski, who had imposed martial law in Poland in 1981, observed, "His great sensitivity to Poland's sovereignty ... that this was a Slav pope who sensed better than others the realities of our region, our history, our dreams ..." (Bernstein & Politi, 1996:452).

Another important social encyclical of John Paul II was *Sollicitudo rei Socialis* ("The Church's Social Concern") (1987). It tackled the problem of poverty and political corruption. According to Aquiline Tarimo, S.J., in an interview with this author, John Paul II's humble beginnings in Poland, a seemingly developing country, helped him understand the yoke of poverty in Africa and Latin America. Idiosyncratically, Hans Köchler deciphered Karol Wojtyła's earlier philosophical convictions and his *personalistic* commitment to the building of a just world order in the encyclical *Sollicitudo rei Socialis*. Very much in tune with his approach in *The Acting Person* and with his anthropological notion of self-determination, the pope emphasized, in the concluding chapter, that "human beings are totally free only when they are completely themselves, in the fullness of their rights and duties" (*Sollicitudo rei Socialis*, 1987).

Interestingly, it has been argued that Karol Wojtyła's pre-papal philosophical writings have in turn been influenced by Catholic magisterial texts. Perhaps this explains why in his article, "The Fundamental Themes of *Laborem Exercens*," Australian legal philosopher John Finnis elucidates the influence of *Gaudium et spes* on Karol Wojtyła's philosophical work. According to professor of philosophy Gregory R. Beabout, it is not fallacious to interpret *The Acting Person* as a meditation on human action inspired by the Pastoral Constitution *Gaudium et spes*, which was promulgated by Pope Paul VI as an official document of the Second Vatican Council (1965).

Noteworthily, Beabout's interpretation is confirmed by Wojtyła's own brief reference in a note in *The Acting Person* to the circumstances under which the book was written. Wojtyła confirmed that while writing *Osoba i czyn*, his participation in the proceedings of the Second Vatican Council "stimulated and inspired his thinking about the person." In the same connection, he states that *Gaudium et spes* "not only brings to the forefront the person and his calling but also asserts the belief in his transcendent nature ..." (1969:302). The language and phraseology in *Gaudium et spes* is indeed very similar to the approach in *The Acting Person*. Article 3 of the Pastoral Constitution's Preface is a case in point: "For the human person deserves to be preserved; human society deserves to be renewed. Hence the focal point of our total presentation will be man himself, whole and entire, body and soul, heart and conscience, mind and will" (*Gaudium et spes*, 1965).

Article 35 of *Gaudium et spes* states, *inter alia*, "When a man works he not only alters things and society, he develops himself as well.... A man is more precious for what he is than for what he has." In the analysis of Hans Köchler, the first sentence of Article 35 resonates with Wojtyła's 1974 article, "The Personal Structure of Self-Determination." Reflecting on the human will, Wojtyła explains that "every act of will effects a modification of the human subject as well" (Köchler, 2006:15). While acknowledging that *The Acting Person* and Wojtyła's anthropology in general articulate the basic humanistic aspirations of *Gaudium et spes*, Köchler disagrees with researcher Samuel Gregg, who sees Wojtyła's philosophical conception absorbed by the theological tradition of Catholicism. Köchler argued that for Samuel Gregg, John Paul II's pre-pontifical writings merely acknowledge "insights into the truth which emerge outside the Church," using language that is familiar to contemporary audiences, as if the writing of *The Acting Person* was a mere tactical move by a theologian and Church politician. In the hermeneutical understanding of Gregg, "*The Acting Person* reads like neo-Thomism couched in Husserlian language" (Köchler, 2006:15). Rocco Buttiglione in his biography, *Karol Wojtyła: The Thought of the Man Who Became Pope John Paul II*, also distanced himself from Gregg's interpretation that John Paul II's philosophical sagacity is of a mere *apologetic* nature. Hans Köchler concluded:

His (John Paul II's) personalistic-phenomenological approach enabled him to reach out to mankind as such, an attitude he brought to hitherto unknown perfection in his global pilgrimage as *pontifex maximus*, addressing men and women of virtually all cultures and civilizations. Thus, having remained loyal to his philosophical origins and true to his commitment to the dignity of the human being, John Paul II has proven the *universal mission* of phenomenology even in a realm that goes far beyond philosophical reasoning (Köchler, 2007:17).

Saint John Paul II could eventually be accorded the title "Doctor of the Church" because of his profound crystal-clear cascades of writings and teachings. Doctors of the Church are particularly known for the depth of understanding and orthodoxy of their theological teachings. He could even be called "Doctor of Light" since he introduced the Mysteries of Light.

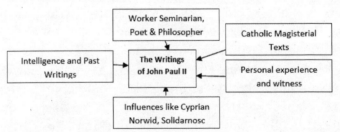

Fig. 5. Author's illustration of John Paul II's past experience and personality on his written Magisterium

Over This, Your White Grave

Over this, your white grave
the flowers of life in white—

so many years without you—
how many have passed out of sight?
Over this your white grave
covered for years, there is a stir
in the air, something uplifting
and, like death, beyond comprehension.
Over this your white grave
oh, mother, can such loving cease?
for all his filial adoration
a prayer:
Give her eternal peace—
(Krakow, spring 1939)

(Written by Karol Wojtyła when he was in his twenties)

The Quarry

He wasn't alone.
His muscles grew into the flesh of the crowd, energy their pulse,
As long as they held a hammer, as long as his feet felt the ground.
And a stone smashed his temples and cut through his heart's chamber.
They took his body and walked in a silent line
Toil still lingered about him, a sense of wrong.
They wore gray blouses, boots ankle-deep in mud.
In this, they showed the end.
How violently his time halted: the pointers on the low voltage
dials jerked, then dropped to zero again.
White stone now within him, eating into his being, taking
over enough of him to turn him into stone.
Who will lift up that stone, unfurl his thoughts again under
the cracked temples?
So plaster cracks on the wall.
They laid him down, his back on a sheet of gravel.
His wife came, worn out with worry; his son returned from school
Should his anger now flow into the anger of others?
It was maturing in him through his own truth and love

Should he be used by those who came after, deprived of su
stance, unique and deeply his own?
The stones on the move again; a wagon bruising the flowers.
Again the electric current cuts deep into the walls.
But the man has taken with him the world's inner structure,
where the greater the anger, the higher the explosion of love.

(In memory of his experience as a worker in the quarry and
one of his deceased worker friends, Wojtyła had written a
poem entitled *The Quarry* in 1956. *The Quarry* is reflected in
Laborem Exercens).

Actor

So many grew round me, through me,
from myself, as it were.
I became a channel, unleashing a force
called man.
Did not the others crowding in, distort
the man that I am?
Being each of them, always imperfect,
myself to myself too near,
he who survives in me, can he ever
look at himself without fear?
(Written by Karol Wojtyła while he was a parish priest and auxiliary bishop of Krakow.)

Girl Disappointed in Love

With mercury we measure pain
as we measure the heat of bodies and air;
but this is not how to discover our limits—
you think you are the center of things.
If you could only grasp that you are not:
the center is He,
and He, too, finds no love—

why don't you see?
The human heart—what is it for?
Cosmic temperature. Heart. Mercury.

(Written by Karol Wojtyła while he was a parish priest and auxiliary bishop of Krakow.)

CHAPTER TEN
THE MEDIA (TRACK NINE DIPLOMACY)

In Multi-Track diplomacy, the media, or peacemaking through information, is considered Track Nine diplomacy. It is built on the basic assumption that "informed people make good choices and that the media offer an appropriate and necessary forum for public debate and involvement on key issues of global importance" (Diamond & McDonald, 1996:120). The media is one of the most powerful instruments of foreign policy. During the Cold War, Radio Free Europe, Voice of America, the British Broadcasting Corporation (BBC), and Radio Moscow were instrumental in spreading the propagandas and ideologies of the superpowers, the Soviet Union and the United States of America. Indeed, the BBC was an integral part of the British Empire. World leaders use the media to sell their foreign policies, thereby influencing the behavior of other units in the international system.

U.S. President Woodrow Wilson's "Fourteen Point Speech" is seen as the genesis of modern media diplomacy. The first point of his speech stated: "Open covenants of peace, openly arrived at, after which there shall be no private international understandings of any kind but diplomacy shall proceed always frankly and in the public view" (1918). The "CNN effect," which is the instantaneous relay of information from one part of the globe to another, is the embodiment of the role of the media. It has led to the establishment of *virtual embassies*, since news agencies such as the BBC and CNN are a major source of news for everyone, and people can now follow news live on mobile phones and laptops. National governments no longer have the monopoly of information because of the democratization and globalization of news, due to developments in information and communication technologies.

The great Napoleon Bonaparte acknowledged the influence of the traditional media when he said, "Four hostile newspapers are more to be feared than a thousand bayonets." The revelation of phone hacking by the English tabloid newspaper *News of the World*, which led to an unprecedented disbandment of the 168-year-old English paper in 2011, says it all. Indeed, if not properly checked, unscrupulous journalism or war journalism could become a crime against humanity. "The news media is not well disposed to peace" (Spencer, 2005). In 1946, Julius Streicher became the first journalist in the world to be tried under international speech crime law. Streicher was the founder and publisher of *Der Stürmer* newspaper, which spread dangerous propaganda against the Jewish people during the Holocaust. He was tried by the Nuremberg Tribunal, convicted, and hanged. Joshua arap Sang, a young Kenyan journalist, was indicted on January 23, 2012, by the International Criminal Court for contributing to crimes against humanity committed during the 2007/2008 post-election violence, while hosting his talk show *Lene Emet* ("what the nation is saying in Kalenjin") as a presenter at Kass FM. Sang now has the reputation of being the second journalist to face an international tribunal on charges for crimes against humanity. (Mwaura, *Daily Nation*, January 28, 2012.)

One of the major revolutions of Saint John Paul II's papacy was his openness to the media. His use of the media to spread his message of life and respect for human dignity was effective. He had already tested the importance of the media by using Radio Free Europe to speak against human rights abuses by the communist regimes in Eastern Europe. He knew how vital the media was in his attempt to preach the Gospel to the utmost bounds of the earth. Saint John Paul II, against cries of foul play by some within the Vatican, appointed a professional lay journalist to head the Vatican press office, charged with the delicate responsibility of eloquently articulating the policies of the Holy See. The chain-smoking Dr. Joaquin Navarro-Valls was entrusted with the task of reorganizing the information service of the Holy See because of his experience in journalism and not because he was a numerary of *Opus Dei*, a personal Prelature, which was particularly dear to John Paul II.

Navarro-Valls studied journalism at the faculty of Sciences of Communication at the University of Navarra in Pamplona, Spain. In one interview, Navarro-Valls recalled the circumstances leading to his appointment as director of the Vatican press office. One day, without warning, Navarro-Valls got a call from the Vatican that the pope wanted to have lunch with him. Thinking he was being teased, he instructed his secretary to call the Vatican to confirm the veracity of the invitation. The secretary called and received a confirmation that the Holy Father wanted to speak with Navarro-Valls. Navarro-Valls later recounted, "I clearly remember that lunch with the pope who raised the issue on whether I had any idea on how to improve communication." As it is often said, the rest is history. Another crucial appointment was Archbishop John Foley, a former editor of the Philadelphian archdiocesan newspaper, to head the Pontifical Council on Social Communications (Melady, 2002:38). These appointments were succinct evidence of the importance John Paul II gave to the mass media.

The papacy of John Paul II was a media papacy. He was the first pope to allow his image, voice, and theatricalities relayed in people's homes. He was the most visible person in recorded history, and was seen by more people than anyone who ever lived. The Vatican's newspaper *L'Osservatore Romano* was originally founded in 1861, and Pope Leo XIII formally purchased it after the seizure of the Papal States. Pope Pius XI founded the Vatican Radio in 1931. Pius XII used the Vatican Radio to broadcast his Christmas messages in wartime Europe. Pius XII recognized the radio as a weapon of truth and even named Archangel Gabriel as the patron of telecommunications (Coppa, 1998:204).

Pope Saint John XXIII publicized the convocation of Vatican II and allowed the press to cover some of the proceedings. He made one ephemeral appearance on Telstar I, the world's first geosynchronous satellite, in 1962. Archbishop Fulton Sheen is one of the most memorable preachers of the Gospel via Voice of America. The first interview of a pope by a journalist was in 1965, when Pope Paul VI made that history. Paul VI also appeared on a special broadcast for ABC television news when U.S. President John Kennedy was assassinated, although journalist Robert Blair Kaiser argued that he was too modest for the celebrity-prone media (2006:44).

Pope John Paul II's use of the media was more than a mere continuance of a trend. It was idiosyncratic. In 1979, John Paul II was named "Man of the Year" by *Time* magazine. He was dubbed by the media and the youth as a "superstar" and an "icon for our age" (Sanford, 1979:88). On October 16, 1979, with exactly a year in the pontifical office, *The Tablet* called him, "without doubt the outstanding personality in the free world" (Kwitny, 1997:344). Remarkably, Saint John Paul II was the subject of twelve *Time* magazine cover stories within a period of seventeen years, although not always without dubious intentions. The magnitude of that statistic could be drawn from John Galsworthy's assertion of "headlines twice the size of the events." Joaquin Navarro-Valls once said that there is "an objective bond between the pope and the media. We don't know what percentage is due to the pope or what percentage to the media, but they have established this deep mutual bond" (Accattoli, 1998:68).

According to André Frossard, John Paul II sought large gatherings to clarify the biases against him by the media (Kwitny, 1997:641). Paul VI was pope for fifteen years, and during that time he was the subject of the cover story of *Time* magazine on three occasions. John Paul II was *Time* Man of the Year in 1994 because of his use of the world's *bully-est pulpit* (media) for mass proselytizing (Melady, 2005:1). According to academician Margaret Melady, John Paul II's personality and his past experience as an actor in the Rhapsodic Theatre are very important in explaining the use of the media in his diplomacy. However, she added that the personality factor of John Paul II cannot solely explain the media's sustained attention on him. His election to the papacy in 1978 was an event in itself. His numerous international visits continuously kept the media focused on him. No U.S. or communist leader attracted the attention of the media like John Paul II. Idiosyncratically, Margaret Melady held that John Paul II's excellent timing, projection of voice, ease, and confidence before a crowd could be traced back to his days as an actor in the Rhapsodic Theatre. American professor of Unitarian theology George Huntston Williams pointed out that John Paul II's poetic and dramatic leanings very much influenced his way of speaking (1981:72).

Rome-based journalist Robert Mickens opined, "John Paul II was a larger-than-life figure who possessed a Herculean personality and a flair for the dramatic gesture, something Benedict XVI does not have" (2011:11). Even though John Paul II was an eloquent communicator, he also used gestures in his communication. Saint John Paul II's personal attitude toward the media was idiosyncratic. He carried his Polish theatre experience to Rome. In his worldview, visibility took precedence over talk and action over words. He was a pope of presence before he was a man of words (Accattoli, 1998:66). There is a joke that when John Paul II spoke, people looked for gestures, whereas with Benedict XVI, people listened. Kissing the ground and babies, flinging walking sticks like *Charlie Chaplin*, and dancing with the youth are all good recipes for the media.

In an interview with this author, Fr. Tony Murphy, MHM, a keen Irish-born Church historian, pointed out that the English word "hypocrite" is derived from the Greek word for "actor." Tony Murphy, who taught English Literature in Cameroon for many years, stated, "I don't think John Paul II was ever accused of being a hypocrite but certainly, as pope, he was very aware of the crowd and was not ashamed to play to them, especially the youth." Still commenting on John Paul II's acting skills, Tony Murphy added, "… but he did not do this to gain popularity for himself. What he wanted was to present his message in a way that would be accepted by the throngs of people (especially the youth). He very much used his skill and training as an actor to achieve this end."

Archbishop Maurice Muhatia reasoned that John Paul II's gestures were tools for his diplomacy. He opined that kissing the tarmac was a simple gesture, but it captured the sentiment and emotions of the audience, who saw the pope as one of them and identified with him. By their vicarious identification with the pope, people identified themselves with Christ, since the pope is the legitimate representative of Christ on earth. Enabling people to identify themselves with God constitutes part of the diplomacy of the Holy See. John Paul II was a handsome man, with rounded cheeks, which made him very natural in his often smile-wreathed face. His blue eyes radiated joy and confidence. His presence was majestic and electrifying. Stefan Cardinal Wyszyński did talk of John Paul II's facial pleasantness at the end of his famous visit to Poland in June 1979, "Dearest beloved father, your visit to your native Poland is ended ... thank you for your simplicity and warmth ... your open arms, your *Slavonic* face, your smiling eyes, always serene and confident" (Zavattaro, 1999). Tanzanian theologian Laurenti Magessa, talking to this author, said John Paul II's handsomeness cannot be overlooked. Margaret Melady reckoned that possibly John Paul II's greatest asset was his facial pleasantness. Most celebrities are beautiful and handsome, as is the case in Hollywood, Bollywood, and Nollywood.

In his 1979 book, *Pope John Paul II: A Festive Profile,* Ludvik Nemec recorded that Saint John Paul II was probably the first pope since Pius IX to have a fine, well-trained singing voice and, according to some Church historians and Vaticanologists, the first in the twentieth century to sing the difficult *Ite missa est* ("The Mass is ended. Go in peace") in tune (1979:47). His voice was a vibrant musical baritone, strong, resolute, and exceptionally flexible. Among the pentad of necessary qualifications for the diplomatic career which Satow espoused in his theory of diplomacy are: good temper, good health, and good looks (1917:183–4). John Paul II's physical build is another factor which cannot be overlooked. He walked like an athlete and descended stairs of planes in a youthful fashion.

John Paul II was attractively built, unlike some of his immediate predecessors. Behind the soft folds of his papal robes were the real muscles of an athlete, formed in hiking, skiing, and mountaineering (John-Stevas, 1982:137). Pius XII had an ascetic, hermitic, aloof look and personage, tall, thin, with penetrating eyes (Lucker, 2000:21). John XXIII was short and fat and weighed over 200 pounds in 1958. Paul VI was thin, although not as skinny as Benedict XV.

John Paul II's use of the media in his diplomacy could not only be attributed to his personality. He came into office in the age of the media revolution and advancement in informational technology, an epoch when space and time had been compressed by electronic innovations and advancements. The nature of globalization in the last quarter of the twentieth century (Globalization 3.0) was obviously different from globalization in the 19th century (Globalization 2.0). Reputed American political commentator and author, Thomas Friedman, captured that difference by stating that "contemporary globalization goes 'farther, faster, cheaper, and deeper'" (1999:7–8).

The realist school of international relations would argue that the nature of the international system in the age of globalization gifted Saint John Paul II the luxury of the mass media during his pontificate. Bernstein and Politi concluded that "John Paul II was the first pope to understand the television era, the first one who mastered the medium, who could handle the microphone, who was used to improvising, who wasn't afraid of performing in public" (1996:399). During the Council, Cardinal Wojtyła presented a paper on the media, "Means of Social Communication." Pope John Paul II efficiently made use of the media during the 1994 Cairo Conference on Population and Development.

The 1994 Cairo Media Battle

The 1994 Cairo Conference on Population and Development was part of a series of decennial global intergovernmental conferences on population organized by the United Nations. The others were the World Population Conference held in Bucharest, Romania in 1974 and the International Conference on Population in Mexico

City, Mexico, in 1984. Prior to the above-mentioned conferences, there were two other conferences on population, organized by the Population Division of the United Nations in cooperation with the International Union for the Scientific Study of Population (IUSSP)—Rome (August 31 – September 10, 1954) and Belgrade (August 30 – September 10, 1965). Noteworthily, the two conferences were scientific meetings of individual experts (mostly demographers) and did not, therefore, make any substantive global policy on population or development issues (Singh, 1998:2).

Initially, the conference in Cairo had to deal with two variables: population and development. The primary aim of the conference was to formulate ways to keep world population from spiraling dangerously out of control, especially in the Third World, and to help developing countries in their quest to become modernized and developed. But the "development" aspect of the conference quickly faded into relative obscurity as the Vatican's opposition to the draft plan references to abortion hardened into what *The New York Times* characterized as "one of the most vehement crusades" of John Paul II's papacy. Thereafter, the proposed Cairo conference became an ideological battle fought between two superpowers and their respective allies. The Vatican (the moral superpower of the world) led by the vociferous Pope John Paul II versus the United States (the economic and military superpower), led by President Bill Clinton. The allies of the Vatican were mainly several Islamic states and some countries in the developing world, while the U.S. was ably supported by the U.N. Fund for Population Activities (UNFPA), the International Planned Parenthood Federation, and many Western states.

The ideological battle revolved around sexuality, abortion, the family, and the institution of marriage. In contrast to the ideology of the Holy See, the Clinton administration defined sexual expression in terms of pleasure, devoid of any connection to marriage or procreation. The Vatican stood opposed to the imposition of limits on family size, and to the promotion of methods of limiting births, such as abortion. While the Vatican saw abortion as a violation of human rights and a heinous evil act, the U.S. and its allies argued that abortion is an important human right that must be globalized and internationalized. The Clinton administration's slogan was "access to safe, legal, and voluntary abortion is a fundamental human right." A full blown "cold war" was thus in existence.

The superpowers used a plethora of instruments to spread their respective ideologies before and during the conference in Cairo. Chief amongst the instruments was the media. In the 1980s, the Vatican and the United States joined forces and made proper use of the media to bring down the communist empire in Eastern Europe. When juxtaposed with other U.N.-sponsored conferences in the twentieth century, the Cairo conference was unique due to the unparalleled exposure it received through newspapers, radio, television, and the internet. The different forms of media helped to bring issues related to reproductive health, reproductive rights, and women's empowerment to the attention of millions of people around the world (Singh, 1998:1). The media played a major role in covering the dispute between the Vatican and the Clinton administration.

During the 1992 presidential campaigns in the U.S., Bill Clinton and his running mate Al Gore ran on a very radical "social issues" platform, committing themselves to extensive federal funding of abortion-on-demand in the U.S. at any stage of pregnancy, and pledging to fund "greater family planning effort" in the U.S. foreign aid programs. In fidelity to his campaign promises, on his first day in office, which happened to coincide with the twentieth annual "March for Life" in Washington, President Clinton signed five executive orders widening the scope of federal involvement with, and funding of, elective abortion (Weigel, 1995). Four days later, *L'Osservatore Romano*, the Vatican newspaper, published an editorial charging that the "renewal" Clinton had promised in his campaign "comes by way of death (and) by way of violence against innocent beings" (Weigel, 1999:715). This was the commencement of the media battle between Pope John Paul II and the administration of U.S. President Bill Clinton over world population and family planning issues that culminated in Cairo, in September 1994.

A couple of preparatory meetings for the Cairo conference were organized by the U.N. The most decisive and consequential of them was the Third Preparatory Commission meeting, informally called Prep-Com III, which took place in New York from April 4 to 22, 1994. Prep-Com III was the most impactful because it produced the draft document for the September 1994 conference in Cairo. On March 16, 1994, less than three weeks before the commencement of Prep-Com III, U.S. Secretary of State Warren Christopher sent a cable to all U.S. diplomatic missions abroad, stating that "the U.S. believes that access to safe, legal, and voluntary abortion is a fundamental right of all women," and emphasizing that the U.S. objective at Cairo was to get "stronger language on the importance" of "abortion services" into the conference final report (Weigel, 1995:2).

A couple of days before Prep-Com III, Dr. Nafis Sadik, the Pakistani head of the U.N. Fund for Population Activities, went to Rome to see Pope John Paul II. She was following a precedent set by the Secretary General of the 1984 Population Conference, Rafael Montinola Salas, who had gone to see the same pontiff in June 1984. There is no transcript available of the conversation that took place between the pope and Dr. Sadik, but upon her return to New York, she somewhat erroneously told members of the secretariat that the pope's comments revolved around the definition of the family and the role of women in the context of moral and natural laws, and not so much on abortion (Singh, 1998:50). It was Sadik's understanding that there would be no press conference after her meeting with the pope, but on March 18, 1994, the Holy See's press office released to the media the text of the pope's message for the Cairo conference addressed to Nafis Sadik. *Inter alia*, the pope said:

> In defence of the human person, the Church stands opposed to the imposition of limits on family size, and to the promotion of methods of limiting births which seek the unitive and procreative dimensions of marital intercourse, which are contrary to the moral law inscribed on

the human heart, or which constitute an assault on the sacredness of life. Thus, sterilization, which is more and more promoted as a method of family planning, because of its finality and its potential for the violation of human rights, especially of women, is clearly unacceptable; it poses a most grave threat to human dignity and liberty when promoted as part of a population policy. Abortion, which destroys existing human life, is a heinous evil, and it is never an acceptable method of family planning, as was recognized by consensus at the Mexico City UN International Conference on Population.

Prep-Com III produced a 118-page document, littered with reproductive rights and abortion on demand expressions. Abortion on demand was, to an extent, the centerpiece of the Cairo draft document. The draft document was strongly criticized by many Moslem leaders in the Arab world. The different forms of media in the Arab world carried reports of Muslim clerics criticizing the document, and even calling upon Muslim countries to boycott the conference. In the end, Libya and Sudan boycotted the conference, while Saudi Arabia and Lebanon politely notified the conference secretariat at the eleventh hour that they were not going to attend.

Perhaps in a show of defiance and a direct moral statement to the organizers of Prep-Com III, two days after the end of Prep-Com III, Pope John Paul II beatified a woman whose life and death stood in sharpest contrast to the Cairo draft document's image of life, sexuality, marriage, and the family. In 1961, Gianna Beretta Molla, a pediatrician and mother of three, was two months pregnant with her fourth child when a fibroma developed on her uterus. After some medical examination, the doctors gave her three options. First, surgical removal of her ovary and uterus (hysterectomy) would save her life but kill the unborn child, because the uterus is where a baby grows when a woman is pregnant. The Catholic Church forbids all direct abortion but traditional Catholic teaching on the principle of double effect would have allowed her to undergo a hysterectomy, which might have caused her unborn child's death as an unintended consequence or concomitant effect of the surgery. Second, the tumor alone could be surgically removed and the unborn child aborted, and she could probably bear more children later. Third, the tumor could be removed while attempting to save the pregnancy, an option that posed serious risks to her own life. She opted for the removal of the fibroma and instructed the surgeons to operate on her in such a way that the pregnancy was saved. She selflessly told the doctors that her baby's life was more important than hers.

The tumor was successfully removed, but as Gianna Molla knew, she faced a dangerous delivery. Her fourth child, Gianna Emanuela, was born on April 21, 1962, Holy Saturday of that year. Seven days after successfully giving birth by caesarean section, Gianna Beretta Molla died of complications from birth (septic peritonitis) on April 29, 1962. Molla was beatified on April 24, 1994, in the presence of her husband and children, including thirty-two-year-old Gianna Emanuela who is now a doctor of geriatrics. Ten years later, she was canonized by Pope John Paul II in the presence of her husband and children, the first time in the history of the Church that a husband witnessed his wife's canonization (Weigel, 1999:720–21). St. Gianna is a patron saint for mothers, physicians, and unborn children.

Given their arrogance and smugness displayed in the preparatory meetings, the U.S. and its allies were very confident of brushing aside abortion critics during the conference in Cairo. It is strange to think that the most consequential factor the planners of the Cairo conference failed to properly consider was the moral and soft power of Pope John Paul II. They were suffering from historical amnesia and were not good students of history, since they forgot to draw some lessons from the role played by John Paul II in the fall of the Berlin Wall and demise of communism in Eastern Europe. Inevitably, the sine qua non of the setback suffered by the international advocates of the sexual revolution, which reduced sex to a recreational activity of no moral consequence and abortion on demand, was the moral public campaign of opposition to the Cairo draft document mounted throughout the summer of 1994 by John Paul II.

On June 30, 1994, John Paul II began a sustained campaign in the court of public opinion against the Prep-Com III document. It consisted of a series of ten twelve-minute reflections on the issues to be discussed in Cairo. The pope eloquently argued out the positions of the Church and the Vatican at his public audiences during the months of June, July, and August of 1994. George Weigel stated that by identifying the fundamental ethical errors of the draft document, and by defining a compelling moral alternative to U.N. -sponsored libertinism, John Paul II set in motion a resistance movement with considerable potency (1995:3).

In his summer reflections, Pope John Paul II emphasized that the right to life is the basic human right, "written in human nature," and the foundation of any meaningful scheme of "human rights." He spoke of the family as the "primary cell" of society and as a "natural institution" with rights that any just state must respect. He defined marriage "as a stable union of a man and a woman who are committed to the reciprocal gift of self and open to creating new life, [which] is not only a Christian value, but an original value of creation." He also defended the equal human dignity of women, and insisted that women must not be reduced to being objects of male pleasure (Weigel, 1995:III).

While conducting his weekly addresses on the ethics of sexuality and family life, John Paul II was urging his press spokesman, Joaquin Navarro-Valls, to get into the public debate and to tell the world the Church's understanding of sexuality and marriage. "You should say clearly what we think," was Navarro-Valls' instruction from his boss about the role he was to play before and during the conference. Ipso facto, Navarro-Valls started a series of briefings at the Vatican press office, eloquently elucidating the Church's positions of the moral issues at stake in Cairo. "Nobody around the world, reading papers or watching television, has any doubts about the main topics regarding the doctrine of the church nowadays regarding family life," Navarro says. "They know what is our position, the position of the Catholic Church" (Shaw, 1995).

By the end of the summer, the pope's decisive clarification of the moral issues at stake in Cairo had not only put the impending conference on the front pages of the prestige press, it had also had a powerful political effect. U.S. Undersecretary of State Timothy Wirth continued to insist, against all the evidence, that the administration had "no fight with the Vatican." Wirth's office ordinarily featured a "condom tree" as a desk ornament. The tree was only removed when Archbishop Tauran visited his office in November 16, 1993 (Weigel, 1999:716).

On August 25, 1994, due to the sustained public campaign against the pro-abortion Cairo draft document, Vice President Al Gore, who was to lead the U.S. delegation to the Cairo conference, gave a speech at the National Press Club in Washington in which he stated "the U.S. has not sought, does not seek, and will not seek to establish any international right to abortion." Any attempt to suggest otherwise was a "red herring." Joaquin Navarro-Valls quickly pointed out at a press conference in Rome a few days later that Gore's statement did not tally with the draft document, whose definition of "reproductive health care" as including "pregnancy termination" had been a U.S. coinage.

Perhaps apart from his 2005 emotional press conferences, during which time his expertise in medicine was important in communicating the pope's deteriorating health to the press, never was Joaquin Navarro-Valls' clout more evident than at the September 1994 nine-day, United Nations-sponsored Cairo International Conference on Population and Development. The conference opened on September 5, 1994. Because of the publicity given to various controversies, more than 4,000 journalists descended on Cairo to cover the Conference—a record number for any U.N. Conference. The number of media representatives slightly exceeded the number of official delegates from member countries (Singh, 1998:57).

Navarro-Valls was in his tenth year as the director of the Vatican press office, the *de facto* liaison between the Vatican the world press corps. Pope John Paul II did not make it to Cairo, but he knew what he would get by deploying his media guru to Cairo.

By sending Navarro-Valls, his public voice, to Cairo, the pope ensured that his position would be forcefully, convincingly, and publicly enunciated. Before the Cairo conference began, Navarro-Valls briefed the Vatican press corps on the pope's objections to the manner in which abortion was treated in the "draft programme of action" that the United States was expected to support at the conference. On August 8, a month before the conference opened, *The New York Times* published a Page 1 story about Navarro-Valls' statement that the pope thought that the Cairo proposals on such matters as "fertility regulation" and "reproductive health" would "legitimize abortion."

Even though Al Gore and Archbishop Renato Martin led the U.S. and the Vatican's delegations to Cairo, respectively, "Navarro-Valls was the most important person at the conference," according to Alessandro Magister, who has covered the Vatican for more than three decades for the Italian news weekly *L'Espresso*. Wherever Navarro-Valls went, the world press would follow, according to Alessandro Magister. Kim Murphy, who covered the conference for the *Los Angeles Times*, said Navarro-Valls was probably no more important than other major delegates in shaping the final language of the document, but she agrees that, in media terms, he was "the most interesting, the most watched, the most quoted, the most followed person" in Cairo in September 1994.

Navarro-Valls' active presence in Cairo, making statements, criticizing Gore, answering questions, and even writing an Op-Ed page piece for *The Wall Street Journal*,—shows just how media-savvy John Paul II was (Shaw, 1995:1). In line with the Multi-track diplomacy system which considers the media as the main actor in Track Nine diplomacy, Joaquin Navarro-Valls argued that, "diplomacy is not the only means of relationships between countries.... Now there is also the press. So why not use the press . . . (use) public opinion" (Shaw, 1995:1). Navarro-Valls later said that the use of the media during the conference in Cairo increased pressure on delegates from some other countries to "change their position, not because of a moral consideration but maybe because they are fearing the press." Did not Napoleon Bonaparte, the great French army general, acknowledge that "four hostile newspapers are more to be feared than a thousand bayonets?" With Navarro-Valls exquisite media performance before and during the conference in Cairo, Pope John Paul II was finally vindicated for having appointed him to head the Holy See's press office, against all odds.

During the conference in Cairo, the U.S. and its allies used the media to tarnish the image of the Vatican and disseminate its pro-abortion norms. Some media networks and diplomats even questioned why a tiny, one-religion city-state with fewer than 1,000 residents, none of them women or children, was even permitted to participate in a policy-making conference that would affect women and children of all religions throughout the world. Some Western diplomats and journalists further criticized the Vatican for what *The Guardian* in England called its "hypocritical alliance" with radical Islamic forces who share the pope's opposition to abortion, even as they criticized the Vatican as an agent of "western cultural imperialism." During Prep-Com III, the ineffable Prime Minister Gro Harlem Brundtland of Norway complained bitterly about obstacles placed in the Cairo conference's path by a "small state with no natural inhabitants."

Since 1964, the Holy See has been seated as a non-member observer state in the U.N. General Assembly. The Holy See has no voting rights since she has not ratified the U.N. Charter. However, within U.N.-organized conferences, the emergence of a *consensus* preference permits the Holy See to exercise effective veto over final "outcome" documents. Holy See delegates frustrated the work of the 1994 Cairo conference at the instruction of Pope John Paul II over concerns that an "internationalisation" of access to abortion was afoot. The Holy See was able to obstruct the conference's progress for three days, prompting howls of diplomatic protest (Cussen, 2014:5).

Due to the considerable impact of the Vatican's delegation in Cairo, many journalistic reports depicted the Vatican as having single-handedly "hijacked" the Cairo conference, frustrating and enraging delegates from other nations by delaying deliberations on a wide variety of issues for more than a week with its insistent demands for "minor" changes in the "plan of action" as it related to abortion. *The New York Times* insisted on reporting the debates as a matter of "the Vatican and its few remaining allies" obstructing the course of human progress.

Due to the fiery campaign of the Vatican, the final document of the conference in Cairo, read, "In no case should abortion be promoted as a method of family planning." The notion of enshrining abortion-on-demand as an internationally recognized basic human right—the centerpiece of the U.S. ideology at Cairo —had been abandoned by its proponents, who tacitly conceded that there was no international consensus supporting the claim.

Thanks to John Paul II's powerful public campaign, his media prowess, the indefatigable Navarro-Valls, and the Vatican delegation to Cairo, the view that abortion is a fundamental human right and an acceptable method of family planning was abandoned. Having forced changes in the references to abortion and then withholding its approval from the chapters containing those references, *The New York Times* said the Vatican had "obtained concessions without abandoning its moral position." Philip Pullella, who has covered the Vatican for many years for the London-based Reuters news agency, put it more bluntly, "The Vatican went (to Cairo) with an agenda and they got everything they wanted" (Shaw, 1995:2). Thus, it became clear, to those with eyes to see, ears to hear, and mouths to tell, that the mores of Hollywood, Bollywood, Nollywood, Wall Street, Western theatres of the sexual revolution, and Manhattan's Upper West Side, are not universally shared, admired, or sought.

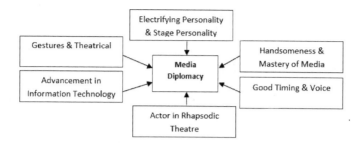

Fig. 6. Author's illustration of John Paul II's idiosyncratic variables and other factors which informed his media diplomacy

CHAPTER ELEVEN
WORLD YOUTH DAY
(TRACK FOUR DIPLOMACY)

Pope Saint John Paul II's papacy was one of innovations. One of the landmark novelties of his papacy was the World Youth Day (WYD). World Youth Day is a biannual event organized by the Roman Catholic Church, which brings together youths from all parts of the globe to journey, interact, and be accompanied by the pope. It is a journey of faith-sharing and mutual encouragement between the pope and youth, in which young people come to discover the ever-young Jesus as their friend and companion along life's uncertain path. It is an important component of Vatican diplomacy. World Youth Day was initiated by Saint John Paul II in 1985. A familiar legal maxim states that *actio personalis moritur cum persona* ("a personal action dies with the person"). WYDs celebrations are more than a personal action since the practice continues way after the death of John Paul II. World Youth Day 2019 was held in Panama City, January 22–27.

Cujusque rei potissima pars est principium ("the principal part of everything is the beginning.") Even though WYD is considered the brainchild of Saint John Paul II, in humility, the pope would credit the youth for the creation of the World Youth Days. Saint John Paul II met with young people in Rome during the International Jubilee for the Young, April 11–15, 1984, and then for the International Year of Youth (March 30–31, 1985). In April 1984, the pope met with the young on the occasion of the Extraordinary Jubilee for Redemption, the Holy Year of 1983–1984. The year 1985 was proclaimed by the United Nations as the International Youth Year. It paid particular attention to issues of concern, and relating to, youth. The proclamation was signed on January 1, 1985, by then-United Nations chief, Javier Pérez de Cuéllar. In the spirit of the International World Youth Day, Saint John Paul II published an Apostolic Letter, *Dilecti amici,* on March 26, 1985, "to young men and women in the world." The saintly pope again had a very exciting, impactful, and meaningful experience with the youth during the International Youth Meeting in Rome (March 30–31, 1985). Thus, Saint John Paul II traced the genesis of World Youth Day to those historic meetings with the youth in Rome in 1984 and 1985: "This was the beginning. *No one invented the World Youth Days. It was the young people themselves who created them.* Those days, those encounters, then became something desired by young people throughout the world. Most of the time these Days were something of a surprise for priests, and even bishops, in that they surpassed all their expectations" (1994:124). In an address to the College of Cardinals and the Roman Curia on December 20, 1985, the pope revealed, "The Lord blessed that meeting (with young people—on the eve of Palm Sunday—30 March 1985) in an extraordinary way to the extent that a World Youth Day was established for forthcoming years to be celebrated on Palm Sunday together with the useful assistance of the Council for the Laity" (Mari, 2007).

Historically, the genesis of World Youth Day could also be traced back to the youth activities of the Taizé Brothers in the 1960s and 1970s. The Taizé Community, a monastic ecumenical order in Taizé, Burgundi, France, was founded in 1940 by Brother Roger Schütz-Marsauche, a Swiss Protestant theologian. Since the late 1960s, thousands of young adults from many countries have found their way to Taizé to take part in weekly prayer meetings. The first international young adults' meeting was organized in Taizé in 1966 with 1400 participants from 30 countries. On March 29, 1971, in response to student protests in Europe and the world, Brother Roger announced a "Council of Youth," whose inaugural meeting took place in 1974 (*Time Magazine*, April 29, 1974). He explained that the first Christians convened councils when faced with difficult questions.

The Council of Youth was meant to affect the lives of all the participants in a direct way, and they would spread the light of Christ by caring for those in their surroundings, wherever they would go. They would work for justice and for the rights of the poor, and the rich would give up their unacceptable privileges (Moed, 2011:40). At the end of the 1970s, the meetings and surrounding activities began to be referred to as the "Pilgrimage of Trust on Earth" by Brother Roger. According to Marjolijn de Moed, the Council of Youth can be seen as a prototype of the Pilgrimage of Faith on Earth (2011:39).

The Pilgrimage of Trust on Earth still goes on today, less spectacular than those of the popes, but with greater spiritual intensity. During a Taizé gathering in Paris in 1995, Brother Roger spoke to more than 100,000 young people who were sitting on the floor of an exhibition hall, "We have come here to search, or to go on searching through silence and prayer, to get in touch with our inner life" (Marlise, 2005). Annually, around New Year's Day (usually from December 28 to January 1), a meeting in a large European city attracts tens of thousands of young adults. It is organized by Brothers of the Taizé Community, Sisters of St. Andrew, and young volunteers from all over Europe and from the host city. The participants stay with local families or in very simple group accommodations. In the morning, they take part in a program organized by the parish closest to their accommodation. For their midday meal, all participants travel to a central location, usually the local exhibition halls. The meal is followed by a common prayer, and the afternoon is spent in workshops covering faith, art, politics, and social topics. In the evening, the participants meet for a meal and prayer. Brother Roger often said, "I will go to the ends of the earth to express my trust in the young generations." Tragically, Brother Roger was stabbed to death during the evening prayer service in Taizé on August 16, 2005, by a young Romanian woman named Luminiţa Ruxandra Solcan, who was later deemed mentally ill.

John Paul II repeatedly acknowledged that one of the important lessons he learned as a young priest, bishop, archbishop, and cardinal was the *fundamental importance of youth*. Saint John Paul II was a celebrity that the media sought. Young people were magnetically attracted to him and incessantly accorded him a rock star reception whenever in their company. Mill Hill Missionary and philosopher Hans Burgman wrote, "The Church needs magnetic personalities. How do we get those? Not through training. They have to be ignited by other magnetic personalities" (2010:31). The secular media could not comprehend the phenomenon of World Youth Day. The media found it difficult to explain why thousands of teens and young adults were magnetically attracted to the pope even in his old age. *Time* magazine explained:

> His appearances generate an electricity unmatched by anyone else on earth. That explains, for instance, why in rural Kenyan villages thousands of children, plus many cats and roosters and even hotels, are named John Paul. Charisma is the only conceivable reason why a CD featuring him saying the Rosary—in Latin—against a background of Bach and Handel is currently ascending the charts in Europe (Evert, 2014:92).

However, chastity speaker Jason Evert does not agree with *Time* magazine's assessment of the rapport between John Paul II and the youth. He sees religious dryness orchestrated by modern secularism as the main reason why young people flocked to Pope John Paul II:

> While some credited 'charisma,' others assumed his popularity among the youth was just a case of youngsters being starstruck by a celebrity figure. But the reason why millions flocked to him was not because they viewed him as a superstar. No, they came because they wished to see Jesus. The more the world deprives young people of what is true, good, and beautiful, the more earnestly will they yearn for it. The vacuum of

modern secularism is actually a fragrant invitation for young people to rediscover the sacred (Evert, 2014:92).

John Paul II ignited the youth. Among the reasons why young people were magnetically attracted to Father Karol Wojtyła were his intelligence, his friendliness, his human sympathy, and his permanent openness (Weigel, 2010:41). Papal historian Luigi Accattoli has examined the many reasons why John Paul II was so well accepted by young people. Among them was his frankness and sincerity. He argued that the pope never modified his message so that it would be well received by the youth; rather, he spoke the truth plainly to them. Journalist Marek Skwarnicki once asked the pope why young people are magnetically attracted to him, even in his old age, at a time when the young generation is rebelling against the old in families and in societies. The pope looked at him and said, "Marek, it is the Holy Spirit" (Hallet, 2002).

In 1992 at Bergamo, Italy, Saint John Paul II spoke ardently to young people in defense of life, "Dear young people, do not be afraid to defend life, all life-life in the womb and life in one's declining years" (June 20, 1992). In the summer of 1980, the pope spent an evening with 50,000 teenagers at Parc des Princes Stadium, France. There were another 35,000 standing outside. During their conversation, one of the teenagers asked him, "In questions of a sexual nature the Church has a rather intransigent attitude. Are you not afraid, Holy Father, that young people will move further and further away from the Church?" Pope John Paul II replied:

If you think of this question deeply, going right to the heart of the problem, I assure you that you will realize only one thing, which is that in this domain the only demands made by that Church are those bound up with true, that is, responsible, conjugal love. She demands what the dignity of the person and the basic social order require. I do not deny that they are demands.

But this is the essential point, that man fulfils himself only to the extent that he knows how to impose demands on himself. In the opposite case "he goes away, sorrowful," as we have just read in the Gospel. Permissiveness does not make men happy. The consumer society does not make men happy. It never has (Evert, 2014:84).

The pope's honest and profound responses to the youth often triggered an examination of conscience and introspection. "For every person, an encounter with the successor of Christ was, and it had to be, a challenge, a moment of reflection on one's self and on one's life. It was really as if one stood in front of one's own conscience, in total truth in front of one's self" (Evert, 2014:96). Saint John Paul II believed in the young people, had confidence in them, and loved them. He always felt happier in their company and was willing to listen to them. The young people understood that they were greatly loved by the pope. When André Frossard told the pope in Paris, "Your Holiness, I think you could lead the young people wherever you want," the pope replied, "On the contrary; it is they who lead me!" (Accattoli, 1998:160).

Laurenti Magesea, the great Tanzanian theologian, in an interview with this author, pointed out that John Paul II understood clearly that the youth were the future of the Church. Indeed, during his inaugural Mass as pope, John Paul II left a precise message to the youth, "You are the future of the world, the hope of the Church, you are my hope" (1994:124). John Paul II understood fully well that the Church needs the enthusiasm and *joie de vivre* of the young. The youth were certainly the hope of the pope since he was aware that in his *Rule*, Saint Benedict asks the Abbot of the Abbey to constantly listen to the youngest monks, for "it is often to a younger brother that the Lord reveals the best course" (*Rule III*, 3, 2001:298–299).

World Youth Days are not sabbaticals or touristic adventures for the youth, but a strategy of evangelization by the late pontiff and the Church. Pope Benedict XVI criticized the tendency to view WYD as a kind of "rock festival." The pope emeritus defended World Youth Day as a "great feast of faith." The "joy" experienced by World Youth Day participants is "not comparable to the ecstasy of a rock festival" because it derives from the presence of God, he said (Rocca, 2008). During WYD, the pope spoke personally to the youth on the need to uphold the ultimate values: respect of life against the culture of death and illegality, sex, virginity, human rights, *inter alia*. Commenting on the impact of WYDs, John Paul II wrote:

> They have become a powerful means of evangelization. In the young there is, in fact, an immense potential for good and for creative possibility. Whenever I meet them in my travels throughout the world, I wait first of all to hear what they want to tell me about themselves, about their society, about their Church. And I always point out: 'What am I going to say to you is not as important as what you are going to say to me. You will not necessarily say it to me in words; you will say it to me by your presence, by your song, perhaps by your dancing, by your skits, and finally by your enthusiasm (1994:124–25).

Archbishop Muhatia M. Makumba, in an interview with this author, advanced that it will be disastrous for the Church not to touch the youth. Youths, he said, in a wider context, are agents of Vatican diplomacy. Some outcomes of WYD prove the efficacy of this pastoral and diplomatic strategy of John Paul II. Inspired by the World Youth Day, a young smiling Canadian lady, Anna Halpine, at the age of 21, began the World Youth Alliance (WYA) at the U.N. in 1999. The WYA is a global coalition of young people below the age of thirty which trains youths to work at regional and international levels. Today, the WYA has at least one million members from over 100 nationalities. Which country has a network of over a million diplomatic agents in every corner of the planet? There is hardly any succinct expression of the goal of the Holy See's diplomacy, other than a statement from the Charter of the Alliance: "World Youth Alliance is committed to building free and just societies through a culture of life ... that affirms the inalienable dignity of the person, defends the intrinsic right to life, nurtures the family, and fosters a social climate favorable to integral development, solidarity, and mutual respect" (Skoggard, 2009).

Why do the WYA members work indefatigably to promote respect for human rights and dignity with conspicuously frugal and meager allowances amidst the vast resources of the organization? Halpine's response shows the extent to which Saint John Paul II had formed the consciences of the youth, "The Holy Father has told us to build a culture of life. We are just following orders" (Weigel, 2005:39). The WYA constitutes Track Four, or citizen, diplomacy, as the ordinary young people in the world are the diplomatic agents. Track Four, or citizen, diplomacy is built on the assumption that power resides not just with the decision makers but at the grassroots level, and that each person can make an impact on international relations (Diamond & McDonald, 1996:60).

Indeed, even as the Holy Father advanced in age, coupled with poor health, he always felt rejuvenated during his meetings with the youth. In Rome in 2000, he joked with the youth, "There is a Polish proverb: 'when you stay with the youth, you remain young.... Rome has heard this noise and it can never forget it." That is why the youth labelled him "the eternal teenager" (Evert, 2014:86). In *Crossing the Threshold of Hope*, Saint John Paul II acknowledged that, *"It is not true that the Pope brings the young from one end of the world to the other. It is they who bring him.* Even though he is getting older, they urge him to be young, they do not permit him to forget his experience, his discovery of youth and its great importance for the life of every man. I believe this explains a great deal" (1994:125). Based on some photographs of the pope, Arturo

Mari, his long-time official photographer, said that Pope John Paul II's face changed literally in the company of the youth. With the youth, he became a youth.

Socrates, the most enigmatic philosopher of all time, drank hemlock in 399 B.C. and died because he was indicted for corrupting the minds of the Athenian youths and for impiety (not believing in the gods of the state). In contrast Pope Saint John Paul II lived on forming and informing the minds and consciences of the youth of the world. No one could more excellently explain John Paul II's rapport with the youth than himself when he pointed out, "And not only in Rome, but anywhere the pope goes, he seeks out the young and the young seek him out" (1994:123). As John Paul II laid in bed in his last moments on earth, he was told by his aides that throngs of young people had gathered outside his window in prayers and singing. The pope then began gesturing in an attempt to communicate with the youth. According to his longtime aide and spokesman, Navarro-Valls, the pope was saying, "I have looked for you. Now you have come to me. And I thank you" (Evert, 2014:202). So, perhaps John Paul's final earthly gesture was to the youth, considering that he slipped into a coma shortly after that.

In the analysis of Christopher Weiler, an orthodox Jew born in South Africa, Europe's *Christophobia* and civilizational suicide is caused by Europe's attempt to jettison God from the life of man, even though Christianity was the main unifying factor of Europe. Perhaps Cardinal Ratzinger's choice of Benedict XVI for his pontifical name was a clear signal of his attempt to re-evangelize Europe, because Benedict of Nursia is the patron saint of Europe. It is a rarity in Europe these days to see huge numbers of young people assembling for religious reasons and functions. Euphemistically, football is a new religion, and only football cathedrals in Europe like the Emirates, Old Trafford, Camp Nou, Anfield, Santiago Bernabeu, Alliance Arena, and San Siro attract thousands of young people to their sanctuaries. During his 2010 successful visit to the United Kingdom, however, Pope Benedict XVI was able to attract more than sixty thousand young people on one occasion. In his typical humility and theology, Pope Benedict XVI would say the young people were attracted to Christ, Our Joy.

It was amazing in an age of totalitarian secularism, atheism, agnosticism, and a tainted image of the Church owing to scandals over sexual abuse by Roman Catholic clergy to see young people in Miami, Trinidad, Tobago, and Manila spending long nights in vigil awaiting the beatification of John Paul II. On May 1, 1989, John Paul II addressed the youth in Madagascar in person. Since he was to be beatified on May 1, 2005, the youth in Madagascar vicariously felt connected to his beatification and spent nights in vigil, followed by celebrations on the day of his beatification.

The youth have an enormous amount of energy, which is sometimes used constructively or destructively by political leaders. Some Cuban youths were used by the U.S. government in 1961 in the abortive "Bay of Pigs" attempt to topple the government of Fidel Castro, the revolutionary leader. The youth in Kenya were at the helm of most of the violence after the disputed 2007/2008 presidential election. They were agents of politicians in Kenya.

Wojtyła's biography is seemingly incongruous with biographies of popes in modern times. While his predecessors, such as Benedict XV and Paul VI, talked of their years in the Pontifical Academy of Diplomacy, or as Pius XI, Pius XII, and John XXIII reminisced about their years in apostolic nunciatures around the world, John Paul II talked with nostalgia about his idiosyncratic experience with the youth in Poland. Reputed Church historian Norman Tanner, S.J., in an interview with the author, pointed out that John XXIII also had a very youthful and vigorous papacy, even though he became pope at the ripe old age of 76. Paul VI was the spiritual assistant of the Federation of Italian University Catholic Students (FUCI), (Rendina, 2002:599).

How idiosyncratic was John Paul II's youthful past? Karol Wojtyła's rapport with young people before 1978 was a harbinger of his Petrine youth diplomacy. From his early priestly assignment in Niegowić, St. Florian University Chaplaincy, to his eventual ascendancy to the offices of bishop, archbishop, and cardinal, Wojtyła more than bonded with the youth, which was a pastoral journey. The youth in his parish, chaplaincy, and diocese called him *Wujek,* "little uncle," (a Stalin-era nom de guerre,) to hide his priestly identity in anti-priestly Nazi and communist Poland. Sometimes as a young priest, *Wujek* was in the company of young unmarried ladies on trains and buses heading hiking, skiing, kayaking, trekking, and acting with old sleeping bags, blankets, and rucksacks as their main camping equipment. Just like Saint Don Bosco, Wojtyła used the passion of young people for sports as an efficient means of apostolic activity. Karol Wojtyła heeded the counsel of Saint Augustine of Hippo that if you wish to attract children and young people, you must share their interests and love what they love to induce them to love what you love.

Father Karol Wojtyła prepared young couples for marriage, and, via his youth groups, which came to be known as "Srodowisko," or "Rodzinka" (the little family), the youth felt totally at ease with him and would discuss a wide range of topics, ranging from sex, love, virginity, masturbation, and spirituality. No subject was too taboo and untouchable in their discussions. One of the "Srodowisko" members once said, "While he [Wujek] was among us, we felt that everything was all right.... We felt that we could discuss anything with him; we could talk about absolutely anything" (Weigel, 2010:41). No pope before him wedded couples. Saint John Paul II wedded Vittoria Janni (daughter of one of the Roman street cleaners) and her husband Mario Maltese. As pope, he often met young couples, and, on one occasion, told them that "getting children is the springtime of the family."

A priest discussing issues of sex with young people was unprecedented in communist-era pious Catholic Poland. It was headline news in Poland for a young priest to celebrate Mass on the riverbanks using overturned kayaks for the altar. On one of his treks, a youth named Zdzislaw Heydel cracked a joke, "Wujek, one day when you're pope, people will get indulgences for walking this trail with you on a moonless night" (Weigel,

1999:103). What a prophesy. Wojtyła took an active part in the chores during camping, such as burying garbage and lugging kayaks. It was therefore no accident or coincidence that during the funeral Mass of John Paul II, many members of Wojtyła's Srodowisko were seated directly behind the heads of state and other official government representatives.

Wojtyła believed that it is not enough for priests to just celebrate Mass. Priests ought to journey and accompany Christians in their search for, and understanding of, God. In Poland, he met with young couples, offered counseling, and baptized their children. As pope, he would continue with the same practice. In a conversation with Weigel in September 1997, John Paul II confessed that the idea of WYD could be traced back to his *Srodowisko* experience with the youth in Poland (1999:493). Yes, the background of a person influences his or her attitudes.

In his book, *Rise, Let Us Be On Our Way*, John Paul II acknowledged the instrumentality of his pre-papal experience with the youth in the innovation of WYD when he wrote, "In a sense, the WYD could be seen as a fruit of that experience" (2004:101). John Paul II was a very consistent person; his whole life had been a preparation for his Petrine office, because God prepares every person for their eventual offices. He carried his efficacious pre-papal youth ministry to the Vatican. In *Crossing the Threshold of Hope*, Saint John Paul II outlined the idiosyncratic character of his youth ministry in the following words:

> As a young priest and pastor I came to this way of looking at young people and at youth, and it has remained constant all these years. It is an outlook which also allows me to meet young people wherever I go. Every parish priest in Rome knows that my visits to the parish must conclude with a meeting between the Bishop of Rome and the young people of the parish. And not only in Rome, but anywhere the Pope goes, *he seeks out the young and the young seek him out. Actually, in truth, it is not the Pope who is being sought out at all* (1994:124).

As a young priest, Woytyla often went skiing and trekking with young intellectuals: physicists, engineers, and other professionals. During those outings with friends such as Jerzy Janik, who had a doctorate in physics, Wojtyła engaged them in intellectual discourses and was open to challenges. This initiative of dialogue with intellectuals also constituted part of his personal diplomacy. He would invite intellectuals such as Jewish philosopher Emmanuel Levinas to his summer residence for intellectual exchanges. Commenting on the early meetings with intellectuals, Saint John Paul II wrote, "Those meetings in Kraków still continue today, from time to time, in Rome or in Castel Gandolfo, thanks to the efforts of Professor Jerzy Janik" (2004:88). Those early experiences with the youth and young intellectuals prefigured some diplomatic initiatives of his pontificate. One of his friends described Wojtyła as a complete man, "he is pious, a scholar, a sportsman, a lover of music and art, and a boy at heart. All generations find they have something in common with him" (Oram, 1979:206).

Karol Wojtyła had a fruitful idiosyncratic experience with the youth in Poland before becoming pope in 1978. The young people called him *Wujek* ("little uncle"), to conceal his identity from the atheistic communist regime in Poland. He used the passion of the youth to help them know and build lasting relationships with God. As a result, skiing, kayaking, trekking, and acting with young people became avenues for evangelization for Karol Wojtyła. After 1978, Pope John Paul II carried his effective youth apostolate to Rome and to the world. During his pilgrimages in Italy and to the world, he sought out the youth and the youth magnetically responded for candid conversations with the man they fondly called *papa*. Together with young people across the globe, the pope initiated the World Youth Day, through which he accompanied them, socialized with them, and persuaded them to lead responsible lives.

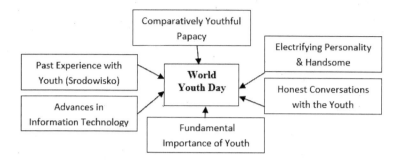

Fig. 7. Author's illustration of factors which impacted John Paul II's youth apostolate

CHAPTER TWELVE

BISHOPS, THE LAITY, AND ACCESSIBLE
PAPACY (TRACKS TWO AND FOUR DIPLOMACY)

There are two facets of Vatican diplomacy, namely the study of the pope as an international actor, and the Holy See's relation with the national branches of the Catholic Church. Just like nuncios, bishops are agents of Vatican diplomacy. Reputed historian Frank Coppa stated, "The Holy See's objectives are attained not only through formal diplomatic relations but also by means of the local bishops who provide another mechanism for communication with Rome" (1998:13). The pope cannot govern the whole Church alone. Some responsibility rests on bishops, who, just like the bishop of Rome, are also legitimate successors of the Apostles.

Popes seldom undo and contradict the teachings and precedents set by their predecessors. Some Church historians believe popes are bound by precedent. This explains why Pope Benedict XVI accompanied the youth in the World Youth Days held in Cologne, Sydney, and Madrid in the footsteps of his immediate predecessor. Pope Paul VI sat in some of the synod deliberations during his pontificate. John Paul II, except when he became very frail, sat in on most of the continental synod deliberations. He had a social personality and wanted to know firsthand the challenges of his brother bishops.

One of the oldest forms of collegiality is found in the quinquennial *ad limina Apostolorum* ("to the threshold of the Apostles") pilgrimages of bishops. During Saint John Paul II's pontificate, the *ad limina* visits became very personal, and visiting bishops had the chance to meet the pope personally on at least three occasions during the pilgrimage. During his morning Mass, breakfast, and dinner, some of the visiting bishops met with the pope, and the discussions continued at an informal level. John Cardinal Onaiyekan, Archbishop Emeritus of the Archdiocese of Abuja, describes his personal experience of the *ad limina* visits during the pontificate of John Paul II:

> He shows very keen interest in the reports that each bishop brings him. I have had three opportunities of such visits with him and each occasion is unforgettable. As you enter to meet him, he already has before him not only the map of the country and precise location of your diocese but also a short summary of the major outlines of the situation of your diocese ... he asks pointed questions which makes it clear that he really knows what you are talking about, that he is genuinely interested in the progress of the Church and appreciates the challenges you are facing (2016:315).

John Paul II knew the importance of bishops in the life of the Church. He had been appointed to many Synods of Bishops after the Council by Pope Paul VI.

One of the major criticisms levied against John Paul II was that he was authoritarian. Jesuit scholar Jean Marie Quenum, S.J., in an interview with this author, said that the pope appointed like-minded bishops who were theologically conservative. A priest confided in me that most of the bishops in John Paul II's long pontificate were chosen because they represented the opinions of the pope. In his opinion, the pope managed to make most of the bishops sing according to his tune and that was then called the Magisterium. This anonymous priest argued that strong alternative voices in the Church (bishops, theologians, and lay people), were all suppressed. People who did not agree with John Paul II's views became disaffected and experienced a cold wintertime. They left the Church because they did not feel welcome anymore. In fact, the view that Saint John Paul II only appointed to the episcopate men who danced according to his tune is not entirely true. He appointed independent-minded bishops who did not always subscribe to his views. Cardinals Carlo Maria Martini of Milan, Godfried Danneels of Belgium, and Walter Kasper are prime examples.

Some critics also hold that bishops were, to an extent, reduced to papal stooges or branch managers of an international non-governmental organization (NGO) during his pontificate. In some instances, it is argued that he bypassed episcopal conferences in his appointments of bishops. His appointment of Wolfgang Haas to the Diocese of Chur in Switzerland is an apt example. His appointment of Jean-Marie Lustiger of Paris was a very bold decision, considering his Jewish background. Archbishop Maurice Muhatia opined that it is the prerogative of the pope to appoint bishops. He said that it is fallacious to talk of the pope bypassing episcopal conferences, since episcopal conferences do not replace the pope but represent him. This explains why Canon 377 § 1 of *The Code of Canon Law* states: "The Supreme pontiff freely appoints bishops or confirms those lawfully elected." Silencing theologians and the withdrawal of licenses of dissidents to teach in Catholic universities, as was the case with Leonardo Boff, Hans Küng, and Charles Curran, *inter alia,* was seen by some as authoritarianism in the pontificate of John Paul II. According to historian John Whale, "Under John Paul II, "the Church was back to the process of anathematizing unorthodox opinions…. He listens to many, speaks with a few, and decides alone" (Whale, 1980:13).

Francis Teke Lysinge, Bishop Emeritus of the Diocese of Mamfe, Cameroon, in an interview with this author, stated that theology is not the faith of the Catholic Church, and theologians ought to be submissive to the faith and the Magisterium. Theologian Robert Murray, S.J. criticized the new *Catechism of the Catholic Church* for not affording a prominent place for theologians in it. John Paul II's appointment of the 80-year old Fr. Dezza as his personal delegate of the Society of Jesus when renowned Superior General Pedro Arrupe suffered a massive stroke and his suppression of the Jesuit Constitution have also been highlighted as grains of authoritarianism and dictatorship. Reflecting on the above situations, Bishop Lysinge explained that the pope intervened in crisis situations and sought to give direction, not necessarily because he was authoritarian.

Was John Paul II authoritarian? That has been subjected to a plethora of debates. Tanzanian theologian Laurenti Magessa advances that the word "authoritarian" is harsh when referring to John Paul II's papacy and that perhaps "disciplinarian" or "disciplined" is closer to the truth. Some writers attribute John Paul II's perceived authoritarianism or discipline to his idiosyncratic past. John Whale and Peter Hebblewaite in a way trace Wojtyła's perceived authoritarianism/discipline to his disciplinarian father. Wojtyła's mother died when he was nine, and until his twenty-first birthday, he lived with his father, eating, praying, and playing together. His father was a retired army officer, and since discipline is a martial trait, coupled with regimental training, some scholars think that his disciplined nature emanated from that. However, Wojtyła does not concur that his father was notoriously disciplinarian. Speaking to Andrè Frossard about his father, John Paul II said, "He was so hard on himself that he had no need to be hard on his son; his example alone was sufficient to inculcate discipline and a sense of duty ... the mere fact of seeing him on his knees had a decisive influence on my early years" (1982:14). Some forty-five years after his father's death, John Paul II wrote of his father, "His example was in a way my first seminary, a kind of domestic seminary" (1994:20).

Others contend that the pope took his model from what is contended to be an authoritarian Polish Church and culture. Papal biographer Tad Szulc held that John Paul II learned the rituals of absolute discipline during his time as a poverty-stricken manual laborer in Nazi-occupied Poland (1995:16). The Polish Church is said to be hierarchical and authoritarian. Cardinals Sapieha and Wyszyński, two of Wojtyła's mentors, were authoritarian. Some even argue that democracy and diversity are not really part of the traditional Polish culture and mentality (Turner & Turner, 1978:204–211). Polish researcher Radoslaw Malinowski, in an interview with this author, acknowledged that the Polish

Church was hierarchical but not *per se* authoritarian. Malinowski pointed out that the hierarchical nature of the Polish Church under communism was a strategy of survival, as "there was no time for a priest to question his bishop."

Although John Paul II's perceived authoritarianism has been a source of fierce debate, that his papacy was less aristocratic than that of his predecessors cannot be disputed. His papacy was to an extent accessible. His less aristocratic inclinations could be traced to his past. Most of his Italian predecessors hailed from aristocratic and noble families. In an interview with this author, Church historian Tony Murphy, MHM, explained, "Popes before John Paul II (for some centuries) had been Italian. Many of them came from upper-class families. They tended to treat the ordinary people as nobility treated them, i.e. with a good deal of reserve and aloofness." From birth, some eventual twentieth-century popes were raised with an eye towards the Petrine office. Benedict XV was a skinny, princely mannered prelate. Herman Goering, a top Nazi leader, confided in one of his friends that, for the first time in his life, he felt pangs of trepidation during his audience in 1938 with Pope Pius XI, the former Vatican librarian (Murphy, 1981:59).

Pius XII (Eugenio Pacelli) was like a Roman Melchizedek. He was educated around the Vatican premises. As a seminarian, Pacelli was personally known to Pope Leo XIII. Due to health reasons, Pacelli was granted extraordinary permission by Pope Leo XIII to study at the Almo Collegio Capranica. The Capranica is the oldest Roman college, founded in 1457 by Cardinal Domenico Capranica. Pacelli hailed from a family of lay canon lawyers. "The Pacelli family had been supplying the Holy See with lawyers since the early years of the 19th century" (Rychlak, 2000:3). Pacelli's grandfather, Marcantonio Pacelli, a lay canon lawyer, was an under-secretary in the papal ministry of finances. At the request of Pius IX, Marcantonio became one of the founders of the Holy See's official newspaper, *L'Osservatore Romano* (Rittner & Roth, 2002:15).

Pacelli's father, Filippo Pacelli, a lay canon lawyer, was head of the Bank of Rome and dean of the Sacra Rota Romana, or the

Consistory College. That body was composed of twelve distinguished lawyers of service to the Church (Rychlak, 2000:4). Pacelli's brother, Francesco Pacelli, also a lawyer, was among Pius XI's negotiating team with Italian Premier Benito Mussolini for the signing of the Lateran Treaty of 1929 (Kwitny: 1997:53). It was Francesco Pacelli who actually drafted the Lateran Treaty. Pius XII's father and grandfather were intensely loyal to the Church. Owing to instability and the assassination of Count Pellegrino Rossi on November 15, 1848, Pius IX fled to Gaeta in the kingdom of Naples accompanied by Pope Pius XII's grandfather, Marcantonio Pacelli (Woodward, 1929:286).

Church historian Francis Murphy described Pope Pius XII as "an omniscient, spiritual aristocrat to whose audiences in Saint Peter's or at Castel Gandolfo all the world flocked" (1981:73). In another instance, Francis Murphy also described the pope as "ascetic in his personal habits, omniscient in his intellectual aspirations, endowed with the gift of total recall, unswerving in his devotional activities, affable though reticent, thoughtful of subordinates, and eloquent and impenetrable as a personality" (1981:58). More still, Pope Pius XII "looked like a casting director's dream of a pope, lean, remote, scrupulously ascetic in gesture and expression" (Rychlak, 2000:108). The same pope famously said, "I need executants and not collaborators."

Sociologists hold that culture is learned via socialization. Pius XII's pontificate was, to an extent, inaccessible. As observed during his student days in Rome, Hans Burgman, revealed, "But high on his *Sedes Gestatoria* he was out of reach." (2010:56). Hungarian-born American historian, István Déak, noted that, in recent times, no other pope surrounded himself with more pomp and none enforced a more rigid etiquette than Pius XII (2000:44). A tendency to snootiness is a trait of monarchs. British journalist and academic John Cornwell recorded that "the pontiff's (Pius XII) funeral was no less resplendent than his coronation" (1999:357).

Noticeably, after the death of Luigi Maglione in 1944, Pope Pius XII did not appoint a secretary of state for the last 14 years of his pontificate. His private secretary, Robert Leiber, strangely found it difficult to approach the pope. Because of his proclivity for isolation, he ate with his housekeeper of more than forty years, Josephine Lehnert, known as Mother Pasqualina, or the "powerful virgin" in the Vatican (Coppa, 1998:200). Mother Pasqualina's rule over the papal household in the 1950s earned her the title *la papessa*, the popess. She was scornfully ejected from the Vatican by some cardinals the very day Pius XII died and took refuge in the convent at the North American College, bringing the deceased pontiff's pet parakeets with her (Weigel, 2017:123). Similarly, Paul VI was born into an aristocratic family and was a lifelong Vatican diplomat. Perhaps because of fear of the crowd and ill health, especially in the 1970s, he ate alone and was a forlorn figure, although he made efforts to make his papacy accessible.

All the major themes of John Paul II's papacy could be traced to the defining events in his life, including, most prominently, his experience of living under the Nazi and communist regimes. Records show that Cardinal Wojtyła was a less aristocratic and more down to earth prelate. To see his colleague, Stefan Cardinal Wyszyński, one had to book appointments and sit in queues. To see Cardinal Wojtyła, one only needed to avail himself or herself in front of his office and was received. The saying that "one came to see a cardinal and ended up seeing a brother" applied to Pope St. John Paul II.

One day, while Cardinal Karol Wojtyła was climbing the Tatra Mountains very close to the Czechoslovakia boundary, he was stopped by a policeman guarding the border. His simple alpinist outfit could not distinguish him from any other alpinist, except by the small metal cross on his wind jacket. "Identification," ordered the policeman. The archbishop of Kraków immediately showed him his passport, identifying him as "Karol Wojtyła, Cardinal of the Roman Church." Where did you steal it?" the policeman asked rudely. "I did not steal it, it's mine," he answered softly. When it became apparent that he could not convince the officer that he was a Roman Catholic prelate, the cardinal invited the officer to have a drink in the not-too-distant mountain hut.

"We emptied some drinks and became friends," related Cardinal Wojtyła; "the policeman let me go at the end, but I think that he remained convinced that the document was indeed forged or stolen."

Wojtyła's lack of concern for comfort, coupled by his simplicity, could be traced to the humble background of his family. Franz Cardinal König of Vienna met Wojtyła in 1963, and was particularly struck by the then-archbishop's shabby cassock and battered hat. The pope's popular meal, breakfast, became a working session. Unlike most of his predecessors, he seldom breakfasted alone. Journalists, lay people, women, philosophers, and old friends were invited to his breakfast table and morning Mass. Dr. Jerome Lujeune, who represented John Paul II during Soviet leader Leonid Brezhnev's funeral on November 15, 1982, was a regular visitor to the pope's breakfast table. Lejeune, a lifelong friend of Karol Wojtyła, served as President of the Pontifical Academy for Life for a few weeks before his death in April 1994. Lejeune has been named "Servant of God" by the Catholic Church, and his cause for sainthood is being postulated by the Abbey of Saint Wandrille in France.

Influenced by the Council's documents, and most especially *Lumen Gentium,* which states that the laity in their own distinct vocations are a crucial part of the Church, John Paul II was keen to implement the Council's decisions by calling for more active participation of the laity in the life of the Church. The word laity comes from the Greek term *laos,* meaning *the people.* Generally speaking, it refers to the vast majority of Catholics who are not ordained ministers. English theologian and poet Saint John Henry Newman, when asked for his opinion on the laity, responded simply, "The Church would look strange without them."

As archbishop of Kraków, Karol Wojtyła set up the council for the laity and tried to understand the documents of the Council together with them in his diocese. As bishop, he wrote a book on the role of the laity in the Polish Church, *The Foundations of Renewal.* He worked with the laity, preparing young couples for marriage, even as bishop. Wojtyła had also been the chairperson of the Commission for Lay Apostolate in the Polish Episcopate. Thus, as pope, he sought to relive his earlier experience with the laity.

One of the most important diplomats in the Holy See's diplomatic service during John Paul II's papacy was a lay person, Joaquin Navarro-Valls, head of the Vatican's press office (1984–2006). For the first time in history, a woman, Mary Ann Glendon, the Learned Hand Professor of Law at Harvard University, led the Vatican's diplomatic delegation to the important 1995 Beijing Conference on "Women: Action for Equality, Development and Peace." Fourteen out of the twenty-two members of the Holy See's delegation were women. It was a first time a majority of a Holy See delegation had been composed of women. In traditional bilateral and multilateral diplomatic negotiations, the minister of foreign affairs was the *de facto* and *de jure* leader of the delegation. However, in recent times, the subject matter of a diplomatic meeting is a consequential factor in deciding the leadership of a diplomatic delegation.

Archbishop Maurice Muhatia pointed out that it was only logical and appropriate for a competent woman like Mary Ann Glendon to lead the Holy See's delegation to a conference whose subject matter was women, equality, peace, and development. Her *curriculum vitae* proved that she was better equipped to lead the delegation because she is an expert on comparative family law and international human rights law. Canon 228 §1 of *The Code of Canon Law (Codex Iuris Canonici) states*, "Lay people who are found to be suitable are capable of being admitted by the sacred Pastors to those ecclesiastical offices and functions which, in accordance with the law, in accordance with the provisions of the law, they can discharge."

Mary Ann Glendon was the highest-ranking woman in the Catholic Church when she was appointed head of the Pontifical Academy of Social Sciences, a body created by Pope John Paul II in 1994 and whose findings helped the pope in his social teachings. Professor Werner Arber, President of the Academy, once wrote, "I think that once in a while the pope takes our findings on board and incorporates them into his knowledge. His decisions are then influenced by them." Pope Benedict XVI once asked the Academy for information and scientific guidance on matters relating to evolution, and to the end of life (Mickens, 2011:29). In 2007, U.S. President George W. Bush appointed Mary Ann Glendon as the United States Ambassador to the Holy See.

Even though John Paul II categorically put an end to all talks surrounding the ordination of women to the sacred priesthood, the pope believed in the great potential of women. Idiosyncratically, some papal biographers have noted that he is the only modern pope who grew up around women. He had female friends at school and collaborated with women in his scholarly endeavors before becoming pope. The pope's pontifical motto *"Totus Tuus,"* which means "Totally Yours!" expresses his total devotion to Mary, the Mother of God. Due to his love and respect for women, on the occasion of the Marian Year in 1988, Pope John Paul II wrote a beautiful apostolic letter, *Mulieris Dignitatem*, on the dignity and vocation of women. The pope paid tribute to women for their contributions to the Church:

> Therefore *the Church gives thanks for each and every woman:* for mothers, for sisters, for wives; for women consecrated to God in virginity; for women dedicated to the many human beings who await the gratuitous love of another person; for women who watch over the human persons in the family, which is the fundamental sign of the human community; for women who work professionally, and who at times are burdened by a great social responsibility; for *"perfect"* women and for "weak" women—for all women as they have come forth from the heart of God in all the beauty and richness of their femininity; as they have been embraced by his eternal love; as, together with men, they are pilgrims·on this earth, which is the temporal "homeland" of all people and is transformed sometimes into a "valley of tears"; as they assume, together with men, *a*

common responsibility for the destiny of humanity according to daily necessities and according to that definitive
destiny which the human family has in God himself, in
the bosom of the ineffable Trinity (1988, *par.* 31).

In the patristic era, the laity played designated roles in the
Church. As observed in the markets of Constantinople in 379 A.D.
by one of the Cappadocian Fathers, Gregory Nazianzus, lay people were seen debating complicated Christological and Trinitarian
controversies, such as the divinity and humanity of Christ, and
the concept of *Homoousios* (Jesus Christ is of one substance and
being with God the Father). Saint John Henry Newman recommended that the laity be well educated in the faith and be con-
sulted by the Church before making serious decisions. Vatican II
was very pro-laity, and its document *Apostolicam Actuositatem* was
devoted to the laity.

Pope St. John Paul II's concern for the laity was reflected also
in the canonization of saints during his pontificate. Prior to his
election in 1978, the 262 predecessors of John Paul II canonized
just over three hundred men and women. It is argued that during
John Paul II's papacy, the Church became a saint factory, with
John Paul II canonizing over 300 and beatifying more than 700
men and women (Bernstein & Politi, 1999:393). There is a joke that
he raised many to the altar of sainthood because he was ordained
a priest on the Feast of All Saints, November 1, 1946. Polish Franciscan Maximilian Kolbe, who heroically accepted death in place
of a man who had been sentenced to die of starvation at
Auschwitz in 1940, was the first saint canonized by Pope John
Paul II. Hans Urs von Balthasar, who died two days before he was
due to receive the honorary red Cardinalate hat from John Paul
II, is the theologian of sainthood. Balthasar identified two categories of saints: "exemplars" and "God's prime numbers." Exemplars are persons who attained sanctity by living out their
vocations in exemplary, but not path-breaking, ways. It could be
a mother, father, priest, carpenter or footballer. God's prime numbers are persons declared saints by the Church because of the

exemplary way in which they lived out their idiosyncratic/singular vocations, embodying some previously unexplored or underappreciated aspect of God's design for the Church. The founders of new religious orders, such as Saint Francis of Assisi, whose radical embrace of poverty and nature had not been witnessed before, are notable examples (Weigel, 2001:176). John Paul II canonized both exemplars and God's prime numbers in big numbers.

In an interview with this author, Congolese-born moral theologian Bènèzet Bujo, S.J., argued that the Church declares people saints as role models for others to emulate. Similarly, Karl Rahner, S.J., the great German theologian of the twentieth century, pointed out that saints "are the imitators and the creative models of the holiness which happens to be right for, and is the task of, their particular age. They create a new style; they prove that a certain form of life and activity is a really genuine possibility; they show experientially that one can be a Christian even in 'this' way; they make such a type of person believable as a Christian type" (Ellsberg, 1997:34).

Aquiline Tarimo, S.J., in an interview with this author, strongly opined that holiness and orthodoxy were not the only yardsticks for sainthood during John Paul II's papacy. According to him, the pontiff's desire to raise local heroes and heroines to the altar of sainthood during his pilgrimages also informed some of the beatifications and canonizations. George Weigel expressed a similar sentiment in noting that the beatification of Lorenzo Ruiz of the Philippines was not only based on his holiness and orthodoxy, but because the pope wanted to show his respect for Asian cultures (1999:391).

Remarkably, Saint John Paul II canonized many lay persons, an uncommon practice in the annals of the Church. Among them were Marie-Clémentine Anuarite Negapeta, a Zairean woman killed by Colonel Pierre Colombe, a Simba soldier, while defending her virginity; Peter ToRot, a catechist from Papua New Guinea, murdered because he refused to stop instructing Christian faithful on the island during World War II; and Gianna Berreta Molla, who died because she refused to have a tumor removed, since it would have resulted in the abortion of her child. Molla is a wonderful and laudable example of the dignity of human life (Bernstein & Politi: 1996:393–394).

In the analysis of Bernstein and Politi, John Paul II canonized many because he was eager to show the fecundity of the Church. In line with the assumption of Track Four diplomacy that when the people lead, the leaders will follow, John Paul II's diplomacy cut across the social stratum of society. He met the sick and the elderly in person and wrote to them that old age is not precisely a time for withdrawal. He visited Rome's *Regina Coeli* Prison, where he asked for clemency on behalf of the prisoners.

In his actions, John Paul II built on the example of some of his predecessors in interacting with ordinary people. Early in his papacy, in 1958, Pope Saint John XXIII visited the Bambino Gesu Hospital for children and shortly afterwards, for his first Christmas, he went to *Regina Coeli* Prison in Rome. The newly elected pope, animated and clearly comfortable in this unusual setting, shared with the inmates the somewhat surprising tale of his own cousin, who had been imprisoned in the same jail after his conviction for poaching. After his warm and gracious words to the inmates, the pope promised to remember all of them, as well as their wives and sisters, in his nightly rosary prayers. Upon hearing this, they burst into a heartfelt applause. Very poignantly, those who were imprisoned for life fell to their knees before Good Pope John XXIII (Martin, 2010).

Pope John XXIII was born into a poor peasant family. As pope, he walked on foot with his famous old red hat, greeting the Roman populace in the following words, "First of all, I seek your benevolence for this man who simply wants to be your brother, friendly, approachable, and understanding" (Rendina, 2002:596). Indeed, he dropped the *majestatis* "We" and replaced it with "I" in his famous encyclical *Pacem in Terris* (1963). The pronoun "We" is part of the royal pronoun. Monarchs customarily say, "We are fine," instead of, "I am fine," even when referring to themselves and not to the entire royal household or subjects. Pope John's rounded façade made him easily loved by the people and sometimes he said that he forgot that he was pope.

Paul VI, although intellectually sophisticated, genuinely attempted to be less aristocratic. He abolished the Papal Courts. Although with a very ephemeral 33 days pontificate, John Paul I was the first pope to reject the grandiose coronation of pontiffs, and he also replaced the *majestatis* plural "We" for "I". The smiling pope addressed the Roman populace saying, "I do not have the *sapientia cordis* of Pope John XXIII, nor the education and experience of Pope Paul VI, but I am in their position and I must try to serve the Church" (Rendina, 2002:605).

In summary, Pope John Paul II had an accessible papacy. He opened the Church to all categories of people and went against the grain to entrust important ecclesiastical responsibilities to the laity. He knew the importance of his brother bishops in the life of the Church and always made time for them, especially during *ad limina* pilgrimages and in his pilgrimages to the people of God around the world. His humble background and pre-papal experiences contributed to his very accessible papacy.

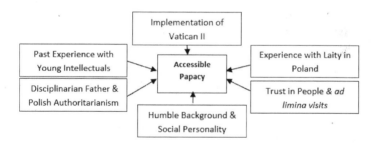

Fig. 8. Author's illustration of the impact of John Paul II's idiosyncratic variables in his relations with bishops and laity (accessible papacy).

CHAPTER THIRTEEN
DIPLOMATIC RELATIONS
(TRACK ONE DIPLOMACY)

The pope is the only Christian religious leader with the prerogative and international obligation to engage fully in bilateral and multilateral diplomacy, by virtue of the fact that he heads the State of the Vatican City and the Holy See. The diplomatic activities of the Holy See are directed by the secretariat of state (headed by the secretary of state), through the section for relations with states. Respect for international law and support for multilateral diplomacy is the fourth principle of papal diplomacy (Lajolo, 2005:26).

The subject-focused multilateral diplomacy gained prominence in the twentieth century because of a plethora of transnational issues of common global concerns. More still, smaller countries gain leverage in diplomacy through multilateral organizations and are able to influence world politics better than when acting on an individual basis (Rouke, 1997:291). Extensive establishment of bilateral diplomatic ties has been considered by some scholars of papal diplomacy, such as Robert Araujo, S.J., as John Paul II's main diplomatic legacy (Zenith, 2005).

One of the main principles of papal diplomacy is that, unlike states, the Holy See's diplomatic actions are not guided and informed by pursuits of national interest. John Paul II explained to the U.N. General Assembly in 1995: "The man who is speaking to you has no temporal power, no ambition to compete with you. As a matter of fact, we have nothing to ask, no question to raise; at most a desire to formulate, that of being allowed to serve you in the area of competence, with disinterestedness, in humility and love" (Lajolo, 2006:29).

The principle of sovereignty is an essential prerequisite for the establishment of diplomatic state relations. Cameroon, for example established diplomatic ties with the Holy See in 1966. That relationship was impossible before 1960 because the then-territories of French and English Cameroun/Cameroon were still being administered by the Anglo-French joint Condominium. They were not yet sovereign states, as French and English Cameroun/Cameroon gained independence in 1960 and 1961, respectively. By October 1978, when Karol Wojtyła became pope, the Holy See had diplomatic ties with 84 juridical personalities. At his death in 2005, the number had more than doubled to 174. Great Britain and the United States reestablished diplomatic ties with the Holy See in 1982 and 1985, respectively. Mali (1979), Denmark (1982), Chad (1988), Mexico (1992), Cambodia (1994), and Cook Islands (1999), are a few examples of countries that established diplomatic relations with the Holy See during the pontificate of John Paul II.

Article 3 of the Vienna Convention on Diplomatic Relations (1961) identified representation as one of the principal functions of diplomacy. In his view, John Paul II saw diplomatic emissaries as representatives of peoples and not just governments (Sylvestrini, 1999:xiii). Article 2 of the Vienna Convention states: "The establishment of diplomatic relations between states, and of permanent diplomatic missions, take place by *mutual* consent." Papal historian Jada Patrisio, in an interview with this author, stated that John Paul II was open-minded, and with respect and solidarity, was willing to establish diplomatic ties with newly independent developing nations such as Mozambique (1995), São Tomé and Principé (1984), Zimbabwe (1980), Eritrea (1995), and Seychelles (1985). In one of his visits to Africa, John Paul II explained, "It is nice to see countries whom a few years ago were under colonial rule and now they are enjoying freedom" (1980:24). Coming from a country which had been partitioned, repeatedly occupied, and victimized, John Paul II understood perfectly well the meaning of freedom and sovereignty. Even at the time of his election, Poland, a particularly Catholic country, had never established diplomatic ties with the Holy See because it was under communist rule.

Pope John Paul II was the most traveled pope and, perhaps, world leader, in reliably recorded history. As Bishop Szczepan Wesoly, a long time Vaticanist, explained, "The difference between the Vatican now and under Pius XII is more than you can imagine. Pius XII left the Vatican two or three times in sixteen years, Paul VI was afraid of the crowds. John Paul II gets rejuvenated by crowds" (Kwitny, 1997:501). Inevitably, Pope John Paul II's visits around the globe played a role in the establishment of diplomatic relations. They facilitated the process that led to diplomatic breakthroughs, since, after his historic visits to countries, many opted for ties with the Holy See.

Leader-to-leader diplomacy achieved via globe-trotting of world leaders normally fosters mutual understanding and friendships between leaders, and subsequently leads to diplomatic relations between states. Because of his numerous meetings with Soviet leader Mikhail Gorbachev (leader-to-leader diplomacy), the late U.S. President Ronald Reagan acknowledged, "There was chemistry between us that produced something very close to a friendship.... I liked Gorbachev" (1990:72). Perhaps, had it not been for the presidential retreat of President Sadat of Egypt, Jimmy Carter of the U.S., and Prime Minister Begin of Israel in Maryland, the Camp David Accords of 1978, which in a way normalized Egyptian-Israeli relations, may not have materialized. John Paul's meetings with leaders during his travels were instrumental in the Holy See's diplomatic relations with states during his pontificate.

After his visit to the Synagogue in Rome in 1986, Chief Rabbi Elio Toaff asked John Paul II to establish diplomatic relations with the State of Israel. In 1982 and 1984, the Holy See reestablished diplomatic ties with Britain and the United States, respectively. Papal diplomacy scholar Robert Araujo, S.J., argued that "these two re-establishments were largely due to the efforts of John Paul II in his apostolic visits to both countries prior to reestablishing diplomatic relations" (2005).

Furthermore, as explained by Bishop Szczepan Wesoly, John Paul II created a revolution via his journeys by pulling down the wall of secrecy that surrounded the papacy (Kwitny, 1997:501). Through his visits, myths surrounding the Holy See were also demystified. World leaders interacted with the pope and got a better understanding of the mission of the Holy See. Through his journeys, people saw the pope in person, world leaders took walks with the pope, others had papal embraces, some saw the pope's eyes wreathed in tears, angry, kissing babies, and came to the resolution or denouement that the pope was also human and one of them. World leaders also took advantage of this demystification of the papacy and flocked to the Vatican in return. As in antiquity, Rome remains the drawing room of international diplomacy, and it was unthinkable for any world leader not to consult Rome before major diplomatic maneuvers. "With Mikhail Gorbachev's pilgrimage to the Vatican a power was acknowledged which far transcends the quantified mass of tank divisions" (McDermott, 1993:xi).

Pope Paul VI started the process of demystifying the papacy through his international journeys (Hebblethwaite, 1978:11). Some outcomes of such visits were the establishment of diplomatic ties. At the end of his visit to the Vatican in 1989, President Mikhail Gorbachev asked Saint John Paul II to reciprocate and establish diplomatic ties with Moscow. The establishment of diplomatic relations of a *Special Nature* with the Russian Federation in 1991 was a fruit of Gorbachev's historic visit.

John Paul II's international visits boosted the prestige and image of the Holy See. His premier visit to Poland in June 1979 held the imagination of the world and held the media hostage for ten days. Furthermore, his efforts towards the demise of communism in Eastern Europe made the image of the Holy See even more esteemed. Due to the great prestige of the Holy See, many world leaders wanted a possible form of association with the pope, either via visits or establishment of diplomatic relations.

Structural realists such as Kenneth Waltz argue that the nature of the international system informs the foreign policies of states.

Ipso facto, the end of the Cold War in 1989 gifted the Holy See with the opportunity to establish diplomatic ties with many former communist allies and satellites. The implosion of Eastern European communism (1989) and the disintegration of the Soviet Union (1991) were prerequisites for the Holy See's diplomatic relations with the communist satellites. Globalization is the most visible post-Cold War feature, and its slogan, "making the world a global village," was an important variable in the establishment of diplomatic ties during John Paul II's papacy. Owing to its transnational character, Archbishop Maurice Muhatia in an interview with this author, explained that the Catholic Church is the fullest expression of globalization; because diplomatic ties strengthen the unity of states, it was only logical for Saint John Paul II to seek diplomatic relations with countries formerly behind the Iron Curtain: Poland (July 1989), Hungary (February 1990), Soviet Union (March 1990), Czechoslovakia (April 1990), Romania (May 1990), Bulgaria (December 1990), Albania (September 1991), and Lithuania (1991).

Pope John Paul's magnetic personality and talents also contributed to the many diplomatic relations established with the Holy See during his papacy. He had a good rapport with many world leaders, and the huge number of dignitaries who showed up for his funeral in 2005 is a testament to that. Reflecting on John Paul's diplomatic legacy, Robert Araujo, S.J. acknowledged that John Paul II's personality played a decisive role. He wrote, "The Holy Father was a gifted man who knew how to work constructively with people from all regions of the world regardless of race, ethnicity, or religion" (Zenit, 2005).

In summation, the ultimate goal of papal diplomacy rests on the protection and promotion of the ultimate values of human existence. This explains why, in most of his addresses to ambassadors and plenipotentiaries accredited to the Holy See, John Paul II repeatedly reiterated the importance of absolute values. According to researcher Bernard O'Connor, "Every repetition adds significant nuance, expands upon detail, broadens an application, deepens and diversifies the basis for perception" (2005:182). The essence of John Paul II's diplomacy is captured in his 1979 address to the U.N. General Assembly:

> This relationship is what provides the reason for *all political activity*, whether national or international, for in the final analysis this activity comes *from man*, is exercised *by man* and is *for man*. And if political activity is cut off from this fundamental relationship and finality, if it becomes in a way its own end, it loses much of its reason to exist. Even more, it can also give rise to a specific alienation; it can become extraneous to man; it can come to contradict humanity itself. In reality, what justifies the existence of any political activity is service to man, concerned and responsible attention to the essential problems and duties of his earthly existence in its social dimension and significance, on which also the good of each person depends.

The above address is an incisive and synthetic description of Christian humanism or, perhaps, theistic humanism. It conveyed the mind and thinking of the Pope John Paul II. It is evident that the human person was the "axis" of John Paul II's thinking, philosophy, and diplomacy. In his thinking, the human person, who is created in the image and likeness of God *(imago dei)*, is the subject and object of every political activity. The essence of politics should be service to humanity. The first foundational principle of Catholic Social Doctrine states that the state has the obligation to defend the inalienable rights of every human being.

Saint John Paul II addressed the United Nations at the height of the Cold War when human rights were seriously curtailed in the Soviet Union. To a great extent, the above excerpt from John Paul II's 1979 address to the United Nations was a direct challenge and political statement to the Soviet Union, where the ideals of communism took precedence over the dignity of the human being. Consequently, just before Pope John Paul II delivered that address, Agostino Cardinal Casaroli, the cautious Vatican secretary of state, meticulously went through the draft text of his speech, eliminating references to human rights and dignity that the Soviet Union and its satellites might have found offensive. The fearless John Paul II simply restored the references which had been chopped off by Casaroli. The inviolable rights of human beings had to be defended. John Paul II's understanding of the human person and politics was different from the inhumane humanism of the atheistic communist regimes that objectivized the human being in the Soviet Union.

Friedrich Nietzsche's *Will-to-Power* perhaps captures best humankind's driving force in life in the twentieth century. Human beings want to lord it over others and take the place of the *Superman*, as Nietzsche postulated. The relationship between human beings has been characterized by tooth and claws, which is based on the jungle policy of the "survival of the fittest." The desire of human beings to subjugate the *Other* finally gave rise to totalitarian systems in the twentieth century. The annihilation of human beings by fellow human beings in the infamous Holocaust says it all. The summit of it all was Nazism, communism, and fascism. Perhaps this explains why George Weigel accorded John Paul II's diplomacy the hearty encomiums of restoring to politics its lost and much trampled upon dignity, and, at the same time, keeping politics within its proper sphere (2000).

Fig. 9. Author's illustration of John Paul II's idiosyncratic variables and factors which impacted the Holy See's establishment of diplomatic ties with states

CHAPTER FOURTEEN
EPILOGUE

The overall objective of this book is to examine the impact of John Paul II's idiosyncratic variables on his diplomacy. This is a historical academic endeavor since it principally digs into biographies, autobiographies, and other literatures to decipher the impact of the pope's early childhood personality formation, past experience, and the history of Poland, on his conduct of pontifical diplomacy. Consequently, I made comprehensive use of historical details in the thematic analyses.

There are many idiosyncratic variables. However, according to my findings via primary and secondary sources, some of the idiosyncratic variables which conspicuously impacted the image, nature, function, and character of John Paul II's diplomacy include his Polish nationality, Cracovian experience, experience as a clandestine seminarian, clandestine membership in the Rhapsodic Theatre, clandestine membership in the "Living Rosary," pre-papal youthful experience, pre-papal travels, extrovert personality, fearlessness, experience of Nazism and communism, distinct worldview, knowledge of Marxism, poetic history, youthful age, Jewish camaraderie, *Slavonic* spirituality, early writings, and influential figures in his life (Cyprian Norwid and Jan Tyranowski).

In his *Erasmus Lecture* "Papacy and Power," George Weigel, appraised the important role of Pope Saint John Paul II's idiosyncratic variables on his diplomacy as follows:

> It is tempting to see John Paul II's public accomplishment as expression of his singular personal experience.

His 'culture-first' view of history and his bold confidence in the political efficacy of moral truth have indeed been deeply influenced by his curriculum vitae. His Slavic sensitivity to spiritual power in history (prefigured in Soloviev and paralleled in Solzhenitsyn); his Polish convictions about the cultural foundations of nationhood (shaped by lifelong immersion in the literary works of Mickiewicz, Norwid, and Slowacki); his experience in the underground resistance during World War II and his leadership in a cultural based resistance to communism from 1947–197—all of these are, if you will, distinctively 'Wojtyłan' experiences (2000).

From available data and inferences, I arrived at the denouement, resolution, and illative sense that John Paul II's idiosyncratic variables influenced his conduct of papal diplomacy. Saint John Henry Newman, an Anglican convert to Catholicism, in his most technically dense work, *Grammar of Assent*, defined illative sense as how the convergence of factors reaches a point where probabilities, added together, drive us to certainties. The extent to which the various idiosyncratic variables of John Paul II impacted his pontifical diplomacy varied. The relationship between the two main variables of the book, namely idiosyncratic variables and pontifical diplomacy, is not tangibly or empirically verifiable. Thus, in the study of diplomacy, just like in other social sciences, researchers often experience a methodological quagmire because of the lack of empirical verification as cogently exemplified in the physical sciences. However, from interviews and available secondary data, it is evident that John Paul II's idiosyncratic variables indubitably shaped the conduct and character of his diplomacy.

The second objective of this book is to examine the various tracks of diplomacy in the pontifical diplomacy of John Paul II. In their Multi-Track diplomatic system, Louise Diamond and John McDonald uniquely identified nine distinct tracks of diplomacy. I analyzed Pope John Paul II's conduct of diplomacy within the framework of those nine tracks. John Paul II was not a career papal diplomat like most of his predecessors. He may not have been very conscious of the expression of the elements of the different tracks of diplomacy in his papal diplomacy. However, students of diplomacy and international relations can analyze his diplomacy within the framework of the Multi-Track diplomatic system.

John Paul II's diplomacy was an intermittent interplay of all nine tracks of Multi-Track diplomatic theory. However, most of his diplomatic initiatives were conspicuously a combination of Track One and Track Two diplomacy (dual diplomacy). His diplomatic endeavors were unofficially informed by his idiosyncratic variables and personal initiatives and not *per se* by virtue of his office as head of a juridical personality under international law (the Holy See). Saint John Paul II's premier mediation in the Beagle Channel boundary dispute between Argentina and Chile (1978) is an example of unofficial diplomacy. His diplomacy was predominantly Track One and a Half and Track Four via his World Youth Days, although other tracks to a lesser extent were expressed in his pontificate.

Note worthily, John Paul II's Multi-Track diplomacy was very potent and provided an avant-garde in the history of papal diplomacy. Reflecting on the potency of John Paul II's public diplomacy, George Weigel wrote in his *Erasmus Lecture* in New York in 2000, "John Paul II's accomplishment has provided empirical ballast for intellectual and moral challenges to several potent modern theories of politics, including French revolutionary Jacobinism, Marxism-Leninism, and utilitarianism" (2000). By conducting international diplomacy via persuasion, Saint John Paul II civilized and ethically edified international diplomacy.

The third objective of the study aimed at examining the innovations in the conduct of pontifical diplomacy initiated by John Paul II. The hallmark of pontifical diplomacy is continuity in diversity. Popes seldom undo precedents set by their predecessors. However, every incumbent pope idiosyncratically pursues the diplomacy of his predecessors, since no pope is a photocopy of another pope. Pope Benedict XVI was in Madrid in August 2011 for the World Youth Day, a strategy of evangelization and diplomatic initiative commenced by his immediate predecessor, John Paul II. Popes customarily build on the foundation laid by their predecessors in their own unique ways, as informed by their unique histories, experiences, and personalities.

In an interview with this author, Archbishop Alain Paul Lebeaupin, a seasoned papal diplomat, pointed out that Pope John Paul II did not *per se* change the diplomacy of the Holy See, but his idiosyncratic variables and personality impacted the image of pontifical diplomacy during his papacy. There were conspicuous innovations in John Paul II's pontifical diplomacy, even though one can see decipherable antecedents and prefiguration in the diplomacies of his predecessors. Pope John XXIII exhibited a very vigorous and youthful papacy. Pope Paul VI was chaplain of the Federation of Italian University Catholic Students. World Youth Day was an innovation of John Paul II. His idiosyncratic past experience with young people was instrumental. The hallmark of John Paul II's public diplomacy was his papal travels. However, he built on the precedent set by Paul VI, who in the modern era, began the tradition of the semi-itinerant papacy.

The prime role played by the laity in John Paul II's diplomacy was, to an extent, a novelty. It was only during his pontificate in 1995 that a lay woman led a Vatican diplomatic delegation to the Conference on Women and Development in Beijing. It was during his pontificate that a lay person (Joaquin Navarro-Valls), and not the traditional Roman collared man, was in charge of articulating the policies and mission of the Holy See. However, lay persons also played some role in the diplomacy of previous pontiffs. Francesco Pacelli, a sibling of Pope Pius XII, was among the Vatican team that negotiated the signing of the Lateran Treaty in 1929.

Pope Saint John Paul II's papacy was accessible and less aristocratic. However, his immediate predecessor, Pope John Paul I, had a much less aristocratic papacy, even though it lasted only thirty-three days. That he did not yield to the majestic coronation ceremony and objected to being carried around on the *sedia ges-tatoria* tells it all. Paul VI made intentional efforts to have his pa-pacy accessible, although he seemingly had a phobia for the crowd. Conclusively, there were innovations in the conduct of pontifical diplomacy by John Paul II, although not without prece-dents.

Lessons from John Paul II's Diplomacy
Efficacy of Soft Power in International Diplomacy

The strategist paradigm, a component of the realist school of in-ternational diplomacy, sees hard power as the major instrument of foreign policy. Unlike soft power, states invest enormous ener-gies and resources in hard power politics. The U.S. is considered the only superpower because of her superior military, economic, diplomatic, and cultural might. In contemporary diplomacy, power comes from the barrel of a gun. Contrary to the realist school, scholars such as Joseph Nye Jr. assert that hard power alone does not suffice in international diplomacy. The old adage goes, "He, who conquers by force, conquers partly." The assassi-nation of Osama Bin Laden did not guarantee an end to interna-tional terrorism. The U.S., with all her military power, was sent to her knees after the unfortunate 9/11 ordeal. States seldom in-vest in soft power.

Former British Prime Minister Lord Salisbury once observed that posterity does not treat kindly the achievements of a diplo-mat, "[A] diplomatist's glory is the most ephemeral of all the forms of that transient reward" (1905:11). However, upon the death of John Paul II, the most scrupulous adorers of hard power, such as Mikhail Gorbachev, Henry Kissinger, and Helmut Kohl, levied encomiums on him as the most influential political figure of the last quarter of the 20th century. The territorial surface of the Vatican is 108.9 acres. The Vatican works on a small budget. Yet, under John Paul II, the Vatican became the drawing room of in-ternational politics, where world leaders queued up like clients to diplomatically consult with him. Just as the U.S. is the sole economic superpower, the Vatican under John Paul II was the indisputable moral superpower in the world. John Paul II was without any notable hard power, using rather his precious asserts of soft power: public evangelism, the prestige of the Holy See, and an electrifying and attractive personality. The dream of every legal personality became the establishment of diplomatic ties with the Holy See. Policy makers should invest in twisting the minds of states (soft power) and not just twisting the arms and legs of other units in the international system (hard power). Other than boots on the ground, soft power will inevitably play a key role in any successful fight against terrorism, radicalization and ISIS in Syria and Iraq. Implanting the culture of peace and life against the culture of illegality and death, with real security being relationships rather than forceful persuasion (hard power), could make the world peaceful and safe for democracy.

John Paul II believed in *plus ratio quam vis* ("reason rather than force"). States should think of investing both in hard and soft power, because a combination of both powers, which Joseph Nye Jr. calls "smart power," would definitely yield greater dividends (Nye, 2007:393). The United States will be more successful in influencing the behavior of most units in the international system and in making the world safe for democracy if she can invest much in "the second face of power," or soft power, in her foreign policies.

Humanitarian and Catholic Interests as Complements of National Interest

In *realpolitik,* national interest is the overriding principle informing the behavior of states in the international system. The international system is merciless and anarchical because there is no legitimate international government or *Leviathan* (although the U.N. is closest to that.). States would surely not engage in any activity which jeopardizes their interests. However, the conduct of Vatican diplomacy under John Paul II shows that national interest must not be the only goal of international diplomacy. Kissinger and Gorbachev described John Paul II as the most consequential actor of the second half of the 20th century, although his diplomacy was informed not by national interest but by the Catholic interest. If John Paul II's diplomacy was so effective, even though it was not informed by national interest, international diplomacy would be more effective if other interests such as universal and Catholic interests are also incorporated as major informing variables of diplomatic practices.

The Vatican is still the diplomatic nerve center, even though its priority is not national interest. Cuban strongman Fidel Castro confessed during his visit to the Vatican in 1997 that, as a boy, he never dreamt of wining and dining with cardinals and popes. In his *Structure of Scientific Revolutions*, Thomas Kühn affirmed that new theories emerge because of anomalies in previous ones. Thus, I recommend National-Catholic interests as underlying goals of international diplomacy. Due to the unique *modus operandi* of John Paul II's potent paradoxical public diplomacy not informed by national interest and hard power, George Weigel deduced five lessons for the institution of diplomacy, researchers, academicians, political analysts, policy makers, and states:

> That the power of the human spirit can ignite world-historical change; that tradition can be as potent a force for social transformation as a self-consciously radical rupture with the past; that moral conviction can be an Archimedean lever for moving the world; that 'public life' and 'politics' are not synonymous; and that a genuinely humanistic politics always depends upon a more fundamental constellation of free associations and social institutions in which we learn the truth about ourselves as individuals and as members of communities (2000).

In recent times, there is an emerging school of international diplomacy known as humanitarian diplomacy, whose ultimate objectives (humanitarian interests) are the provision of relief and protection of human rights of victims of human-made and natural disasters. Some prominent humanitarian agencies include U.N. World Food Program, Oxfam International, the International Committee of the Red Cross, Jesuit Refugee Services, and Doctors without Borders. Scholars such as Larry Minear contend that humanitarian diplomacy is of paramount importance since it curbs the weaknesses of official diplomacy. In Minear's analysis, some special representatives of the U.N. secretary general dispatched to war-torn areas are unaware of humanitarian principles, and that culpable ignorance jeopardizes peace talks and processes in many areas (2007:32). The operational principles of humanitarianism are humanity, impartiality, neutrality, and independence. The principles are derived from the seven principles guiding the works of the Red Cross and Red Crescent societies. States should make use of humanitarian agencies, which often are better informed than *ad hoc* special representatives deployed to troubled areas. Papal diplomacy is proposed as a model for civil or secular diplomacy because of its admirable ideals and goals. Informed by Giovanni Battista Montini's (future Pope Paul VI) discourse on the occasion of the 250th anniversary of the Pontificia Accademia Ecclesiastica in 1951, John Morley writes, "The ideal of ecclesiastical diplomacy is the brotherhood of men, and, whether or not it succeeds in achieving this goal, it serves as a guide for civil diplomacy which attempts to make reason prevail over force and to contribute to the growth of individual states in harmony with all others" (1980:12).

The Importance of Dual Diplomacy

In diplomatic practices, there is a marked insistence on Track One diplomacy and hard power in conflict management and transformation. International conflict management is an integral part of diplomacy. The efficacy of Track One diplomacy with mechanisms such as mediation, negotiations, and arbitration, as enumerated in Article 33 of the U.N. Charter, cannot be underestimated. However, word verbatim, interfaith thinker, Edward Kessler described John

Paul II as the "tikkun olam pope," because of his quest for peace and ability in conflict management and reconciliation of peoples (2011). *Tikkun olam* is a Hebrew phrase, which means "healing the world." His quest for peace in every corner of the globe was achieved via dual diplomacy.

Most of John Paul II's diplomatic maneuvers were not carried out on an official basis but by his personal initiatives and *fiat*. Because of John Paul II's genius in combining Track One and Track Two diplomacies in changing the last quarter of the twentieth century, Cardinal Roger Etchegaray deservedly branded John Paul II as a man "above" and not "outside" politics (1997). Thus, based on the successful and efficient dual diplomacy of John Paul II, policy makers and world leaders should invest in dual diplomacy in conflict management rather than a prickly insistence on Track One diplomacy.

Multi-Track Diplomacy

The nine tracks of the Multi-Track diplomatic theory found expression in the public diplomacy of Saint John Paul II. The process leading to the establishment of diplomatic ties with the State of Israel was predominantly Track One and a Half diplomacy. During the pontificate of John Paul II, the Vatican partnered with Quest-net, an international multimillion-dollar company, to produce coins of John Paul II and Mother Teresa of Calcutta (exclusive editions). That was an apt example of Track Three diplomacy. American business tycoon Armand Hammer used business diplomacy to promote East-West détente. Even though the Soviet Union and the United States never established diplomatic ties, Hammer used his vast wealth and tireless energy to mitigate the East-West hostilities (Berridge, 2005:201).

John Paul II's youthful diplomacy and the role of the laity as agents of the Holy See's diplomacy constituted Track Four or Citizen diplomacy. Track Four diplomacy played a pivotal role in the peaceful transition from white unilateral minority rule in Rhodesia (present day Zimbabwe) to black majority rule in 1980. In 1975, Alec

Smith, son of Ian Smith (then prime minister of Rhodesia), be-friended a Black Nationalist leader named Arthur Konoderkeka at a Moral Re-Armament conference. The fruit of their enduring friend-ship was a meeting between Robert Mugabe and Ian Smith on the night before the announcement of the victory of Mugabe in the Zim-babwean elections. As a result of that unprecedented meeting, a planned coup by the Rhodesian army was called off, and Mugabe and Smith made reconciliatory statements to their constituencies, which ushered in a peaceful transition in 1980. Jesuit educated Robert Mugabe went on to rule Zimbabwe for thirty-seven years.

In line with Marxist inclined peace researchers, John Paul II's support and empowerment of the Solidarity Movement was part of Track Six diplomacy, or peacemaking through advocacy or ac-tivism. The pope's extensive writings, drawn from his personal experiences, to uphold the ultimate values of life, and to influence the behaviors of not only Catholics, constituted part of Track Seven diplomacy. The John Paul II Foundation in the Sahel coun-tries, created in 1984 to provide basic resources such as water, is an apt example of Track Eight diplomacy. Via John Paul II, the funding for the Foundation came from rich countries such as Ger-many, Italy, and the U.S. John Paul II's seemingly unintentional use of the tracks of the Multi-Track diplomatic theory was very potent. Perhaps a holistic diplomacy (Multi-Track) should be taken into consideration by world leaders. Peace research centers in the world should pay more attention to the Multi-Track diplo-matic community of Diamond and McDonald and perhaps incor-porate elements which could be helpful in the management of conflicts in the world.

The Importance of Idiosyncratic Variables in Policy Making and Formulation (The Idiosyncratic Theory of Papal Diplomacy)

The thematic analyses clearly demonstrate that Pope John Paul II's idiosyncratic variables strongly influenced many aspects of his diplomacy. One of the functions of theories and paradigms is to predict and explain the actions of people. Based on President Barack Obama's African roots, since his father was a Kenyan citizen, political analysts predicted that Africa would constitute a vital component of his diplomacy. Due to the influential role of John Paul II's idiosyncratic variables in his pontifical diplomacy, as well as the historical role of the idiosyncratic variables of secular leaders on their diplomacies, policy makers should take into consideration the idiosyncratic variables of leaders in foreign policy formulation, analysis, and implementation. More so, electorates around the world should also pay close attention to the idiosyncratic variables of potential leaders during elections.

In Roman Catholic Tradition, upon the death of a pope, cardinals aged eighty and below go into the Sistine Chapel to discern the will of God and decipher the one God has chosen as Vicar of Christ on earth. Thus, in a way, one can say the election of a pope in the Sistine Chapel is a discernment of the will of God by the College of Cardinals. However, the human factor, or unsavory politicking (*Prattiche*) in the election of a pope, cannot be disregarded. From some premises, John Paul II's idiosyncratic variables (Slavic roots) were instrumental in his election to the Petrine office in 1978 (at the height of the Cold War). Cardinal Joseph Ratzinger (Pope Benedict XVI), in an April 15, 1997 interview on Bavarian television, clarified the often-misunderstood role of the Holy Spirit in the conclave:

> I would not say so in the sense that the Holy Spirit picks out the pope, because there are too many contrary instances of popes the Holy Spirit would obviously not have picked. I would say that the Spirit does not exactly take control of the affair, but rather like a good educator, as it were, leaves us much space, much freedom, without entirely abandoning us. Thus, the Spirit's role should be understood in a much more elastic sense, not that he dictates the candidate for whom one must vote. Probably the only assurance he offers is that the thing cannot be totally ruined.

Saint John Paul II's idiosyncratic variables positively shaped his public diplomacy. It is a recommendation of the author that amidst the orthodoxy and rituals surrounding the election of a pope, the Princes of the Church (cardinals), should consider, when possible, the personality of the candidates and the nature of the international environment. This explains why I hereby postulate the *Idiosyncratic Theory of the Conduct of Papal Diplomacy*, since the idiosyncratic variables of popes shape their conduct of papal diplomacy.

AFTERWORD BY GEORGE WEIGEL

In canonizing John Paul II on April 27, 2014, the Catholic Church was not recommending the Polish pope as a model of statesmanship: as, for example, later generations of scholars and political leaders might lift up prime minister Benjamin Disraeli or U.S. secretary of state Dean Acheson as models of statesmanship. Still, John Paul II's heroic exercise of the chief virtue of statecraft—prudence—contains important lessons for those practicing the arts of governance on a global stage in the twenty-first century. As St. John Paul II always insisted, correctly, that he was neither diplomat nor politician; he was, rather, a pastor, who in exercising his pastoral responsibilities had some things to say to the world of political power, because the things he said had to do with the Church's defense of human dignity, the protection of which gives the exercise of public authority a distinctive "excellence" (to borrow from Aristotle) and a fundamental moral purpose. John Tanyi's study of John Paul's diplomacy underscores this point. Yet the Polish-born pastor who refused to don the mantle of politician or diplomat, choosing instead the role of moral witness, was the most politically consequential pope in centuries, a pope whose evangelically-inspired action changed history and left a deep impression on the future, so that the footprints of his distinctive statecraft can be found all over the world: in central and eastern Europe, which he helped liberate from communism; in Latin America, Asia, and Africa, where men and women formed by John Paul II's social doctrine are striving to make freedom for excellence work in the political and economic fields; in the United States, Canada, and western Europe, where John Paul II's robust defense of religious freedom as the first of human rights has taken on new, and perhaps unexpected, salience in post-modern societies threatened by what Benedict XVI called the "dictatorship of relativism."

To be sure, the responsibilities of a pope and the responsibilities of presidents, prime ministers, members of legislatures, diplomats, and other public officials are not identical. Popes no longer deploy "hard power" in the form of armies, as they once did; democratic leaders charged with the defense of the common good must calculate the interests of the people they represent and serve in ways that popes don't. Which is to say that popes and public officials deal with international politics out of different toolkits. Still, at a time in which statecraft is often misunderstood as a form of psychotherapy, what might statesmen who seek to defend freedom and advance the cause of human rights and democracy learn from the distinctive global statecraft of a saint who had a real impact on what punditocracy call the "real world"?

Seven such lessons suggest themselves to me, as Tanyi's analysis confirms.

The first lesson: Culture comes first.

John Paul II's statecraft rejected the fallacies that had made political modernity a slaughterhouse. He rejected the Jacobin fallacy, born in 1789, that history is driven by politics, understood as the quest for power, understood as my ability to impose my will on you. He rejected the Marxist fallacy that "history" is merely the exhaust fumes of the means of production. And he rejected the liberal fallacy that if a society only gets the machinery of democracy and the free economy right, those machines can run by themselves. Rather, drawing on both Catholic and Polish sources, John Paul II insisted that culture was, is, and always will be the most dynamic force in history, both defensively (in terms of resisting tyranny) and positively (in terms of building and sustaining free societies). Moreover, he understood that at the center of culture is cult, or religion: what people believe, cherish, and worship; what people are willing to stake their lives, and their children's lives, on.

This culture-first approach to history and statecraft was on full display during John Paul's epic first papal pilgrimage to Poland: nine days in June 1979 on which the history of the twentieth century pivoted. Those nine days are often described as a moment of national catharsis, and there is undoubtedly something to that: the pent-up frustrations, sorrows, and angers engendered by Poland's awful experiences over two centuries—its vivisection in the late 19ᵗʰ century, its demolition by Nazis, and its desecration by communists—began to be healed by the triumphant return to his homeland of Poland's papal son. But a lot more went on during the Nine Days than catharsis. What went on then is more properly described as *transformation*: the revitalization of culture in a revolution of conscience, ignited by John Paul II's summons to the people he knew so well—"You are not who *they* say you are. Reclaim who you really are, own the truth of your history and your culture, and you will find tools of resistance that totalitarianism cannot match."

The Nine Days of John Paul II in June 1979 were, arguably, the most politically potent papal intervention in world affairs since the High Middle Ages. Yet during those nine days the Pope didn't mention politics or economics *once*. Rather, the Pope spoke the truth of Poland's history, its culture, and its national self-understanding, in dozens of variations on one great theme. And by returning to his people the truth about themselves, he helped them forge tools of liberation that were essentially moral and cultural in nature. Deployed over a hard decade of struggle that led to the triumphs of the Revolution of 1989, those tools proved more than adequate in answering Stalin's cynical question, "The Pope? How many divisions does he have?"

The second lesson: Ideas count, for good and for ill.

I doubt that John Paul II ever read John Maynard Keynes, but he certainly understood the truth of what the Cambridge economist meant when Keynes wrote that "Both when they are right and when they are wrong, ideas are more powerful than is commonly understood. In fact, the world is ruled by little else. Practical men, who believe themselves to be quite exempt from any intellectual influences, are usually the slaves of some defunct economist. Madmen in authority, who hear voices in the air, are distilling their frenzy from some academic scribbler of a few years back.... Soon or late, it is ideas ... which are dangerous for good or evil."

The dangers of false ideas John Paul knew from experience: he had seen the lethal effects of Lenin's, Stalin's, and Hitler's wicked ideas in the deaths of tens of millions of human beings, including his friends and classmates. But he also knew from experience the regenerative power of noble ideas: for example, the ideas of Christian Democracy deployed by men like Konrad Adenaur, Alcide de Gasperi, and Robert Schuman in rebuilding postwar Europe and laying the foundations of today's European Union. In both cases—the wicked, false, and death-dealing ideas, and the good, true, and ennobling ideas—what was most crucial, in John Paul II's view, was the idea of the human person being proposed. Or to use a social science term in its philosophical sense, what counted was *anthropology*.

And here we find the connection between Karol Wojtyła, Polish philosopher, and John Paul II, statesman. In the first decade of his pontificate, John Paul II, statesman, saw that the division of Europe decreed by the Tehran and Yalta conferences during World War II was not only wrong but fragile and unsustainable, because Karol Wojtyła, Polish philosopher, knew that Stalin's power-grab was in service to a false idea of the human person: a warped anthropology that led inevitably to the Gulag, the KGB, and all the rest of the apparatus of Soviet repression. In the last years of his papacy, John Paul II, statesman, knew that 21st-century Europe risked dissolving into incoherence because Karol Wojtyła, Polish philosopher, had accurately measured the deficiencies of the atheistic humanism and soul-withering secularism that were at the root of Europe's post-Cold War crisis of civilizational morale.

Thus, the democratic statesman who wishes to learn from the example of John Paul II will take ideas, and the war of ideas, with as much seriousness as he or she takes indices of gross national product or measures of military capability. Why? Because all three are connected. Neither wealth nor military power will be usefully deployed in the cause of freedom in the twenty-first century if the will to do so is not present. And it seems unlikely that such a will—the will to challenge the lies and propaganda of the forces of disorder as an essential component of restoring a measure of order to world affairs—will be formed if the political culture of the West continues to be eroded from within by skepticism, relativism, and irony, by an anthropology that reduces the human person to a mere bundle of desires, and by a nihilism that mocks all religious and moral conviction.

The third lesson: Don't psychologize the adversary.

One result of the decline of philosophy and the concurrent rise of social science in the late-modern and post-modern West has been the emergence of psychological approaches to statecraft, as political theory has sadly disappeared from many university curricula and "political science" has been debased into a subset of statistics. In American terms, one can trace this back to the social science theories popular among the "best and brightest" of the Kennedy/Johnson years: the mandarins who believed that a naval blockade of Cuba in 1962 was a form of "communication," and who imagined that "signaling" North Vietnam by turning the spigot of air power on and off could change Ho Chi Minh's behavior. The Obama-era's analogue to this psychologization of statecraft was the famous "reset:" first with Russia and the Arab Islamic world, then with Cuba and Iran. The premise here is that malign actors in world politics behave badly because of what *we* do, so that if we behave differently *their* behavior will change and become less disagreeable, if not downright praiseworthy.

John Paul II knew this for the foolishness it was and is. As a keen student of the human condition, he understood that malign actors behave badly because of who they are, what they espouse, and what they seek, not because of anything "we" did to "them."

Thus he could focus on the issues at hand—religious freedom and other basic human rights in the communist world, for example—without tying himself up in knots over whether the Cold War division of Europe was, somehow, Harry Truman's fault; unlike western revisionist historians, John Paul understood that Stalin, his heirs, and their Polish epigones did what they did because of who they were, what they believed, and what they sought, not because good old Uncle Joe had been offended by the haberdasher from Independence, Missouri, at the Potsdam conference in July 1945.

The 21st-century lessons to be drawn from this papal clarity about the sources of conflict should be obvious. To take one urgent case: Vladimir Putin does what he has been doing in Ukraine, Moldova, the Baltic states, and elsewhere, not because of anything Ukraine, Moldova, or other post-Soviet states did to him or to Russia, but because of who he is, what he believes, and what he seeks. Thus "narratives" of the ongoing low-grade war in Ukraine that seek to "balance" responsibilities for the conflict or describe it as a "civil war" distort reality and in doing so make creative and sensible policy virtually impossible. The same is true of the Shia totalitarians who hold ultimate authority in Tehran. Unless their behavior in seeking a nuclear capability is understood on its own terms, as an expression of their own apocalyptic ideas and ambitions rather than as a reaction to pressures from the Sunni world, the West, or both, the world will remain vulnerable to Iranian dissembling and stalling, and the likelihood of an Iranian bomb will grow accordingly.

The fourth lesson: Speak loudly and be supple in deploying whatever sticks, large or small, you have at hand.

When John Paul II was elected the 264th Bishop of Rome on October 16, 1978, Vatican diplomacy was well into the second decade of its *Ostpolitik*, an approach to the problems of local Catholic churches behind the Iron Curtain that avoided public condemnation of communism's human rights violations for the sake of reaching diplomatic agreements with Warsaw Pact countries. Those agreements were supposed to guarantee the Church's freedom to live its sacramental life by its own standards. But in the event, what limited agreements were achieved demoralized the resistance Church in several Eastern bloc countries, turned the Catholic Church in Hungary into a subsidiary of the Hungarian party-state, did nothing to relieve the condition of Catholics in the Soviet Union, and opened the Vatican to further penetration by communist intelligence services, a process that had begun in the early 1960s.

Yet John Paul was shrewd enough not to dismantle the *Ostpolitik* of Pope Paul VI and his principal diplomat, Archbishop Agostino Casaroli. Rather, he made Casaroli his own Secretary of State, named him a cardinal, and gave him full rein to pursue his diplomacy east of the Elbe River. Thus, no communist leader could publicly accuse the Church of reneging on its previous commitments because of a "reactionary" Polish pope in league with NATO (although Soviet and Eastern bloc propaganda and disinformation campaigns worked overtime to sell precisely that message throughout the West, not without some success). But while Casaroli continued his bilateral diplomatic efforts, John Paul II restored the Catholic Church's "voice" in challenging human rights violations and calling upon communist states to honor their human rights commitments under "Basket Three" of 1976 Helsinki Final Act—and did so by making his own voice the Vatican's principal voice. Time and again, in venue after venue, John Paul II lifted up the first freedom, religious freedom, and brought his case before the world in his 1979 address to the U.N. General Assembly. And because of that papal megaphone (and its amplification by Radio Free Europe and Radio Liberty), the resistance Church behind the Iron Curtain knew it had a champion; those in the West committed to supporting the resistance Church in central and eastern Europe were inspired to expand their efforts; and all the while, the Soviet rationale for the Cold War was being systematically undercut in the order of ideas.

The Polish pope applied the same methods in his efforts to shore up those Catholic leaders working for justice and peace in Central America in the face of Marxist governments and insurgencies there. The Sandinista tide began to recede when John Paul II vocally confronted the adolescent cheerleading of Daniel Ortega and his comrades at a 1983 papal Mass in Managua—and the entire affair, including the Pope demanding "Silence" from Ortega & Co. so that he could preach his sermon, was telecast throughout the region. Yet John Paul was also willing to be the quiet persuader, working behind the scenes while local churchmen did the denouncing of injustice, when that seemed appropriate: a method that worked well in Argentina, Chile, and the Philippines, as the Pope met with (and thus gave his tacit blessing to) local human rights activists and political reformers while he worked privately on the Argentine military, on General Augusto Pinochet, and on President Ferdinand Marcos, urging them to respect human rights and to restore democracy in their countries.

The lesson for the 21st-century statesman: Moral pressure can be an important lever in world politics, but effective human rights advocacy and democracy-promotion require dexterity—diplomatic dexterity, and dexterity in waging the battle of ideas.

The fifth lesson: Listen to the martyrs.

The *Ostpolitik* that set the default positions in Vatican diplomacy for some fifteen years prior to the election of John Paul II did not dishonor the persecuted local Churches behind the Iron Curtain. But it did tend to regard their intransigence as an obstacle to diplomatic accommodation between the Holy See and communist regimes. And such accommodations had to be reached, according to the *Ostpolitik*, because the post-war division of Europe was a permanent reality of world politics, not a temporary aberration. Thus, in the decade prior to John Paul's election, Paul VI removed Cardinals Josef Beran and József Mindszenty from their posts in Prague and Budapest and kept the exiled leader of the

Greek Catholic Church in Soviet-occupied Ukraine, Cardinal Josyf Slipyj, at a distance.

John Paul II had long "read" the witness of the martyr-confessors in the underground Churches behind the Iron Curtain differently. To his mind, the witness of these brave men and women, living and dead, helped strengthen a religiously-informed cultural resistance to communism because it embodied in a unique way the moral pressure that could and should be exerted on communist regimes. So during his time as archbishop of Kraków, Karol Wojtyła clandestinely ordained priests for service in the underground Church in Czechoslovakia, in what amounted to a tacit challenge to the Vatican's *Ostpolitik*. As pope, he made sure that the world (and especially the Kremlin) knew of his meeting with the Ukrainian Cardinal Slipyj, leader of the largest underground Church in the world, a month after his election. That meeting took place a few weeks after he had sent his cardinal's zucchetto to the Ostrabrama shrine at Vilnius in Lithuania as a gesture of solidarity with another long-suffering and bitterly-persecuted local Church—a gesture that was repaid within weeks as the Lithuanian Committee for the Defense of Believers' Rights was formed and became one of the most dogged human rights proponents in the Soviet Union.

This pattern continued throughout the pontificate and was not limited to the Pope's support for fellow Catholics. John Paul II deployed his own private contacts into the USSR to keep himself informed of the views of the hard-pressed human rights resistance there; one result of that clandestine papal intelligence operation was his December 1985 meeting in the Vatican with Elena Bonner, wife of Andrei Sakharov, which was arranged by one of John Paul's informal agents, Irina Ilovayskaya Alberti, former aide to Aleksandr Solzhenitsyn in his Vermont exile.

For John Paul II, the witness of the modern martyr-confessors deserved honor and respect in its own right; just as the Church demeaned itself, he believed, when it accommodated the demands of totalitarian persecutors, so the Church was strengthened by acknowledging the witness of its sons and daughters who took the risk of freedom and paid the price for it. Honoring the persecuted Church also had an important effect on the Holy See's diplomatic action in world politics, John Paul seemed to think: it acted as a brake against the Realpolitik pragmatism that is common to European foreign ministries, but that is neither realistic nor pragmatic over the long haul.

There are lessons here, for both statesmen and churchmen, in dealing with such 21st-century challenges as the transition to a post-communist future in Cuba and China, and in responding to the lethal threats posed by jihadist Islam to Christian communities in the Middle East and Africa. Listening to the voices of the martyr-confessors of these regions will clarify the obstacles to a better future posed by the Cuban and Chinese regimes and by jihadists. Lifting up the witness of the living martyr-confessors publicly and persistently might also afford them a measure of protection, while helping sustain islands of civil society essential to future progress toward justice and peace in Cuba, China, the Middle East, and Africa.

The sixth lesson: Think long-term and do not sacrifice core principles to what seems immediate advantage.

In the mid-1980s, after martial law had been lifted in Poland but while the Solidarity trade union was still legally banned, officials of General Wojciech Jaruzelski's communist regime sounded out Polish Church leaders with a proposal: the regime would open a national dialogue on Poland's future and the Church would act as the regime's interlocutor. Some Polish churchmen were tempted by the offer. But John Paul II refused to take the bait. Solidarity was the proper representative of Polish civil society, in his view, and the Church ought not substitute itself in that role—especially when that meant tacitly acquiescing to Solidarity's legal non-status. The Church could help facilitate a conversation between the regime and the opposition; but the Church ought not replace the opposition.

That decision had theological roots: in John Paul II's ecclesiology, the Church could not be a partisan political actor because that contradicted the Eucharistic character of the Church (a theme he had stressed in his challenge to various forms of liberation theology in Latin America). But it was also based on John Paul II's social doctrine. In that vision of the free and virtuous society, the Church formed the people who formed the civil society and the political institutions that did the work of politics; the Church was not a political agent in its own right, although the Church obviously had a voice in society.

In the event, the Church's refusal to play "opposition party" to the "leading role" of the communist party in Poland increased the pressure on the Jaruzelski regime to recognize the real Polish opposition, which was represented by Solidarity. Thus John Paul II's principled decision helped create the conditions for the possibility of the Polish Roundtable of early 1989 and the partially-free elections of June 1989. And those elections, by delivering an overwhelming victory to Solidarity, made possible the first non-communist government in post-war Polish history the following September.

The lesson here, for both 21st-century statesmen and the diplomats of the Holy See, would seem to be this: The cause of freedom, and the cause of the Church, are both best served when statesmen and churchmen-acting-as-statesmen think long-term and do not bracket or minimize core principles for what can seem to be immediate advantage. That lesson bears on the Church's role in Cuba today, where local Church leaders' understandable concerns to strengthen the Church's institutional infrastructure should go hand-in-hand with a vigorous defense of those dissidents who form the core of the Cuban civil society of the future. This sixth "John Paul II lesson" should also raise cautions about the push for full diplomatic relations between the Holy See and the People's Republic of China. In the present circumstances, any such deal would require the Vatican to sever its diplomatic exchange with the Republic of China on Taiwan—the first Chinese democracy in history. What signal would such a deal, with such a price tag, send about the Catholic Church's vision of China's future? What signal would it send about the Church's concern for the hard-pressed and often-persecuted elements of civil society that exist in China today and are pressing for a non-authoritarian and open future? The evangelical mission of the Church in the Cuba and the mainland China of the future are not going to be materially advanced by accommodating too easily to the regnant regimes in those countries. Neither is the path beyond Castroite communism and Chinese authoritarianism.

There are also lessons here for the Holy See's role in Ukraine. The longstanding Vatican priority given to cordial ecumenical relations and serious theological dialogue with the Russian Orthodox Church ought to be re-examined in light of the unhappy fact that, in the drama of Ukraine since the Maidan revolution of dignity in 2013–2014, the current Russian Orthodox leadership has functioned as an agent of Russian state power, playing its own sorry role in Kremlin propaganda and disinformation campaigns. Neither common ecumenical witness in defense of international legal norms nor serious theological dialogue is possible under those circumstances; pretending otherwise merely reinforces the damage being done by aggressors.

The seventh lesson: Media "reality" isn't necessarily reality, and the statesman cannot play acolyte to such "narratives."

The most unintentionally hilarious commentary on the public impact of Pope John Paul II came from the editorial page of the *New York Times*. John Paul was in the middle of those epic Nine Days of June 1979 when, on June 5, the *Times* ran an editorial on the papal pilgrimage with this conclusion: "As much as the visit of Pope John Paul II to Poland must reinvigorate the Roman Catholic Church in Poland, it does not threaten the political order of the nation or of Eastern Europe." Wrong.

Why did the *Times* so badly miss the reality of what was afoot in Poland? In part, I suspect, because it regarded "the Roman Catholic Church in Poland" as of no more political consequence to "the political order of the nation or of Eastern Europe" than the Polish Flat-Earth Society. Then there was the view in the liberal world (for which the *Times* was both mirror and infallible teaching authority) that the Cold War would be resolved when an increasingly social democratic West "converged" with a liberalizing East and the Berlin Wall would simply dissolve—a "narrative" that was also popular in certain European (and indeed Vatican) circles. And then there was the *Times'* concern, shared by many foreign policy "realists" in the United States and western Europe, that any disturbance of the Yalta postwar order threatened nuclear holocaust; so, while it might be too bad for what were once called the "captive nations," the way things were was the way things were going to have to be, lest greater demons be set loose.

These "narratives"—the narrative of the political irrelevance of religion in the late 20th century; the narrative of "convergence;" and the change-risks-nuclear-war narrative—seemed to be reality. But they weren't reality; they were merely simulacra of reality. John Paul II was wise enough to know that and to act according to what was really reality: the reality that a morally-informed human rights resistance, based on a clear and correct conception of the dignity of the human person, attacked communism at its most vulnerable point and thus held one of the keys to settling the Cold War in favor of the forces of freedom.

The problem of confusing reality with "media reality" or "narrative" has intensified since 1979, in no small part because of the ubiquity of social media and instant Internet commentary, both of which readily create "narratives" that seem to be "reality." Yet the statesmen of the 21st century would do well to take a lesson from John Paul II and read the "signs of the times" more closely than is possible through lenses crafted by "narrative." The same lesson applies to churchmen: Church leaders, clerical and lay, who respond to media-generated "narratives" about the Catholic Church rather than to the imperatives of the Gospel are not going to advance either the evangelical mission of the Church or the cause of human dignity and freedom. The Gospel has power, and its power can cut through the densest of false "narratives."

Is there an overarching lesson to be learned from the singular "public" effect of St. John Paul II? While his life displayed many admirable qualities, what is perhaps most compelling as a lesson for the long-term future is his refusal to submit to the tyranny of the possible, when thinking about both public affairs and the life of the Church.

The great hopes that followed the Revolution of 1989, the collapse of the Soviet Union, the various color-revolutions in the post-communist world, and the Arab Spring, have often been frustrated. "History" is manifestly not over and the forces that stand for ordered liberty in the world seem to be in retreat. Too much of Latin America has reverted to chronic patterns of corruption and authoritarianism, or corruption and incompetence, or corruption, incompetence, and authoritarianism. Europe—incapable of putting its fiscal house in order, responding forcefully to the threats posed by a revanchist Russia, or dealing with home-brewed jihadist terrorism and anti-Semitism—remains paralyzed by a crisis of civilizational morale than only the willfully ignorant or fanatically secular will fail to recognize as spiritual in character. Africa is beset by a host of troubles, and China is becoming ever more aggressive on the world stage. That religious freedom came under assault in the West within two decades of its vindication in the formerly communist world was not something than many expected in 1989—or at the turn of the millennium, for that matter. What Pope Francis has aptly described as a "throwaway culture," in which the disposable are not just consumer goods but people, is eroding the moral-cultural fabric of civilization. Drastically different ideas of the human person, human community, and human destiny are in conflict throughout the world.

In the mid-21st century, it is imperative that we take a lesson from John Paul II and not bind ourselves with the self-imposed shackles of low expectations, submitting to the tyranny of the possible as the conventional wisdom of the day defines the possible. Had Karol Wojtyła, on becoming John Paul II, accepted the conventional wisdom of the moment, he would have settled down to manage the inevitable decline of the Catholic Church in a world permanently divided along geopolitical and ideological fault lines defined in the late 1940s. Because he believed more deeply, and thus saw more clearly, he discerned sources of renewal in the Church where others saw only decay, and he saw openings for freedom whether others only saw impenetrable walls. By refusing to bend to the tyranny of the possible, he helped make what seemed impossible, not only possible, but real.

Events proved that his signature challenge on October 22, 1978—"Be not afraid!"—was not romanticism. It was the deepest, truest realism. Or as he put it to thousands of young people in Kraków in June 1979, as they gathered near the site of the martyrdom of St. Stanisław, "Be afraid only of thoughtlessness and pusillanimity." The world would do well to heed that summons and that challenge.

George Weigel is Distinguished Senior Fellow of Washington's Ethics and Public Policy Center, where he holds the William E. Simon Chair in Catholic Studies. His two-volume biography of Pope St. John Paul II, *Witness to Hope* and *The End and the Beginning*, has been widely translated and is complemented by a memoir, *Lessons in Hope: My Unexpected Life with St. John Paul II.*

BIBLIOGRAPHY

Abbott, E. (1988). *Haiti: An Insider's History of the Rise and Fall of the Duvaliers*. London: Simon & Schuster.

Accattoli, L. (1998). *When a Pope Asks Forgiveness: The Mea Culpas of John Paul II*. New York: Alba House.

_____ (1998). *Man of the Millennium: John Paul II*. Boston: Pauline Books and Media.

Akonga, E. et al. (eds) (1999). *The African Bible: Biblical Text of the New American Bible*. Nairobi: Paulines Publications Africa.

Albert of Aachen. (1879). Historia Hierosolymitana,' Recueil des historiens des croisades. *Historiens occidentaux* (RHC. OCC). Paris: Imprimerie Nationale.

Allen, J. (2001). "Cardinals Debate Church's Future." In: *National Catholic Reporter,* June 1.

_____ (2002). Conclave: The Politics, Personalities, and Process of the Next Papal Election. New York: Doubleday.

_____ (2004). All the Pope's Men: The Inside Story of How the Vatican Really Thinks. Sydney: Doubleday.

_____ (2005). The Rise of Benedict XVI: The Inside Story of How the Pope Was Elected and Where He Will Take the Catholic Church. New York: Doubleday.

Andrew, C., & Mitrokhin, V. (1999). The Sword and the Shield: The Mitrokhin Archive and the Secret History of the KGB. New York: Basic Books.

Araujo, J. R. (2005). *John Paul II's Legacy in Diplomacy*. Retrieved November 2, 2020, from http://www.zenit.org/article-12769?I=english.

Araujo, J. R., & Lucal, A. J. (2004). *Papal Diplomacy and the Quest for Peace: The Vatican and International Organizations from the Early Years to the League of Nations.* Florida: Sapientia Press of Ave Maria University.

_____ (2010). *Papal Diplomacy and the Quest for Peace: The United Nations from Pius XII to Paul VI.* Philadelphia: Saint Joseph's University Press.

Arinze, F. (2002). In: Hallet, J. D. (writer & director). "Witness to Hope." A documentary.

_____ (2008). *Reflecting on Our Priesthood: Letter to a Young Priest.* Nairobi: Paulines Publications Africa.

Art, R. J. & Cronin, P. M. (2007). "Coercive Diplomacy." In: Crocker, C. A & Hampson, O. F &

Aall, P. (eds). *Leashing the Dogs of War.* Washington: United States Institute of Peace Press.

Barnes, J. & Whitney, H. (1995–2014). "John Paul II: His Life and Papacy." In Frontline's *John Paul II: The Millennial Pope.*, from https://www.pbs.org/wgbh/pages/frontline/shows/pope/etc/bio.html. Accessed September 7, 2020.

Baylis, J. & Smith, S. & Owens, P. (2008). *The Globalization of World Politics: An Introduction to International Relations.* Oxford: Oxford University Press.

Beabout, G. (2001). "Review Essay" [Challenging the Modern World: John Paul II/Karol Wojtyła and the Development of Catholic Social Teaching by Samuel Gregg]. In: Journal of Markets & Morality, Vol. 4, No. 2, Fall 2001, www.acton.org/publicat/m_and_m/2001_fall/beabout2.html.

Bernstein, C., & Politi, M. (1996). *His Holiness: John Paul II and the Hidden History of Our Time.* New York: Bantam Doubleday Dell Publishing Group, Inc.

Berridge, G. R. (2001). "Machiavelli." In: Berridge, G. R., & Keens-Soper, M., & Otte, T. G. Diplomatic Theory from Machiavelli to Kissinger. New York: Palgrave.

_____ (2001). "Richelieu". In: Berridge, G. R., & Keens-Soper, M.,

& Otte, T. G. *Diplomatic Theory from Machiavelli to Kissinger.* New York: Palgrave.

_____ (2002). *Diplomacy: Theory and Practice.* New York: Prentice-Hall.

Berridge, G. R., & Keens-Soper, M., & Otte, T. G. (2001). *Diplomatic Theory from Machiavelli to Kissinger.* New York: Palgrave.

Binchy, D. A. (1941*). Church and State in Fascist Italy.* London: Oxford University Press.

Bokenkotter, T. (2005). *A Concise History of the Catholic Church.* London: Doubleday.

Bull, H. (1985). *The Anarchical Society: A Study of Order in World Politics.* London: Macmillan.

Bunderson, C. (2012). "In first tweet, Pope blesses his million-plus followers." (EWTN News). http://www.ewtnnews.com/catholic-news/Vatican.php?id=6709. Accessed on December 18, 2018.

Burgman, H. (2010). *Words of Passage.* Cambridgeshire: Melrose Books.

Cardinale, I. (1962). *The Holy See and Diplomacy: An Historical, Juridical, and Practical Survey of Pontifical Diplomacy.* Paris: Desclee & Cie.

Calvocoressi, P. (2008). *World Politics, 1945–2000.* New Delhi: Dorling Kindersley.

Cardinale, H. E. (1976). *The Holy See and the International Order.* Colin Smythe: Gerrards Cross. Casaroli, A. (1990). "Ostpolitik: Chipping Away at Marxism's Crumbling House," *L'Osservatore Romano* (English weekly Edition).

Chadwick, O. (1986). *Britain and the Vatican during the Second World War.* Cambridge: Cambridge University Press.

Charter of the United Nations (1945). Http://www.un.org/en/documents/charter/index.shtml. Retrieved on May 17, 2011.

Chimamanda, N. A (2009). "The Danger of a Single Story." In: *African Cultures and Issues, Art Making, Contemporary Literature, Non-Fiction and Politics.* Accessed on January 7, 2022.

China, People's Republic of 1993. *China's Foreign Policy*. Beijing: New Star Publishers.

Chittister, J. (2006). *The Rule of Benedict: Insights for the Ages*. New York: The Crossroad Publishing Company.

Confalonieri, L. (2012). *Democracy in the Christian Church: An Historical, Theological and Political Case*. London: Bloomsbury Publishing Plc.

Congregation for the Doctrine of the Faith (1985). *Notification on the book "Church: Charism and Power"* by Father Leonardo Boff O.F.M. http://www.vatican.va/roman_curia/congregations/cfaith/documents/rc_con_cfaith_doc_19850311_notif-boff_en.html. Retrieved on November 29, 2019.

Cohn-Sherbok, D. (2006). *The Paradox of Anti-Semitism*. London: Continuum International Publishing Group.

Coppa, F. J. (1998). *The Modern Papacy since 1789*. New York: Addison Wesley Longman Limited.

Coppen, L. (2021). "Cardinal Wyszyński and Mother Elżbieta Beatified in Poland." In: *National*

Catholic Register. *https://www.ncregister.com/cna/cardinal-wyszynski-and-mother-elzbieta beatified-in-poland*. Retrieved on October 17, 2021.

Cornwell, J. (1999). *Hitler's Pope: The Secret History of Pius XII*. New York: Viking Press.

Craig, G. A., & George, A. L. (1995). *Force and Statecraft: Diplomatic Problems of Our Time*. 3rd ed. New York: Oxford University Press.

Creswell, J. (2003). *Research Design: Qualitative, Quantitative, and Mixed Methods Approaches*, 2nd ed. London: Sage Publications.

Crocker, C. A. & Hampson, O. F. & Aall, P. (2007). *Leashing the Dogs of War*. Washington: United States Institute of Peace Press.

Cussen, G. J. (2014). *The Church-State(s) Problem: The Holy See in the International Theoretical (or Theological Marketplace)*. The

International Symposium on Religion and Cultural Diplomacy, Rome, March 31– April 3, 2014. National University of Ireland.

Dalin, D. (2007). "John Paul and the Jews." In: *First Things Magazine*. New York.

_____ (2020). "A Righteous Gentile: Pope Pius XII and the Jews." https://www.catholiceducation.org/en/controversy/common-misconceptions/a-righteous-gentile-pope-pius-xii-and-the-jews.html. Retrieved 12/8/2020.

De Lubac, H. (1963). *The Drama of Atheist Humanism*. New York: The World Publishing Company.

Diamond, L., & McDonald, J. (1996). *Multi-Track Diplomacy: A Systems Approach to Peace*. West Hartford: Kumarian Press.

Dickey, C. (2019). "Jacques Chirac Stood Up to George W. Bush on Iraq, and Made Paris Shine." In: *Daily Beast*. https://www.thedailybeast.com/jacques-chirac-stood-up-to-george-w-bush-on-iraq-and-made-paris-shine?ref=scroll. Accessed on January 13, 2022.

Dougherty, J. E. & Pfaltzgraff, R. L. (2001). *Contending Theories of International Relations: A Comprehensive Survey*. New York: Addison Wesley Longman, Inc.

Dupuy, A. (2004). *Pope John Paul II and the Challenges of Papal Diplomacy: Anthology* (1978–2003). New York City: The Path to Peace Foundation.

Dziwisz, S. (2008). *A Life with Karol: My Forty-Year Friendship with the Man Who Became Pope*. New York: Doubleday.

Ellsberg, R. (1997). "Taking saints seriously for the needs of our time." In: *Sojourners*, September-October 1997. In: Rittner, C. "What kind of Witness." In: Rittner, C., & Roth, J. K. (eds) (2002). *Pope Pius XII and the Holocaust*. New York: Leicester University Press.

Emilewicz, J. (2018). In: Anderson, C. "Liberating a Continent: John Paul II and the Fall of Communism." A documentary.

Evert, J. (2014). *Saint John Paul the Great: His Five Loves*. New York: Totus Tuus Press.

Fisher, E. J. & Klenicki, L. (ed) (1995). *John Paul II, Pope, Spiritual Pilgrimage: Texts on Jews and Judaism 1979-1995*. New York: Crossroad.

Fitzjames, S. J. (1883). *History of the Criminal Law of England*. Oxford: Oxford University Press.

Formicola, J. R. (2002). *Pope John Paul II: Prophetic Politician*. Washington: Georgetown University Press.

Frey, L. R. & Botan, & G. L. Kreps (2000). *Investigating Communication: An Introduction to Research Methods*. London: Allyn and Bacon.

Friedman, T. (1999). *The Lexus and the Olive Tree: Understanding Globalization*. New York: Farrar, Straus & Giroux.

Frossard, A. (1982). *Be Not Afraid: André Frossard in Conversation with John Paul II*. Paris: Redwood Burn Ltd.

_____ (1990). *Portrait of John Paul II*. San Francisco: Ignatius Press.

Fukuyama, F. (1992). *The End of History and the Last Man*. New York: The Free Press.

_____ (2012). *The Origins of Political Order: From Prehuman Times to the French Revolution*. London: Profile Books.

_____ (2014). *Political Order and Political Decay: From the Industrial Revolution to the Globalization of Democracy*. New York: Farrar, Straus and Giroux.

Fuller, T. (1639). *The Historie of the Holy Warre*. Cambridge: Cambridge University Press.

Gaddis, J. L. (2005). *The Cold War: A New History*. New York: Penguin Press.

Gaudium et spes, 1965 (Pastoral Constitution on the Church in the Modern World). Rome.

Garner, B. A. (ed). *Black's Law Dictionary*. Oxford: West Publishing Co.

Gibbs, D. (1995). "Secrecy and International Relations." *Journal of Peace Research*, 32:213:238.

Goodstein, L. (1998). "How Boyhood Friend Aided Pope with Israel." New York Times 29th March 1998, Ai and 10. In: Formicola, J. R (2002). *Pope John Paul II: Prophetic Politician.* Washington, D.C., Georgetown University Press.

Goldstein, D. M., & Williams, P., & Shafritz, J. M. (2006). *Classic Readings and Contemporary Debates in International Relations* (3rd ed). Belmont: Thomson Worth.

Graham, R. (1959). *Vatican Diplomacy: A Study of Church and State on the International Plane.* Princeton: Princeton University Press.

_____ (1987). *Pius XII's Defense of Jews and Others: 1944–45.* Milwaukee: Catholic League Publications.

_____ (2000). "Church, Shoah, and Anti-Semitism" in *Pope Pius XII: Architect for Peace.* New York: Paulist Press.

Green, J. C., & Caracelli, V. J., & Graham, W. F. (1989). "Toward a Conceptual Framework for Mixed-Method Evaluation Design." In Educational Evaluation and Policy Analysis, Vol.11. n3. Pyana, M. S. (2010). *Peacebuilding and Education: Promoting a Culture of Peace in Eastern Democratic Republic of Congo.* Master's thesis (published).

Greenstein, F. (1992). "Personality and Politics." In: Hawkesworth, M., & Kogan, M. *Encyclopedia of Government and Politics.* New York: Routledge.

Gregg, S. (1999). *Challenging the Modern World: Karol Wojtyła/John Paul II and the Development of Catholic Social Teaching.* Lanham, Md.: Lexington Books.

Grossman, C. (2012). "Twitter Faithful Awaits Pope Benedict's First Words". http://www.usatoday.com/story/tech/2012/12/10/pope-twitter-wednesday/1758409/. Assessed on December 18, 2020.

Hahn, S. (2003). *The Lamb's Supper: The Mass as Heaven on Earth.* London: Darton Spencer Court.

Hamilton, K. & Langhorne, R. (2005). *The Practice of Diplomacy: Its Evolution, Theory and Administration.* London: Routledge.

Haron-Feiertag, J. (2009). *Eulogy to Papal Diplomacy.* Retrieved November 2, 2019, from http://www.diplomaticourier.org/kmitan/articleback.php?newsid=299.

Hawkesworth, M., & Kogan, M. (1992). *Encyclopedia of Government and Politics.* New York: Routledge.

Hazel, S. (2007). "Humanitarian Diplomacy: Theory and Practice." In: Minear, L., & Hazel, S. (eds). *Humanitarian Diplomacy: Practitioners and Their Craft.* New York: United Nations University Press.

Hebblewaite, P. (1978). *The Year of Three Popes.* London: William Collins.

Hegel, G. W. F. (1956). *The Philosophy of History.* New York: Dover Publications.

_____ (1973). *Lectures on the Philosophy of World History: Introduction.* Cambridge: Cambridge University Press.

Holy See Press Office (2012), "Synod of Bishops." http://www.vatican.va/news_services/press/documentazione/documents/sinodo/sinodo_documentazione-generale_en.html. Retrieved on July 16, 2019.

Hume, B. (1976). *Searching for God.* London: Hodder & Stoughton.

Huntston, G. W (1981). *The Mind of John Paul II: Origins of His Thought and Action.* New York: Seabury Press.

Inter Mirifica (Decree on the Media of Social Communications). Solemnly Promulgated by His Holiness Pope Paul VI on December 4, 1963. Rome.

István, D. (2000). "The Pope, the Nazis, and the Jews." In: *New York Review of Books.* March 23, 2000.

John Paul II, (1978). "Letter of His Holiness John Paul II to the People of Poland." Libreria Editrice Vaticana.

_____ (1979). "By the Communion of Persons Man Becomes the Image of God" (General Audience). Wednesday 14 November 1979.

_____ (1980). *Africa: Apostolic Pilgrimage.* Boston: Daughters of Saint Paul.

_____ (1981). *Laborem Exercens (On Human Work)*. Nairobi: Paulines Publications.

_____ (1986). "Address of John Paul II to the Representatives of Christian Churches and Ecclesia Communities gathered in Assisi for the World Day of Prayer." Basilica of St. Mary of Angels, October 27, 1986.

_____ (1988). "Hello from John Paul II to Msgr. Emery Kabongo Kanundowi and to his Family." Liberia Editrice Vaticana.

_____ (1988). *Pastor Bonus* (Apostolic Constitution). Liberia Editrice Vaticana.

_____ (1988). *Mulieris Dignitatem* (Apostolic Letter). Liberia Editrice Vaticana.

_____ (1990). *Redemptoris Missio* (On the Permanent Validity of the Church's Missionary Mandate). Nairobi: Paulines Publication Africa.

_____ (1992). "Speech of His Holiness John Paul II to the Catholic Community of Gorée Island in the Church of Saint Charles Borromeo." https://www.vatican.va/content/john-paul-ii/fr/speeches/1992/february/documents/hf_jp-ii_spe_19920222_isola-goree.html. Assessed January 15, 2022.

_____ (1994). *Crossing the Threshold of Hope*. London: Jonathan Cape.

_____ (1998). Ad Limina Addresses: The Addresses of His Holiness Pope John Paul II to the bishops of the United States, February 1998 – October 1998.

_____ (2004). *Rise, Let Us Be On Our Way*. Nairobi: Paulines Publication Africa. Johnson, P. (1981). *Pope John Paul II and the Catholic Restoration*. New York: St. Martin Press.

Kaiser, B. R. (2006). *A Church in Search of Itself: Benedict XVI and the Battle for the Future*. New York: Alfred A. Knopf.

Kedar, B. (1998). "Crusade Historians and the Massacre of 1096." In: *Jewish History*. Milan.

Kemen, H. (2014). *The Spanish Inquisition: A Historical Revision*. New Haven: Yale University Press.

Kellerman, B. (ed) (1986). *Political Leadership: A Source Book*. Pittsburgh: University of Pittsburg Press.

Kelly, J. D. (1990). *The Oxford Dictionary of Popes*. Oxford: Oxford University Press.

Kent, P. C., & Pollard, J. F. (eds) (1994). *Papal Diplomacy in the Modern Age*. New York: Praeger Publishers.

Kessler, E. (2011). "Hope Will Be his Legacy." In: Pepinster, (ed). *The Tablets*. London: Special edition on the beatification of John Paul II. April 30, 2011.

Kissinger, H. (1977). "The Permanent Challenge of Peace: US Policy Toward the Soviet Union." In: Kissinger, *American Foreign Policy*. (3rd edition). New York: Norton.

_____ (1979). *The White House Years*. Boston: Little, Brown.

Kipling, R. (1929). *"The White Man's Burden: The United States & The Philippine Islands, 1899."* New York: Doubleday.

Kluger, J. & Di Simone, G. (2012). *The Pope and I: How the Lifelong Friendship between a Polish Jew and Pope John Paul II Advanced the Cause of Jewish-Christian Relations*. MaryKnoll: Orbis Books.

Kojève, A. (1969). *Introduction to the Reading of Hegel*. New York: Basic Books.

Korchler, H. (2006). "Karol Wojtyła's Notion of the Irreducible in Man and the Quest for a Just World Order." International Conference on *Karol Wojtyła's Philosophical Legacy*. West Hartford, Connecticut, USA: Saint Joseph College.

Kunz, J. L. (1952). "The Status of the Holy See in International Law." *The American Journal of International Law* 46, no. 2: 308–14.

Lajolo, G. (2005). *Nature & Function of Papal Diplomacy*. Singapore: Institute of Southeast Asian Studies.

Lapide, P. (1967). *Three Popes and the Jews: Pope Pius XII Did Not Remain Silent*. New York: Hawthorn Books.

Leguey-Feilleux, J. R (2009). *The Dynamics of Diplomacy*. London: Lynne Rienner Publishers.

L'Etang, H. (1970). *The Pathology of Leadership*. New York: Hawthorne Books.

Lewis, J. P (2007). *Fundamentals of Project Management*. Toronto: American Management Association.

L'Osservatore Romano, March 21, 1919. In: Rubenstein, R. L. (2002). "Pius XII and the Shoah." In: Rittner, C., & Roth, J. K. (eds). *Pope Pius XII and the Holocaust*. New York: Leicester University Press.

Lukas, R. (1986). *The Forgotten Holocaust: The Poles under Nazi Occupation 1939–1944*. Lexington, Ky: University Press of Kentucky.

Luker, R. (2000). "The National Catholic Reporter" (March 31, 2000). In: Fleischner, E. "The Spirituality of Pius XII." In: Rittner, C., & Roth, J. K. (eds). *Pope Pius XII and the Holocaust*. New York: Leicester University Press.

Lumen Gentium (Dogmatic Constitution on the Church). Solemnly Promulgated by His Holiness, Pope Paul VI on November 21, 1964. Rome.

Madison, (1961). "The Political Testament of Cardinal Richelieu: The Significant Chapters and Supporting Selections." In: Berridge, G. R (1994). *Richelieu*. In: Berridge, G. R., & Keens-Soper, M., & Otte, T. G. (2001). *Diplomatic Theory from Machiavelli to Kissinger*. New York: Palgrave.

Magister, S. (2004). "From Rome to the World: The Globe Offensive of the Catholic Media." Vatican (August 20, 2004).

Maimbourg, L. (1675). *Histoire des croisades pour la delivrance de la Terre Sainte, 1675*. D ed., vol. Paris.

Makori, H., Kodi, B., Muroki, F., Anataloni, L., Wainaina, F. (2005). *The Seed: A Magazine of Missionary Concern* (May 2005–Vol. 17 No. 5). Special Issues in Memory of Pope John Paul II. Nairobi.

Malishi, L. (1987). *Introduction to the History of Christianity in Africa*. London: Mission Book Service.

Marjolijn de Moed (2011). "Reuniting the Body of Christ: The ecumenical movement called community of Taizé." Department of Religious Studies and Theory: University of Utrecht. Published Bachelor Thesis.

Marlise, S. (2005). "Brother Roger, 90, Dies; Ecumenical Leader." *International New York Times*. Retrieved September 18, 2013).

Marrus, R. M. (2002). "Ten Essential Themes." In: Rittner, C., & Roth, J. K. (eds). *Pope Pius XII and the Holocaust*. New York: Leicester University Press.

McCool, G. (1993). "The Theology of John Paul II." In: McDermott, J. M (ed). *The Thought of Pope John Paul II: A Collection of Essays and Studies*.

McDermott, J. M. (1993). *The Thought of Pope John Paul II: A Collection of Essays and Studies*. Rome: Editrice Pontificia Universita Gregoriana.

Melady, T. P. (1994). *The Ambassador's Story: The United States and the Vatican in World Affairs*. Huntington, IN: Our Sunday Visitor.

Melady, M. B. (1999). *The Rhetoric of Pope John Paul II: The Pastoral Vocabulary of the Sacred*. New York: Praeger Publishers.

Meredith, M. (2011). *The Fate of Africa: A History of the Continent Since Independence*. New York: Public Affairs.

Messori, V. (2015). *Kidnapped by the Vatican? The Unpublished Memoirs of Edgardo Mortara*. San Francisco: Ignatius Press.

Metzger, Y. (2005). "Yesterday, Today and Tomorrow: Catholic-Jewish Relations 40 Years after *Nostra Aetate*." *America*, 193, no. 12 (October 24, 2005).

Mickens, R. (2011). "This is What is Pleasing to the Lord." In: Pepinster (ed). *The Tablet*. London: May 7 issue on the Beatification of Pope John Paul II

Mickens, R., & Luximoore, J. (2011). "Faith of a Titan Recalled at John Paul II Beatification." In: Pepinster (ed). *The Tablet*. London: May 7 issue on Beatification of John Paul II.

Minear, L., & Hazel, S. (eds) (2007). *Humanitarian Diplomacy: Practitioners and Their Craft*. New York: United Nations University Press.

Minerbi, S. (1990). *The Vatican and Zionism*. New York: Oxford University Press. Modern History Sourcebook: Woodrow Wilson: Speech on the Fourteen Points Jan 8, 1918. http://www.fordham.edu/halsall/mod/1918wilson.html. Retrieved on May 15, 2018.

Morley, J. F. (1980). *Vatican Diplomacy and the Jews during the Holocaust 1939–1943*. New York: KTAV Publishing House.

Mufson, S. "Bush Nudged by the Right over Rights," *International Herald Tribune,* January 27 28, 2001, 3. See also "American Power—For What? A Symposium," *Commentary,* January 2000, 21n.

Murphy, F. X. (1981). *The Papacy Today: The Last 80 Years of the Catholic Church from the Perspective of the Papacy*. New York: Macmillan Publishing Co., Inc.

Murray, J. C. (2003). "The Declaration on Religious Freedom." In: Curran, C. (ed). *Change in Official Catholic Moral Teaching*. New York: Paulist Press.

Nan, S. A. (2002). "Complementarity and Coordination of Conflict Resolution Efforts in the Conflicts over Abkhazia, South Ossetia and Transdniestria" (Published Doctoral Dissertation). George Mason University: Fairfax.

_____ (2004). "Track One and a Half Diplomacy: Searching for Political Agreement in the Caucasus." In Fitzduff & Church (eds). *NGOs at the Table: Strategies for Influencing Policies in Areas of Conflicts*. Oxford: Rowman & Littlefield Publishers.

Newsweek Magazine. *John Paul II: Special Double* Issue. April 18, 2005. New York.

Nemec, L. (1979). *Pope John Paul II: A Festive Profile*. New York: Catholic Book Publishing CO.

Noonan, P. (2005). *John Paul the Great: Remembering A Spiritual Father*. New York: Penguin Group.

Nye, J. S. (2002). *The Paradox of American Power: Why the World Only Superpower Can't Go It Alone*. Oxford: Oxford University Press.

_____ (2007). "The Place of Soft Power in State-Based Conflict Management." In: Crocker, C. A., Hampson, O. F., & Aall, P. *Leashing the Dogs of War*. Washington: United States Institute of Peace Press.

_____ (2008). *Understanding International Conflict*. Toronto: Dorling Kindersley Publishing, Inc.

O'Brien, D. (1998). *The Hidden Pope: The Untold Story of a Lifelong Friendship That Is Changing the Relationship Between Catholics and Jews – The Personal Journey of John Paul II and Jerzy Kluger*. New York: Integrated Media.

O' Connor, B. J. (2009). *Papal Diplomacy: John Paul II and the Culture of Peace*. New York: Praeger Publishers.

Onaiyekan, J. (2016). *Theology in Context: Inculturation and Evangelization in Africa*. Abuja: Paulines Publications Africa.

Otte, T. G. (2001). "Kissinger." In: Berridge, G. R., Keens-Soper, M., & Otte, T. G. (2001). *Diplomatic Theory from Machiavelli to Kissinger*. New York: Palgrave.

_____ (2001). "Nicolson." In: Berridge, G. R., & Keens-Soper, M., & Otte, T.G. (2001). *Diplomatic Theory from Machiavelli to Kissinger*. New York: Palgrave.

_____ (2001). "Satow." In: Berridge, G. R., Keens-Soper, M., & Otte, T. G. (2001). *Diplomatic Theory from Machiavelli to Kissinger*. New York: PALGRAVE

Palmer, R. (1980). *John Paul II: A Pictorial Celebration*. Indiana: Our Sunday Visitor.

Park, B. E. (1994). *Ailing, Aging, Addicted: Studies of Compromised Leadership*. Lexington: University Press of Kentucky

Paul VI (1969). *Sollicitudo Omnium Ecclesiarum* [The Care of All the Churches], the Apostolic Letter of Pope Paul VI on the Duties of Papal Representatives, June 24, 1969.

_____ (1971). *Octogesima adveniens* (Apostolic Letter on the occasion of the Eightieth Anniversary of *Rerum Novarum.*

_____ (1967). *Populorum Progressio.* Nairobi: Paulines Publication.

Peterkiewicz, J. (translator) (1982). *The Place Within: The Poetry of Pope John Paul II.* New York: Random House.

Rashid, A. (2011). "How Obama Lost Karzai." In *Foreign Policy: Global Politics, Economics and Ideas.* New York. March 2011 edition.

Ratzinger, J./Benedict XVI. (2007). *John Paul II: My Beloved Predecessor.* Boston: Pauline Books & Media.

Reagan, R. (1990). *An American Life.* New York: Simon & Shuster.

Reese, J. T. (1998). *Inside the Vatican: The Politics and Organization of the Catholic Church.* Cambridge: Harvard University Press.

Rendina, C. (2002). *The Popes: Histories and Secrets.* California: Pharos Publication Ltd.

Riccards, M. P. (1998). *Vicars of Christ: Popes, Power, and Politics in the Modern World.* New York: The Crossroad Publishing Company.

Riley-Smith, J. (1986). *The First Crusade and the Idea of Crusading.* Cambridge: Cambridge University Press.

Rittner, C., & Roth, J. K. (eds) (2002). *Pope Pius XII and the Holocaust.* New York: Leicester University Press.

_____ (2002). "A Chronology about Pope Pius XII and the Holocaust." In: Rittner, C., & Roth, J. K. (eds). *Pope Pius XII and the Holocaust.* New York: Leicester University Press.

Rocca, F. (2008). "Pope Defends World Youth Day as More 'Than Rock Festival.'" *Religion* News Service.

Rosenau, N. J. (1971). *The Scientific Study of Foreign Policy.* New York: Collier Macmillan

Rostow, E. (1970). "The Vatican and its Role in the World Order." In Sweeney, F. (1970). *The Vatican and World Peace.* Montreal: Palm Publishers Limited.

Roth, J. K. (2002). "An American Protestant Reflections." Rittner, C., & Roth, J.K. (eds). *Pope Pius XII and the Holocaust*. New York: Leicester University Press.

Rubenstein, R. L. (2002). "Pius XII and the Shoah." In: Rittner, C., & Roth, J. K. (eds). *Pope Pius XII and the Holocaust*. New York: Leicester University Press.

Russett, B. & Starr, H. (1986). *World Politics: The Menu for Choice*. New York: Worth Publishers.

Rychlak, R. (2000). *Hitler, the War, and the Pope*. Indiana: Our Sunday Visitor.

Sacco, U. C. (1999). *John Paul II and World Diplomacy: Twenty Years of Search for a New Approach 1978:1998*. Leuven: Peters Bondgenotenlaan.

Salisbury, G. K. (1905). "Essays by the Late Marquess of Salisbury. 2 vols. Vol. 1." In: Otte, T. G. (2001). "Satow." In: Berridge, G.R., & Keens-Soper, M., & Otte, T. G. (2001). *Diplomatic Theory from Machiavelli to Kissinger*. New York: Palgrave.

Satow, E. (1911). "The Immunity of Private Property at Sea: II. Theoretical." In: *Quarterly Review*, vol. CCXV, no.428. In: Otte, T. G (2001). *Satow*. New York: Palgrave.

_____ (1917). *A Guide to Diplomatic Practice*. London: Longmans, Green & Company.

Scola, A. (2014). *Let's Not Forget God: Freedom for Our Faith*. New York: IMAGE.

Shaw, D. (1995). "Coverage of the U.N. Conference Shows Vatican Media Savvy Influence: Office Stress Pope's position in advance of the gathering on population, then sent its articulate spokesman to put Church doctrine in world spotlight." *Los Angeles Times*. Retrieved on June 9, 2016

Sheets, J. R. (1993). "The Spirituality of Pope John Paul II." In: McDermott, J. M. (1993). *The Thought of Pope John Paul II: A Collection of Essays and Studies*.

Singer, J. D. (1961). "The Level of Analysis Problem in International

Relations." In: Khorr, K, and Verba, S. (ed). *The International System: Theoretical Essays*. Princeton: Princeton University Press.

Singh, J. S. (1998). *Creating a New Consensus on Population: The International Conference on Population and Development*. London: Earthscans Publication Ltd.

Skollarg, I. (2009). "Faith and Intellect: Preparing Leaders for Church and World." Anna Halpine 'O8.M.Div: Crusading for Human Dignity. http://www.yale.edu/divinity/080220_news_halpine.shtml"

Sliwinski, C. (1982). "John Paul II in Africa," in Wierzbianski, ed., *The Shepherd for All People*. New York: Bicentennial Publishing Corporation.

Soltis, A. (2005). "Magic 'Spell' Unites Bush and Chirac," in *New York Post*. April 8, 2005.

Stake, R. P. (2009). "The Holy See and the Middle East: The Public Diplomacy of John Paul II." (Master Thesis).

St. John-Stevas, N. (1982). *Pope John Paul II: His Travels and Mission*. London: Faber and Faber Limited.

Stoessinger, J. G. (1985). *Crusaders and Pragmatists: Movers of American Foreign Policy*. 2nd ed. New York: Norton.

Sybel, V., H. (1981). *Geschichte des ersten Kreuzz?* Leipzig.

Szulc, T. (1995). *Pope John Paul II: The Biography*. New York: Scribner.

Tanner, N. (ed) (1990). *Decrees of the Ecumenical Councils: Nicaea I to Lateran V*. Vol. 1. London: Sheed & Ward and Georgetown University Press.

Tanner, N. (2000). *The Councils of the Church: A Short History*. New York: The Crossroad Publishing Company.

Taborski, B. (1987). *Introduction to Karol Wojtyła: The Collected Plays and Writings on Theatre*. Berkeley: University of California Press.

Tashakkori, A., & C. Teddie (1998). Mixed *Methodology: Combining Qualitative and Quantitative Approaches*. London: Sage Publication.

Thavis, J. (2011). "On the World Stage and Behind Closed Doors, Vatican Works Diplomatic Levers." In: *Catholic News Service. June 17, 2011.* http://www.catholicnews.com/data/stories/cns/1102426.htm. Retrieved, June 25, 2020. The Code of Canon Law (1983). "New Revised English Translation." Bangalore: Theological Publications in India.

Thomas, P. C. (2005). *A Compact History of the Popes.* Mumbai: ST. PAULS.

Turowicz, J. (1991). "Karol Wojtyła" In: Zbigniew Baran, ed., *Cracow: The Dialogue of Traditions.* Krakow: Znak. "Testament of the Holy Father John Paul II." The Holy See. Retrieved July 24, 2021. United Nations, Vienna Convention on Diplomatic Relations (1961), art. 14, sec. 1, and art. 16, sec. 3, online at http://www.un.org/law/ilc/texts/dipfra.htm (accessed October 2020). 24, 1964. Vienna.

Valeri, V. (1956). "International Relations of the Holy See after the Second World War." Rome: Banco di Roma.

Vischer, L. (1974). "The Holy See, the Vatican State, and the Churches' Common Witness: A Neglected Ecumenical Problem," in Journal of Ecumenical Studies 11, no. 4 (Fall 1974)

Wallace, R. (1992). "International Law" (2nd ed). In: Araujo, J. R., & Lucal, J. *Papal Diplomacy and the Quest for Peace: The Vatican and International Organizations from the Early Years to the League of Nations.* Florida: Sapientia Press of Ave Maria University.

Washington's Farewell Address 1796. *The Avalon Project Documents in Law, History and Diplomacy.* http://avalon.law.yale.edu/18th_century/washing.asp Retrieved on May 15, 2021. Washington, C. T. (2015). *The Participation of non-Catholic Christian Observers, Guests and Fraternal Delegates at the Second Vatican Council and Synods of Bishops: A theological Analysis.* Rome: Editrice Pontificia Universita Gregoriana.

Walters, R. A. (2009). *Historical Dictionary of United States-Africa Relations: Historical Dictionaries of U.S .Diplomacy,* No.9. Toronto: Scarecrow Press, Inc.

Weigel, G. (1992). *The Final Revolution: The Resistance Church and the Collapse of Communism*. Oxford: Oxford University Press.

_____ (1995). "What Really Happened at Cairo and Why." In: Michael Cromartie, ed., *The Nine Lives of Population Control*. In: Weigel, G. *Soul of the Word: Notes on the Future of Public Catholicism*. Washington: Ethics and Public Policy Center and Wm. B. Eerdmans Publishing Co.

_____ (1995). "What really happened at Cairo." In: *First Things*. New York City.

_____ (1996). *Soul of the Word: Notes on the Future of Public Catholicism*. Washington: Ethics and Public Policy Center and Wm. B. Eerdmans Publishing Co

_____ (1999). *Witness to Hope: The Biography of Pope John Paul II*. New York: HarperCollins Publishers, Inc.

_____ (2001). *The Truth of Catholicism: Inside the Essential Teachings and Controversies of the Church Today*. New York: HarperCollins Publishers.

_____ (2001). "Papacy and Power." In: First Things Magazine (Essay adapted from his Erasmus Lecture, delivered in New York in November 2000).

_____ (2005). *God's Choice: Pope Benedict XVI and the Future of the Catholic Church*. New York: HarperCollins Publishers, Inc.

_____ (2005). *The Cube and the Cathedral: Europe, America, and Politics without God*. New York: HarperCollins Publishers, Inc.

_____ (2010). *The End and the Beginning: Pope John Paul II — The Victory of Freedom, the Last Years, the Legacy*. Auckland: Doubleday.

_____ (2017). *Lessons in Hope: My Unexpected Life with St. John Paul II*. New York: Basic Books.

Weigel, G., Gress, C., & Weigel, S. (2015). *City of the Saints: A Pilgrimage to John Paul II's Krakow*. New York: Image.

Whale, J. (1980). *The Man Who Leads the Church*. New York: Harper & Row, Publishers.

Wight, M. (1977). *Systems of States*. Leicester: Leicester University Press.

Willey, D. (1992). *God's Politician: Pope John Paul, the Catholic Church, and the New World Order*. New York: St. Martin's Press.

Wills, G. (2000). *Papal Sin: Structures of Deceit*. New York: Doubleday.

Wiseman, T. P. (2013). *The Death of Caligula*. Liverpool: Liverpool University Press.

Wlodzimierz, R. (2014). *Accanto a Giovanni Paulo II: Gli Amici & i Collaboratori Raccontano*.

Wojtyła, K. (1969). *Osoba i czyn*. Kraków: Polskie Towarzystwo Teologiczne.

Wolterstorff, N. & Audi, R. (2000). *Religion in the Public Square: The Place of Religious Convictions in Political Debate*. Boston: Rowman & Littlefield Publishers, Inc.

Woodrow, A. (1998). "Superstar or Servant?" In: MacEoin, G. et al. The *Papacy and the People of God*. New York: Orbis Books.

Woodward, E. L. (1929). *Three Studies in European Conservatism: Metternich-Guizot-The Catholic Church in the Nineteenth Century*. London: Constable.

Wozniack, F. E. (1984). "Byzantine Diplomacy." In *Dictionary of the Middle Ages*. In Hamilton, K. & Langhorne, R. *The Practice of Diplomacy: Its Evolution, Theory and Administration*. London: Routledge.

Yallop, D. (2007). *The Power and the Glory: Inside the Dark Heart of John Paul II's Vatican*. New York: Carroll & Graf Publishers.

Zavattaro, F. (1999). *A Quarter of a Century with Pope John Paul II*. Rome: Pauline Audiovisuals

Zenit. Papal Homily for John Paul II Beatification. http://www.zenit.org/article-32440?/=202105-01. Retrieved on May 2, 2021.

Zucotti, S. (2002). "Pope Pius XII and Rescue of Jews during the Holocaust: Examining Commonly Accepted Assertions." In: Rittner, C., & Roth, J. K. (eds) (2002). *Pope Pius XII and the Holocaust*. New York: Leicester University Press.